WOMEN, THE STATE, AND DEVELOPMENT

SUNY Series in Feminist Political Theory
Marion Smiley, editor

WOMEN, THE STATE, AND DEVELOPMENT

Sue Ellen M. Charlton
Jana Everett
Kathleen Staudt
editors

STATE UNIVERSITY OF NEW YORK PRESS

Published by
State University of New York Press, Albany

For information, address State University of New York
Press, State University Plaza, Albany, N.Y., 12246

Library of Congress Cataloging-in-Publication Data

Women, the state, and development / Sue Ellen M. Charlton, Jana
    Everett, and Kathleen Staudt, editors.
        p.   cm. — (SUNY series in feminist political theory)
    Bibliography: p.
    Includes index.
    ISBN 0–7914–0064–6.   ISBN 0–7914–0065–4 (pbk.)
    1. Women in development—Cross-cultural studies. 2. Women–
–Government policy—Cross-cultural studies. 3. State, The— Cross
–cultural studies. I. Charlton, Sue Ellen M. II. Everett, Jana
Matson, III. Staudt, Kathleen. IV. Series.
HQ1240.W663   1989
320'.088042—dc19   88-8531
                                                                    CIP

10 9 8 7 6 5 4 3

CONTENTS

Preface   vii

1. Women, the State, and Development   1
   Sue Ellen M. Charlton, Jana Everett, and
   Kathleen Staudt

2. Female Welfare and Political Exclusion   20
   in Western European States
   Sue Ellen M. Charlton

3. Women and the State in Eastern Europe   44
   and the Soviet Union
   Sharon Wolchik

4. The State and Gender in Colonial Africa   66
   Kathleen Staudt

5. Women and the State in Islamic West Africa   86
   Barbara Callaway and Lucy Creevey

6. Gender and the State: Perspectives   114
   from Latin America
   Susan C. Bourque

7. Subversive Mothers: The Women's   130
   Opposition to the Military Regime in Chile
   Patricia M. Chuchryk

8. Incorporation versus Conflict: Lower Class   152
      Women, Collective Action, and the State in India
      Jana Everett

9. Conclusion   177
      Jana Everett, Kathleen Staudt, and
      Sue Ellen M. Charlton

Notes   *191*

Index   *241*

PREFACE

The editors and principal authors of this book are political scientists and feminists with particular interests in comparative politics, area studies, feminist theory, and development. We began communicating with each other through mutual involvement in the interdisciplinary field of women and development. We shared the recognition characterizing this field that the process of development affects people differently, depending on their class and ethnicity and, of course, their gender. We also recognized that the insights that have emerged from both feminist theory and from women and development studies, whether conceptual or applied, have remained largely isolated from much new thinking in the social sciences. In particular, the "rediscovery" of the state by political scientists in the 1980s occurred with virtually no reference to the differential impact of state ideology, institutions, and policies on women and men. Overall, studies in comparative politics are especially devoid of sensitivity to gender issues.

This book, then, is designed to be a catalyst for the belated process of feminist reconceptualization of the state, with particular attention given to the linkage between states, women, and socioeconomic development. Our collective work began in 1984, when Jana Everett and Sue Ellen M. Charlton drafted the initial proposal of a comparative politics panel on women, development, and the state for the 1985 American Political Science Association Annual Meeting in New Orleans. The earliest drafts of our chapters on Western Europe and India, along with Kathleen Staudt's on colonial Africa, were presented at that time. The panel, chaired by Judith

Stiehm, and for which Lois Wasserspring was our able and enthusias-
tic discussant, was the beginning of a collaborative effort that has
lasted about four years and that we hope will carry us well into the
future.

This has been a genuine collaboration, one that has been feminist both in content and in process. Despite similar interests, we
have different styles and academic strengths and we have sought to
build on our respective abilities while working in an integrative fashion. We did not allocate the necessary labor by task, but shared in
the efforts of communicating with authors, writing, and editing. We
are divided by miles and institutional affiliation and each of us has
been through her own period of personal and professional turmoil in
these past four years. Our discussions have gone forward through the
mail, in hotel rooms, restaurants, offices, and over telephones and
kitchen tables—often with Jana's and Kathleen's children sharing the
conversation. Nonetheless, the cooperation has been worth it and,
we recognize, something of a luxury. In a profession that rewards individual more than collaborative scholarship, our relative security at
our respective institutions facilitated the project and has made it
possible for us to test our ideas against each other.

We are grateful for the studies from our contributing authors,
each of whom has responded to our deadlines and requests for revi-
sions while juggling the other demands on her time. We have benefit-
ted from Lois Wasserspring's thoughtful critiques, as well as from
those of SUNY's anonymous reviewers. Support staff at three insitu-
tions have handled our numerous requests for drafts and more drafts:
Earlene Bell, Carol Cran, Donna Bahr and Patsy Smith at Colorado
State University; Gerry Darr and Juanita Ramirez at the University
of Colorado at Denver; and Jill Bonar at the University of Texas at El
Paso. As in all such efforts, family and friends have sustained us, and
we have appreciated their encouragement and patience. Kathleen
Staudt, in particular, thanks her husband, Robert Dane'el, and her
children, Mosi and Asha, and Jana Everett thanks her daughter,
Carson.

Kathleen Staudt
Jana Everett
Sue Ellen M. Charlton

WOMEN, THE STATE, AND DEVELOPMENT

Sue Ellen M. Charlton
Jana Everett
Kathleen Staudt

The 1980s is a decade of rediscovering the state as a concept meriting sustained examination in the social sciences. The state has preoccupied Marxists and non-Marxist scholars to varying degrees since the nineteenth century, but its centrality lay dormant in the United States until relatively recently. As contemporary scholarship seeks to bring the state back into our understanding of social, political, and economic reality,[1] political scientists are rethinking both classical and modern state theories for their cross-cultural and empirical utility. This book is part of the broad-gauged revival of interest in the state.

Parallelling, but seldom intersecting, the recent state studies has been a revival of Western feminist scholarship. This scholarship, like that on the state, is frequently interdisciplinary, and although its American roots lie in the issues raised by the civil rights and feminist movements of the 1960s and early 1970s, it has moved rapidly in new directions. Contemporary feminist thought challenges fundamental concepts, theories, and paradigms of traditional academic disciplines as it seeks to understand the inequalities imbedded in gender relations. The studies in this book are part of this scholarship: they seek both to extend feminist theory and to enrich political science by proposing gender-sensitive perspectives for analysis of the nature of the state and state-society relations. For despite the creativity that characterizes the new scholarship on the state, there is little in that scholarship that helps us understand questions such as the differential impact of state structures and policies on women and men, or the unequal female and male influence on state actions which, regardless of class structures, exists in virtually all societies.

The past two decades have produced a major rethinking of development—what it means, what fosters it, what impedes it. Development studies range from the micro- to the macrotheoretical; they may be based in a single discipline, or they may be interdisciplinary. It is beyond the scope of this book to critique or transform these disparate approaches, but we try to foster linkages between the development literature on the one hand, and the statist and feminist literatures on the other. Conventional approaches to development have no lack of critics, and women around the world are frequently prominent among them. However, their voices are still largely isolated, primarily because they are absent from the state and international agencies that bear responsibility for formulating and implementing development policies.

A gender-sensitive approach to states and development requires that central problems in the statist, feminist, and development literatures be linked and extended to reformulate questions with an eye toward more complete understanding of political and socioeconomic reality. To illustrate, much theorizing on the nature of the state addresses the degree of state autonomy, or the degree to which states may act independently of the interests of specific groups or classes in society. What is the relevance of the autonomy question for the efforts of women's organizations to influence public policy? Feminist theory in the social sciences has a special interest in what has become known as the public-private dichotomy: the relationship between the realm of family and household on the one hand, and the sphere of public or civic affairs on the other. What is the role of the state in defining the changing boundaries between public and private, and how susceptible are these boundaries to state control? As the boundaries between public and private are created or redefined in the course of development, what are the implications of this for women's productive and reproductive lives? For example, how does the state seek to control reproduction as part of a development strategy?

This collection builds on state, feminist, and development theories as it seeks to improve our understanding of the relationship between states and women. The next section summarizes the dominant perspectives that have emerged in social science literature on the state. With rare exceptions, none of these addresses women or gender. Subsequent sections look first at some implications of development for both states and women; a closer look at feminist theory on the state follows, and then a discussion of some broader issues concerning states and gender. For purposes of analyzing these issues, we propose a conceptual approach that focuses on state officials, state policies, and state definitions of politics. This allows us to address both the explicit and implicit role of the state: explicit as in the decision makers who act in the name of the state, and the policies they formulate and implement; and implicit in terms of the way in which state structures and ideologies condition the nature of politics. State ideologies set the tone and acceptable boundaries of political discourse and also nourish assumptions about gender. This approach contributes to the debate about state autonomy, as our authors look at the linkages between state and society, including economic interests and women's organizations.

PERSPECTIVES ON STATES

The state can be seen as government; as ruling class; as a bureaucratic, coercive, and legal order; and as a normative order.[2] These definitions overlap with the three dominant theoretical approaches to the state in the social sciences: liberal-pluralist, Marxist, and statist. The pluralist approach has typically equated state with government, or the decision-making apparatus that ostensibly is the arbitrator between competing social and economic interests. This interpretation has been modified to accommodate the reality of the unequal strength of interests and interest groups,[3] but continues to be grounded in the assumption that politics is largely a matter of allocation in response to citizen demands or inputs. Gender, like class, does not structure politics in any significant way: the state, presumably, is blind to gender. In effect, the liberal-pluralist views of the state imply that women are potentially equal competitors in the politics of allocation and that the challenge for women is to foster organizations and tactics that will provide access to, and control over, decision making.

Historically, Marxist theory argues that the state is the apparatus of the dominant capitalist class. This instrumentalist argument was muted, however, even in Engels' classic formulation, in which the state might mediate between classes and even be independent of them for a time.[4] Structural Marxism views the state as preserving the coherence of capitalist society and from this tradition come more recent insights into the question of state autonomy. Confronting the critical issues that instrumental Marxists have not explained well—the internal divisions within the capitalist class and the occasional victories of noncapitalist groups, for example—structural Marxists see the state as forging compromise to cope with inherent contradictions and to maintain the viability of the capitalist state, even if it means opposing the capitalist class.[5] Thus it is in what Engels foresaw as a mediator's role that the state comes to assert its relative autonomy from the capitalist class.

Engels himself was interested in the way in which the division of labor within the family was linked to the growth of private property and ultimately to the subordination of women,[6] and it is from his successors that we have our appreciation of the way in which the control of female labor sustains both family and state power. What Marxist feminists have not adequately provided is much understanding of other issues raised by women and addressed in this book, such as the vitality of gender ideologies, conflict between men and women of the same class, the distinctiveness of women's organizations, or gender conflicts in socialist countries.

Although the studies in this book draw on both pluralist and Marxist assumptions, they fit more comfortably within the statist tradition, where the state is viewed simultaneously as a bureaucratic, coercive, legal, and normative order. Statist orientations

> place greater emphasis on institutional constraints, both formal and informal, on individual behavior. . . . Actors in the political system, whether individuals or groups, are bound within these structures, which limit, even determine, their conceptions of their own interest and their political resources.[7]

Statist approaches have revived appreciation for continental European, and particularly Weberian, theories. Weber emphasized qualities of organization and compulsion in his analysis of the state, but he also left room for normative and legitimizing characteristics. For Weber, primary among a state's formal characteristics are that it possesses "an administrative and legal order subject to change by legislation" and that it claims "binding authority over all action taking place in the area of its jurisdiction. It is thus a compulsory organization with a territorial basis."[8] Although Weber in particular, and contemporary statists in general, have not been concerned with the specific implications of this legal and normative order for the differential impact of the state on women and men, the studies in this book build on the Weberian tradition in two important ways: they understand the state to be simultaneously administrative, coercive, and legitimizing; and they assume that analyses of states and state policies must be historically specific.

Although the preference in these studies is for a statist approach, we have some concerns about that approach insofar as it tends to reify the state. Appropriate modifications of statist literature will be sensitive to the ways in which individuals and communities resist or cope with the expansion of state power, and will look more closely at the nature of state-society linkages. It is in this context that the view of states as relatively autonomous, with the degree of autonomy varying in time and place, can clarify the state's effect on gender in more compelling ways. In fact, the assumption of relative state autonomy is the only way to integrate gender into analysis without casting women as merely one more pressure group or pushing gender far into the background of class relations. Institutionalized male privilege exists independently of the dominant class, and it means that women occupy a different, and subordinate, role in intergroup competition (when it exists). The challenge is to locate the boundaries that define state autonomy and to explain those forces that both enhance and limit autonomy, whether international or domestic. For example, the dependency and world systems theoretical approaches provide frameworks for understanding how international economic accumulation and inequity limit the power of nation-state institutions and even impinge upon households and women.[9] In this perspective, however, it is tempting simply to view women as the last victims in one great chain of exploitation, with little or no recognition of the ways in which women respond to both national and international forces. The studies in this book suggest that there are strategies available to those who would insulate themselves from state policy or, alternatively, attempt to shape that policy. These strategies, in turn, say something about the domestic limitations on state autonomy.

STATES AND DEVELOPMENT

Historically, states have developed in response both to internal opportunities and challenges, and to international conditions. Particularly in Western Europe, interstate competition has been pervasive, with the result that state development has been inseparable from the preoccupation with territorial integrity and security. For Gianfranco Poggi, this historical reality conditioned continental European views of politics as inherently antagonistic and the state as primarily charged with protection from outside danger.[10] Drawing on her analysis of historical cases, Theda Skocpol summarizes the dual purposes of states in the light of interstate competition: "The state normally performs two basic sets of tasks: It maintains order, and it competes with other actual or potential states."[11] The necessity of responding to both internal and external threats and opportunities often leads to conflicting state policies which in turn contribute to the broader conflict in political life. Under these competitive conditions, the state seeks to enhance its autonomy by controlling political participation and by making extractive and distributive decisions to achieve various goals, including the promotion of economic growth and ideologically defined social and cultural preferences.

The process of development as it is understood and practiced throughout the world is inseparable from the process of state development. Ideologies (whether secular or religious), institutions, policies, and state officials all contribute to protecting the state from internal and external challenges, and socioeconomic development is an important protective strategy. The critical question for women is the degree to which this state enhancement serves their interests, and it is clear from the studies in this book that the answer depends both on a definition of interests and on the characteristics of states as they develop at different times and places.

The recognition that there is a dynamic and symbiotic relationship between socioeconomic development on the one hand, and the development of state institutions and ideologies on the other, is critical for efforts to synthesize statist and feminist theories. Beginning in the 1970s, the U.N. Decade for Women served as a catalyst to stimulate cross-cultural, international exchanges between feminist and women's rights activists of very different philosophical and political persuasion. These exchanges have, in turn, enriched the debates about the nature of development. Third World feminists have politicized the development debates and have also shown just how political presumably apolitical development strategies are as they reinforce gender, class, and race privileges, ravage the environment, or contribute to militarism.[12] The studies in this book acknowledge this debate by extending the assumptions about development as politically significant and by asking questions about the way in which development reinforces state authority and legitimacy and the way in which the state manipulates development to its own ends.

The U.N. Decade also stimulated what has become known as the "women-in-development" (WID) literature, which examines the role of women in Third World development and development projects. Many of the case studies which inform this literature have been ahistorical and descriptive, or even incidental to larger studies having little to do with gender. There is a second and more serious problem with some of the women-in-development literature: inspired (or even financed) by the major national and international development agencies, it has been captured by the priorities, concepts, and data of nation-states. As Adele Mueller points out, "WID knowledge" has the effect of continuing to conceptualize the Third World in a relationship of dependence with the First World of dominant capitalist countries.[13] Despite the problems with the women and development field, however, its case studies are part of the factual information that, along with more traditional historical and anthropological works and newer studies by Third World scholars, contributes to the effort at theory building that this book represents.

FEMINIST THEORY AND THE STATE

Feminist theory has been preoccupied with gender relations, but only belatedly has it attended to the state in ways that would help explain the differences and inequalities between men and women. Human societies are marked by a nearly universal division of labor and cultural roles by gender: specific human characteristics and responsibilities are viewed as either masculine or feminine, although "the actual content of being a man or woman and the rigidity of the categories themselves are highly variable across cultures and time."[14] The control that men exercise over women's sexuality, labor, and mobility results in gender inequality, with women and men having differential access to economic resources, political power, and social value. States reflect this gender inequality insofar as their institutions are staffed and controlled by men and their policies reflect male domination of women's lives.

Feminist theory and action have long criticized mainstream politics and government and attacked policies that disadvantage women. Until the 1980s, however, relatively little attention was paid to the structure of state bureaucracies and ideologies in terms of their impact on gender relations. Despite this gap, Western feminism has made a pivotal contribution to our understanding of the role of states by viewing politics and power as central to gender relations, even in the family. To see the personal as political means to see the private as public,[15] notes Catharine MacKinnon, and this insight then becomes a bridge to conceptualizing the ways in which the state, as it fosters development, also structures gender relations.

There are, of course, as many feminist theories as there are state theories, and increasingly feminist theories are distinguishing between types of states as to their effects on gender relations. For Western Europeans and North Americans, the debate about the impact of the liberal democratic state on women is particularly important. What purposes does the state serve and in whose interests does the state operate? Are these purposes antithetical to the feminist project of gender equality? Can feminists transform the state so that it promotes women's interests? Or will such efforts by feminists result in failure, cooptation and/or an undermining of women's interests? No consensus exists; there are both pro- and antistate tendencies in feminist theory. For example, Wendy Sarvasy categorizes feminist state perspectives on the basis of answers to two questions: whether the state can be a positive force for women and whether the state is inherently patriarchal.[16] Judging the state as a positive (or negative) force requires scrutiny of state actions both on a case-by-case basis and over time, in the light of women's interests. This scrutiny, in turn, is linked to the evaluation of the state as patriarchal—that is, as replicating in the public sphere male control over female sexuality and labor in the private (family) sphere.

But the question of what constitutes women's interests remains. To answer this question, Maxine Molyneux proposes the distinction between "strategic gender interests" and "practical gender interests."[17] The former are derived deductively from the analysis of women's subordination and the formulation of strategic objectives to overcome that subordination, such as abolishing the sexual division of labor, alleviating the burden of domestic labor and child care, and attaining political equality. "Practical gender interests" arise from the concrete conditions of women's location within the gender division of labor and respond to immediately perceived needs. Thus, strategic and practical interests may conflict, and women disagree about which women's interests to pursue and when.

The emerging feminist debate on the state is a welcome development, but certain shortcomings in the existing literature should be noted. Feminist perspectives on the state tend to be reductionist and one dimensional, recapitulating earlier liberal and Marxist perspectives on the state. For example, Frances Fox Piven views the state as an arena of conflict in which women can make gains because "the structure of the welfare state itself has helped to create new solidarities and generate the political issues that continue to cement and galvanize them."[18]

Another variant of this perspective can be seen in the argument of Zillah Eisenstein that because of conflicts between patriarchy and capitalism, the state becomes an arena in which conflicting class and gender interests are mediated and where women's struggles can make a difference.[19] In contrast, Eileen Boris and Peter Bardaglio perceive the state to be an instrument of male control over women and suggest any policy reform affecting gender relations merely means a trade-off between family patriarchy and state patriarchy.[20] A structural feminist perspective can be seen in the work of Catharine MacKinnon who emphasizes the role of law in the construction of gender relations: "The state will appear most relentless in imposing the male point of view when it comes closest to achieving its highest formal criterion of distanced aperspectivity."[21]

Using Cynthia Daniels' critique of liberal and Marxist theories of the state, we can identify certain weaknesses in the feminist state perspectives discussed above.[22] Liberal feminist views assume the neutrality of the state and fail to take into account the political ramifications of gender subordination in social life. Instrumental feminist views associate the state with rule by men, and thus cannot easily account for the actions of Margaret Thatcher or Jeane Kirkpatrick. Structural feminist views maintain that the state reproduces patriarchy and sketches a scenario which assumes that human agency is nonexistent and that the power and knowledge of the state is omnipotent. Neither of these assumptions is tenable. Each of these feminist perspectives on the state represents only a partial understanding of the relationship between the state and gender.

Furthermore, Western feminist perspectives have tended to devote insufficient attention to the relationship between gender and the other forms of structural inequality (class, race, ethnicity, religion) in the modern state. There are several aspects of this issue that merit attention. First, as women of color and Marxist feminists have pointed out, "women" should not be considered as an undifferentiated category.[23] Maxine Molyneux states, "A theory of interests that has an application to the debate about women's capacity to struggle for and benefit from social change must begin by recognizing difference rather than by assuming homogeneity."[24] Second, state action should not be assumed to have uniform effects across class or racial lines. There has been some investigation of the ways in which the impact of states on women differs by class and the ways in which the impact of the state on class differs by gender in particular historical circumstances, but the findings have not been integrated into a general framework.[25] Third, there is the important question of the overall impact of the growth of the liberal democratic state on race, gender, and class relations. Among the feminists who have addressed this question in terms of class and gender relations, most paint a picture of increasing social control.[26] Exceptions include Zillah Eisenstein and Michele Barrett, who see the state "as a site of struggle."[27]

Feminist theorizing on the state has mainly focused on the liberal democratic welfare state of North America and Western Europe. This has meant that the theorizing has been somewhat ethnocentric, even though the experiences of these states are relevant to non-Western states because the influence of Western norms and institutions is worldwide. An examination of socialist and Third World states from a feminist perspective increases the range of variation and should yield new insights, thereby enriching theory.

Revolution, the classic instance in which the state is presumably transformed, offers the potential of serving strategic gender interests. Old structures and ideologies crumble, authority is unstable in both the public and the private spheres, and women can play new roles. Here state autonomy comes into full play.

> In such a situation, women have easier access to political roles, since dominant institutional patterns are weak. Moreover, social change affects women directly in every aspect of their lives.

Hence, there is a greater likelihood of political interest and political response . . . role differentiation according to sex tends to diminish as women find they have to perform tasks formally considered male, such as waging guerilla warfare or working in armaments factories . . . Finally, because the new order has not yet been established the real possibility of change still exists.[28]

Revolutionary regimes are typically unstable, however, and in the face of this instability, the new leaders may have ambivalent or contradictory attitudes about the desirability of mobilizing women. The aim of maintaining or expanding the power base of the state may be balanced by the perception that women are conservative) and potentially represent a drag on the process of radical social, economic, and cultural transformation. It is the suspicion that revolutionary states, including socialist states that lay claim to egalitarian priorities, are little different from nonrevolutionary states in their subordination of women's interests to other goals that increasingly characterize feminist analysis of postrevolutionary societies.[29] Revolutionary leaders invariably rely on bureaucratic institutions in attempts to socialize both the economy and services in ways that redistribute resources to more than the privileged.[30] Those who man the bureaucracy, and particularly its decision-making positions, are often the same people with the same gender ideologies as those who manned them before the revolution. Of course, perennial shortages of resources typically plague postrevolutionary regimes. Such shortages seem to have dire consequences for achieving public policies that might meet women's needs. Troubling, too, are state tendencies to *use* women to transform the economy: lower value for female labor has long been easily justified, as has women's unpaid household labor.

For Third World women, expansion of the state may offer attractive, or even the only viable, alternatives to oppressive family or kin relationships that prevent them from realizing either strategic or practical gender interests. Fatima Mernissi, for example, argues that the traditional private-public, female-male distinctions that exclude women from extrafamilial activities in Muslim societies are an anachronism in a society that professes to want to develop.[31] Women look to the state for opportunity and benefit in moving away from family control and in laying claim to resources generated by development.

. . . a North African woman of today usually dreams of having a steady, wage-paying job with social security and health and retirement benefits, at a State institution; these women don't look to a man any longer for their survival but to the State. While perhaps not ideal, this is nevertheless a breakthrough, an erosion of tradition.[32]

Forward Looking Strategies, the final document of the Nairobi conference which concluded the U.N. Decade for Women, is filled with recommendations that depend on government for implementation. The Nairobi experience suggests that state action continues to hold considerable allure for serving women's interests in many different societies.

STATES AND GENDER

Feminist analyses of the state must recognize historical variations in order to appreciate the relationship between states and gender. The studies in this book illustrate both the pervasiveness of Western state norms and variations in the way those norms are implemented through specific institutions and policies. To a considerable degree these variations are responsible for the differences in the way women view states. All over the world women confront state-determined bureaucracies, public policies, ideologies, and socioeconomic changes, and the states in which women confront these forces are more or less autonomous with varying capacity to achieve their goals. But to say that a state is relatively autonomous provides as little guidance for comparative purposes as to say that it responds to societal interests (pluralism) or to the dominant class (Marxist). The chapters in this book illustrate the variations in state autonomy and capacity, and the diversity of women's responses to the state. In the conclusion we look at the implications of these variations for our agenda of synthesizing statist, feminist, and development theories.

In general terms, the links between states and gender exist at three levels. The first level is that of the elites who occupy the official positions of the state. The second is that of state action and the intended and unintended consequences of state policies for strategic and practical gender interests. The third and most complex level, yet perhaps ultimately the most critical for women, is the collectivity of norms, laws, ideologies, and patterns of action that shape the meaning of politics and the nature of political discourse. It is at this fundamental level that gender ideologies operate in their most powerful form.

STATE OFFICIALS

Public officials draw on both the inherent and the potential authority of their institutions to formulate and implement policy. Through their activities, these individuals simultaneously seek to strengthen the state and to enhance the power and prestige of the officeholders. They also bring their ideologies, conventional wisdom, and personal material realities to bear on the decision-making process.[33]

Analysts who focus on state officeholders with an eye to gender relations invariably note the absence of women in positions of state power.[34] In fact, women are *never* central to state power. Anthropological and historical accounts that fail to specify women as actors in state formation are not simply suffering from researcher bias. Women do not occupy decision-making roles, institutions, or individual offices in more than insignificant or symbolic terms. This is so universal a fact that more theorists of the state take it for granted rather than try to explain it.

Feminist studies that have been inspired by the dominant pluralist paradigm emphasize the conditions within society that prevent women from achieving positions of prominence within state structures,[35] but precisely because these studies emerge from pluralist assumptions, they tell us little about the gender-based distinctions that are institutionalized and legitimized in the very construction of the state bureaucratic and legal order. And without this kind of gender focus, we cannot effectively discuss whether or how more women in public office affect the fundamental nature and policies of the state.[36] This should be a central issue, for two reasons. First, in some Third World states, educated women are well placed to occupy strategic positions in their state bureaucracies, bureaucracies which may be more open to institutional change than those with much older traditions and patterns of socialization, as found in Western Europe. Second, as the number of educated women grows, so does the insistence that they play a more prominent role in policy making on development issues. Will the integration of substantial numbers of women into state structures as policy makers alter planning in such a way as to include women as equal participants and beneficiaries in the process of development? Might women, in fact, find themselves in a position to redefine the prevailing meaning of development in less destructive directions?

STATE POLICIES AND INSTITUTIONS

State actions provide the clearest link to gender concerns, for here we can see state policies that benefit and disadvantage women, or that benefit some and disadvantage others. Women may be the direct object of state policies, or their interests may be (and typically are) subordinate to goals such as international security or economic growth. Though subordinate to those goals, women's interests are nevertheless significantly affected by their pursuit. For example, the state can promote female employment or female subsistence production as part of a strategy for economic growth, or a growth strategy can completely overlook women's productive roles and even effectively undermine productive activities. The source of contradictory policies for women can be found in the pursuit of goals such as enhancing stability through maintaining female dependency on men in families, while at the same time supporting female education, wage labor, and family planning. The institutionalization of male interests helps us to understand that seemingly irrational policies are not simply temporary aberrations from reason or fairness principles but are historically grounded.

STATE DEFINITION OF POLICIES

States independently affect policies in two ways, Ann Shola Orloff and Theda Skocpol argue. "First, states may be sites of autonomous official action . . . Secondly . . . the organizational structures of states indirectly influence the meanings and methods of politics for all groups in society."[37] The most challenging level of state-gender analysis is the inquiry into the way in which the state defines the very nature and scope of politics.

> States matter not simply because of the goal-oriented activities of state officials. They matter because their organizational configurations, along with their overall patterns of activity, affect political culture, encourage some kinds of group formation and collective political actions (but not others), and make possible the raising of certain political issues (but not others).[38]

The state defines the parameters of politics both through its institutions and through ideology. The state is typically the chief promoter of the accepted political reality; it also fosters certain relations of production that reinforce that reality. Ideology is significant not just because it is dominant, but because it is frequently so pervasive that it passes for the natural order of things. To illustrate, the distinction between a private and a public sphere, with the former female-dominated and the latter male-dominated, may be taken as a reflection of natural biological differences, that is, as a physical inevitability rather than as a *social* construct.[39] But this social construct can have and has had grave consequences for the meaning of states for women. Public-private distinctions which derive from Western political theory and state development have described Third World women as having solely or primarily family concerns. The cruel irony is that these distinctions serve to exclude women from public affairs even as the scope of those affairs broadens. At the same time, the definition of family as private serves to justify the paucity of policies which would provide women greater equity and freedom within the private sphere. Even where the official ideology purports to support practical (and occasionally strategic) gender interests, the family remains officially private insofar as it serves state interests. Especially under conditions of scarce resource economies, the result of this distinction will be a predictable gap between rhetoric, policy, and effect, with a general tendency to argue that development policy is distinct from "family policy."

We need to know more about the particular nature of male power institutionalized in the state, how state power reinforces and legitimizes the economic, political, and sexual subordination of women, and finally, what strategies are open to women to alter this subordination. The research agenda is all the more challenging because women are subordinated in dependency relationships at multiple levels, from the family to international political and economic systems. The state reinforces female subordination, but it may also displace prestate forms of oppression (and thereby be historically liberating), aggravate or elaborate on those forms of oppression, or operate as a channel through which foreign domination occurs. This agenda in turn requires that we give more attention to the nature of state-society linkages, which could help women devise strategies vis-à-vis the state.

Is it possible for state policy and action to reflect female values? Does proactive collective action offer women (and other powerless groups) the opportunity to gain access to the state? Can it challenge not only the composition of the political elite and their policies, but also the prevailing definition of legitimate political activity? Or does collective action by women merely subject them to increased control by male institutions?

CHAPTER OVERVIEW

The selections in this book begin to answer these questions by drawing on several social science disciplines. In some areas we attempt a synthesis; in others we raise questions that challenge theory but leave us open to criticisms. While each author is writing with a particular region or country in mind, she suggests generalizations that are useful for comparison and that we address further in our conclusion.

The dominant state forms in the past several centuries have been those developed in Europe and subsequently exported to most of the rest of the world through colonialism. Charlton, Everett, and Staudt all assume European derived states to be central to their analysis, while Charlton makes the European experience the focus of her narrative. In stressing the European state, Charlton returns to two feminist concerns introduced above: the relationship between the public-private dichotomy and the liberal-democratic state on the one hand, and the debate about the implications of the twentieth century welfare state on the other. She notes that there is an apparent contradiction between the state as benefactor and the state as institutionalization of oppression, but suggests that this contradiction can be resolved by distinguishing between the state as the sum of its structures and ideologies, and the state seen through discrete policies or political acts. Charlton concludes by emphasizing the international importance of European state experiences and discussing some implications of this for women in underdeveloped countries.

There is diversity among both West European and East European states, although common patterns of political institutions, values, and policies will, in turn, introduce common patterns in gender relations. The role of the state in shaping gender relations is immediately evident for the Soviet Union and East European nations, where the state's ideological commitment to gender equality is balanced by the periodic mobilization of women as a source of labor aiding the social, economic, and cultural transformations that accompany development. Sharon Wolchik notes that formal goals of gender equality have produced certain measures that benefit women by serving their "practical gender interests," such as maternity leave. At the same time, the existence of a single, officially approved framework for analyzing gender relations preconditions debate, and state development policies exacerbate tension between women's reproductive and productive roles in society.

Two chapters on Africa approach the question of state power, colonialism, and gender ideology, and illustrate the difficulties in generalizing about these linkages. Kathleen Staudt addresses the primary question of the way in which male power becomes state power. Staudt's particular concern is gender ideology in the colonial state in Africa: colonialism drew the boundaries between public and private spheres in ways that allowed colonial administrators, missionaries and "native authorities" to vest men with control over female labor and sexuality. Her argument does not presume that pre-state societies were egalitarian, but that the new state eliminated earlier options available to women to moderate or escape specific controls by men. Missionaries and colonial officials were extensions of European norms regarding appropriate sexual and marital behavior, male and female productive activities, land tenure, and legal rights. The effect of colonial policy was to create a public sphere administered by men.

Barbara Callaway and Lucy Creevey share with Staudt an interest in the impact of colonialism on indigenous African societies, but they focus on the relationship of Islam, the rule of law, colonial and postcolonial state power, and gender relations in Senegal and Nigeria. Both in Senegal, which is overwhelmingly Muslim, and in Nigeria, where Muslims are a simple, not an absolute, majority, the effect of colonialism was to consolidate the political subordination of women and a public-private split in gender roles that had roots in traditional society and had been reinforced by Islam. Women in pre-Islamic societies were second class citizens; Islamic law exported from rural and paternalistic societies modified some elements of their traditional status but did not overturn it. Both in Senegal and in northern Nigeria, Muslim leaders were part of the system of colonial control and their influence not only persists, but has grown in the postindependence period. A secular state in Senegal initiated some improvements in the status of women from the 1960s to the

1980s, but in Nigeria, political turmoil and ethnic cleavages resulted in a constitutional order that left its states free to determine whether secular or religious law would prevail in matters of vital concern to women, such as family and property rights. At the same time, there are increasing signs that the socioeconomic and political dislocations caused by development encourages anti-Western, pro-Islamic movements which enforce traditional gender norms as part of their nationalism.

Two studies of Latin America explore the changing relationships between gender and the state stemming from the intended and unintended consequences of the state's manipulation of gender ideologies. Susan C. Bourque discusses important points of intersection between research on the state and research on gender. She examines the explicit and implicit theoretical questions raised by recent work in Latin American studies on the origins of sexual subordination, state policies toward women and agriculture, the responses of military regimes to protest, and the conditions created for political participation by military regimes. Bourque argues that a systemic approach to the study of gender and the state should pay attention to four levels of analysis: "The symbolic use of 'gendered' symbols of state authority and their manipulation," the role of state policies in structuring access by gender to control social resources, the role of state policies toward sexuality and its control, and the state's use of competing and intersecting hierarchies of class, gender, and ethnicity or race to achieve social control.

Patricia H. Chuchryk provides a case study of Chile after the 1973 military coup, where we can see the importance of state fostered ideologies promoting motherhood and family life and shaping the very nature of politics. As an ideological precept, "preservation of the family" argues for the maintenance of the family in general, and women in particular, outside of politics. General Pinochet did not invent this image, but his government has used state institutions and policies to reinforce it. Comments Chuchryk: ". . . Pinochet is, in effect, using the state to manipulate women's reproductive roles for its, and his, own purposes and, at the same time, attempting to depoliticize women and situate them outside the realm of that which is traditionally considered political." Yet it is motherhood that motivates women to participate in politics in Chile, as elsewhere in Latin America. Taken together with Everett's and Staudt's case studies, Chuchryk's suggests innovative ways in which women attempt to resist the state, in part by redefining politics. As women in North America and Western Europe have also suggested, private-public distinctions are increasingly irrelevant as the power of the state expands.

Jana Everett's chapter draws on her study of women's organizations in India, and focuses on the ability of collective action strategies to gain access to the state for lower class women. The Western feminist debate about the welfare state is relevant to countries such as India insofar as it raises questions about the way in which poor women can gain resources from different states during different historical periods. The answer to these questions depends, in turn, on the nature of the state. Everett's discussion of the postcolonial Indian state shows that, despite some differences of interpretation, observers see the Indian state as having been consolidated and transformed by the process of economic development. A comparison of urban women's associations and rural grass roots movements sheds light on state-society relations by contrasting strategies designed to increase benefits from the state with those endeavoring to redistribute economic and political power through direct action. Overall, these strategies appear to enhance the potential for state autonomy vis-à-vis the dominant classes. Both reformist and confrontational strategies maximize benefits for women as long as women's organizations maintain an independent base while seeking benefits from state agencies.

The chapters that follow provide generalizations drawing on historical patterns and case studies that illustrate the specific impact of state ideologies, laws, institutions, and policies. The concluding chapter returns to three questions that have guided our thinking about the relationships between development, women, and the state: What roles have states played in the maintenance and/or transformation of gender relations? How have women responded to the imposition and/or expansion of the state? As women respond to state imposition and/or expansion, how do their responses affect their practical and strategic gender interests?

2

FEMALE WELFARE AND POLITICAL EXCLUSION IN WESTERN EUROPEAN STATES

Sue Ellen M. Charlton

The principal forces contributing to the development of the modern state derive from economic and political changes originating in Europe and transmitted throughout the world. Inextricably linked to state development in Europe is the distinction between private and public, a distinction with critical ramifications for women. The distinction has been omnipresent, but not uniform: it has changed as the European societies themselves have changed. What has been consistent is the absence of women from the public realm of politics, or the civic society, and from the state itself as it became more differentiated from society. This is the origin of the dilemma for women that will be explored in this chapter: women may benefit from specific state policies in both industrialized welfare states and also in underdeveloped states, but they are objects or targets of those policies, with little or no say in their formulation and implementation. To change this situation in any fundamental way requires that women, like any disadvantaged group, have access to and influence over that state apparatus which is primarily responsible for devising strategies of economic and social development. But to gain access without transforming the apparatus—as all those who seek basic change acknowledge—is to be coopted, in this case by a political institution whose primary goal is its own maintenance and expansion.

The first section of this chapter reviews the process of European state development by emphasizing those elements that reinforce the asymmetrical nature of political authority between women and men in the contemporary nation-state. The discussion draws on the public-private distinction which is found in Western political theory, both liberal and Marxist. The distinction is particularly significant for women because tradition sees the reality of women, including the reality of their work, as largely constrained to the private sphere. Insofar as the private sphere lies outside the authority of the state (in theory) and historically outside the realm of politics, the female reality of subordination to men and male institutions eludes most theorizing about states. Yet to understand the significance of state development for women in Europe or elsewhere, we need to link it explicitly to the reality of private lives. This linkage becomes more urgent because the policies pursued by most nation-states as part of their development strategy entail expanded control over the national society. Any viable distinction between public and private spheres wanes in practice as the state legitimizes itself as the official embodiment of the civil society, and as its policies penetrate the traditionally private sphere. At the same time, state ideologies maintain the private-public dichotomy and these ideologies continue to justify the myth of women as private creatures having little or no political relevance.

Following an historical overview, the chapter evaluates the impact of the sweeping forces of the nineteenth and twentieth centuries that have molded the administrative and legal order of the state, while reinforcing its claims to legitimacy. Nationalism and capitalism, together with the development of the bureaucratic and military structures of the state, have produced a political hierarchy that occasionally responds to the specific, practical interests of certain classes of women, while remaining antagonistic to the long-term gender interests of women in general.[1] The discussion also looks briefly at the impact of religion on state development, both because religion is historically important in Europe, and because it is central to our understanding of some non-European states in the late twentieth century (such as those of the Middle East). Religion, like capitalism, militarism, and the other forces described, has helped to circumscribe the lives of women in the private and public spheres alike.

The contemporary European states are, to a greater or lesser extent, welfare states, capable of and committed to improving the socioeconomic welfare of their respective citizens. The implications of welfare state development for women are complex, and consequently are vigorously debated by feminists. On the one hand, nineteenth and twentieth century feminists encouraged the establishment and expansion of welfare policies as part of a liberal-democratic agenda of socioeconomic and political reform. Simultaneously, however, the growth and elaboration of the bureaucracies essential to implement these policies strengthened male power in the public sphere and failed to overturn the sources of gender inequality. The fourth section of the chapter looks at the resulting contradiction of the welfare state for women, and the feminist debate about this contradiction.

The chapter concludes with some observations about the significance of European state development for the non-European world, particularly underdeveloped countries. The European experience has not been replicated elsewhere, but its pattern of state development has had an undeniable impact around the globe, directly through colonial control and indirectly through education, ideology, and example. As a result, Third World women share with European women the historical experience of subordination to male-controlled state development, as well as sporadic examples of state support for specific gender interests.

STATE DEVELOPMENT AND THE PUBLIC-PRIVATE DISTINCTION

The public realm is the realm of politics and community beyond the family (the private). The exact meaning, scope, or range of public and private vary with societies and history, but the distinction is central in the Western political tradition.[2] As Jean Bethke Elshtain has argued, in the earliest Western theorizing about politics, the household realm of women was defined as outside of, and excluded from, the realm of *polis*, culture, citizenship, or the larger community.[3] The *polis* was the realm of politics and, as such, inaccessible to women.

The European state developed in response to both internal and external pressures: seen from the vantage point of the state's coercive and legitimizing capacity, in fact, these pressures combined in a kind of creative tension for the growing states. The early kings constructed an administrative and coercive apparatus in order to assert their supremacy over regionally based nobles, and simultaneously they constructed doctrines of legitimacy to sustain the state's right to monopolize large-scale violence.[4] Both the structures and the doctrines of coercion would later be used to maintain the state in the face of revolts by other classes, such as the peasantry. Interstate competition and war were endemic to the relatively small geographic region in which the European states emerged, and the relationship between war and the development of state bureaucracies, both military and civilian, was dynamically symbiotic. The military imperative created and justified new mechanisms of state policy, such as taxation.

Early modern political theorists, particularly Jean Bodin and Niccolò Machiavelli, helped construct the new state edifices, and in doing so reinforced the split between public and private, as politics—what would become the realm of the state—was identified with the use of force. Indeed, the concept of citizenship as it reemerged after the twelfth century in the context of the new states was inseparable from the military act of loyalty and commitment to the state's rulers, with consequence both for our contemporary notions of citizen obligation and for the twentieth century militarization of the state.

> With the twelfth century revival of the works of Aristotle in the West and the rise of civic humanism, a concept of the public-spirited citizen who embodied, in Machiavelli's phrase, civic *virtu*, was revived. But the resurgence of a notion of a political action merged with the notion of an armed citizen within Machiavelli's thought. Women again were excluded from the public state and citizenship for men was militarized. The private world remained; indeed, its importance was enhanced by the exhortation and example of such Protestant reformers as Martin Luther. The gentler virtues of family life, however, were no match for the bold and forbidding doctrine of *raison détat*, which became the paradigmatic political notion of early modern Europe.[5]

It is no coincidence that the linkage between politics and coercion accompanied the rise of the early dynastic states and the efforts

of theorists to justify the authority of these new states in the concept of sovereignty.[6] While there were significant differences between Bodin and Machiavelli, the combined weight of their arguments contributed to the development of a state conceptualized as
purely masculine realm. Machiavelli's insistence on the centrality
of force as virtually the "constituent element"[7] of the state found
echoes centuries later, particularly in continental theorists.[8] Jean
Bodin, in developing the concept of sovereignty, found the essence of
the state in the existence of supreme legal power. For Bodin, of course,
it was the sovereign monarch who benefited from the conjuncture
of territorial control and national independence. While sovereignty
might ultimately shift to the people, the effect of Bodin's sovereignty
was to gird the physical might of the state with legal sanctity.[9]
Bodin, as well as Machiavelli, distinguished between the rules of
conduct appropriate to the public sphere and those of the private
sphere, with the former the sphere of (amoral) politics. Elshtain argues that as this distinction evolved, politics took on a meaning
which, given the prevailing assumptions about female nature, continually excluded women.

> Politics is the realm of public power, the sphere of justice, and
> systems of law . . . Women are not part of politics *per se,* but
> provide, in their capacities in the private sphere, a refuge from
> public life for men when they share in the private sphere. . . .
> Non-politics is a private realm of feeling and sentiment, or
> moral suasion, not subject to laws and not judged by rational
> standards. . . . This realm is not properly part of the public
> sphere but provides a base for it. Women are part of non-politics
> . . . [10]

In the two centuries following Machiavelli's and Bodin's writing, the absolutist system of rule helped transform law from a set of
givens whose validity rested ultimately on the superhuman agency
of the Deity, to an instrument of rule. Simultaneously, the state became increasingly differentiated from the larger society, even as it
was empowered to affect the whole society: the civil society became
an object of rule. Writing of the period of Frederick William II (1713-
1740) and Frederick the Great, Gianfranco Poggi notes:

> . . . the state was intended to operate as the instrument of its
> own enacted laws, thereby making its activities systematized,
> coordinated, predictable, machinelike, and impersonal . . . Pub-

lic law shaped the state as an artificial, organizational entity operating through individuals who in principle were inter-changeable and who in their official duties were expected to employ their certified abilities in stewardlike loyalty to the state and commitment to its interests.[11]

The process of state differentiation occurred at a different pace and under different conditions throughout Europe, a fact which accounts for the variety in state-society linkages found in contemporary European states. In France, for example, the tradition of Roman law strengthened the distinction between public and private institutions, between civil society and the state, and contributed to the consolidation of the absolutist state, whose legacy persists in contemporary *étatisme*. The development of civilian and military bureaucracies enhanced state autonomy in both France and Prussia, while the limitations on bureaucratic growth until the twentieth century in Britain resulted in a state both less autocratic and less autonomous than several of its continental counterparts.[12] However uneven, the creation of a territorial state occurred throughout Europe and these states were, with only an occasional exception such as Switzerland, reinforced and legitimized by nationalistic sentiment in the eighteenth and nineteenth centuries.

By the eighteenth century, women had been excluded not only from the public domain of politics and citizenship (as were all who owned no property), but also from the new institutions designed by the centralizing monarchs to protect external sovereignty and consolidate internal sovereignty and unity. The rise of capitalism and, concomitantly, liberal theories of state and politics, altered the conditions of political discourse and thereby fostered the early Western feminist movements without, however, creating the conditions for the liberation of women from male institutions. As a reaction to the absolutist system of rule, liberal political theories opposed demands for recognition of a public interest that transcended private concerns and also challenged state monopoly of the public realm. The private sphere continued as the nonpolitical domain of individual and family. Society, theoretically outside state control, was the realm of nonstate economic activities resting on the institution of private property, but this society was also civic or public in the sense of being preoccupied with political issues—most notably the issue of controlling the state itself. By raising individuals from a state of passivity as part of an undifferentiated mass, liberal norms linked belief in human rationality to demands for a redefined political role for a reasoning and reasonable public. Here, seemingly, was a theoretical bridge for women to move from the private to the public or civic sphere, insofar as they could argue successfully that they shared with men the human potential for reason. Standing in their way was (only) flawed social tradition, a tradition that was already being eroded in other ways.

The women's movements of the nineteenth and twentieth centuries were successful in generating state responses to some specific demands, such as those for economic protection. In this way, early feminists stimulated the expansion of the bureaucracies that would sustain the twentieth century welfare state. But neither European nor North American feminists succeeded in challenging the public-private split in a way that would provide a permanent basis for female emancipation. Their failure, in turn, was rooted in their inability to challenge the two forces which had come to provide the wealth and the legitimacy of the state: capitalism and nationalism.

LEGITIMACY AND THE CAPITALIST NATION-STATE

The liberal-democratic state that emerged from nineteenth century Europe was also a bourgeois state, not solely because of the existence of private property and a capitalist mode of production, but also because of the unique circumstances characterizing the rise of the European state. The bourgeoisie was the dominant class in opposition to the aristocracy; with the argument that the public interest could be both served and institutionalized through mechanisms of representation, the chief currents of opinion in the civil society would be the new constituency of the state. As the bourgeoisie became the dominant class in the civil society with the rise of capitalism, representation both reflected and legitimized this dominance. Thus the contradiction of the nineteenth and twentieth century liberal-democratic state was established:

> A state that purports to be the source of all power relations acts in fact as the guarantor of power relations that do not originate from itself, and that it does not control—those engendered by the institution of private control over capital.[13]

The power relations guaranteed by the capitalist state included those of the family, with the prerogative of the male head in property rights, child custody, and so on, finding sanctity in the laws of the state. As Zillah Eisenstein has argued, patriarchal dominance within the family was replicated on the state level, without being identified as such. As the state formalized male rule through laws and other institutions, its ideology characterized the private realm as that of family, female nature, and children, and as therefore outside political life.[14] The origins of patriarchal dominance on the state level, of course, predate the rise of capitalism, and noncapitalist states are also patriarchal.[15] What is distinctive about Europe is that capitalism emerged with the modern state, was encouraged by the policies and laws of the state, and the state in turn came to serve the interests of the dominant capitalist class.[16] For some early modern theorists, such as John Locke, the preservation of property was pivotal to the definition of politics because property was the chief motive for the formation of civil society. How, then, given the patriarchal tradition of European history and the new justification of state and civil society, could women emerge "simply by a grant of formal rights, from a condition of propertylessness and subjection to one of public parity?"[17]

As women moved into the industralized workplace, they occupied the lowest echelons of the labor hierarchy, in part because prevailing norms labelled their nonhousehold work as a temporary aberration. In view of the fact that women were defined as private beings, their public labor was insufficient to legitimize an enduring civic presence for the growing female proletariat. Even the new channels of political participation, such as trade unions and political parties, responded to gender issues only marginally, if at all. Meanwhile, with the growing commodification of human labor, unpaid household work lost the recognition it had in precapitalist society. Since the feminists of the nineteenth and early twentieth centuries came predominantly from the bourgeoisie, they were ill-equipped to analyze or challenge the legitimacy of a state that purported to be distinct from society. They largely accepted the prevailing wisdom that politics and economics were inherently separate and so underestimated the economic sources of female subordination in both the private and public spheres.

Politically articulate women were ill-disposed to challenge the state for another reason: since the late eighteenth century, European states had begun tapping deep human emotions of loyalty and identity, as states around the world continue to do in the late twentieth century. Nationalism has served to galvanize the antagonistic classes of the capitalist states against an external enemy.[18] Historically, nationalist ideologies have both generated demands for strong states and been the products of state development: ". . . national feeling was a weapon in the hands of those who actually held power and, by skillfully using it, laid the foundations of the modern state."[19] Nationalist movements throughout the world have sought to create, defend or expand the nation-state.[20] Once a nation-state has been created, its unity must be continually defended from external and internal threats: the predations of neighboring states, the centrifugal forces of ethnic groups, or the physical challenges of revolutionaries.

The process of identifying and defending the nation-state has always been dynamic and can never be viewed as complete because neither the international nor the domestic situation is static. The state, in fact, stands at the junction of these domestic and international forces, and because its ability to influence the external environment is often limited, the necessity to devise effective internal strategies for economic and social control is all the more pressing. This control, in turn, is both physical and ideological. The physical mechanisms of control vary from one nation-state to another, as do the contents of nationalist ideologies. In advanced capitalist states, ideology tends to be more important than coercion in maintaining social control,[21] but where the legitimacy of the nation-state is less widely accepted, coercion is concomitantly more important. Everywhere, though, economic development policy enhances control and serves to validate claims to national legitimacy.

Educated Third World women, like men, tend to view the nation-state with the same optimism and enthusiasm that nineteenth century liberal nationalists did: the nation-state is the ideal political form for the development of distinctive cultures and modern economies.[22] As Kathleen Staudt points out, even contemporary feminists, whether socialist or liberal, accept the nation-state as a given, and this acceptance makes it more difficult to question the separation of the public and private.[23] The growth of the public-private split is linked historically to the development of the state and one of the chief effects of nationalism is to legitimize the expansion of state policy into areas formerly regarded as private. However, the chief concerns of women are not redefined as political (or civil),[24] so the combined force of state authority and nationalist legitimacy increases public demands on presumably private women without providing the real liberation promised by both nineteenth and twentieth century nationalist politicians.

In Europe, nationalism supplanted religion as the primary source of legitimacy for political authority. Although the state gradually defined itself in opposition to the medieval church, there are nonetheless modern examples of close ties between secular and religious authority, with the church performing legitimizing functions (as in Franco's Spain). More typically, however, the Catholic church, and occasionally Protestant churches, play more circumscribed roles, deploying their influence on specific public policy questions. Church influence is strongest on questions related to the family, and it is no coincidence that this influence works to restrict women, particularly in matters of divorce, contraception, and abortion.[25]

There is an inherent contradiction between the private-public distinction of the modern (secular) state and the universalistic claims of religion, particularly proselytizing and easily politicized religions such as Christianity and Islam. Thus it is not surprising that a reassertive Islam in the Middle East seeks a rejection of a secularized (read: Western) state, and religion and nationalism serve to reinforce each other.[26] Private and public are refused in the ideal as well as in reality, yet it would be hard to argue that women are advantaged by this fusion. In Pakistan and Iran, for example, the policies implemented pursuant to *Sharia*, the heart of which is family law, appear to have disadvantaged women by removing certain kinds of legal protections and by reinforcing the traditionally subordinate role of women in the family.[27] In effect, women are further confined to the private sphere even though politicized religion has the effect of destroying any meaningful distinction between private and public. Family, religious, and state patriarchies are mutually sustaining and reinforcing.

COERCION AND ORDER IN THE NATION-STATE

The relationship between bureaucracy, state, and society varies across time and space; but no state is conceivable today without a bureaucratic infrastructure, and the growth of the bureaucracy is intrinsic to the development of the modern state, even though bureaucracies themselves are not uniquely modern.[28] Bureaucrats, the officials who staff the state, are less than the sum of the structures and ideologies that compose the state, yet are essential to it. Arguments that bureaucrats compete for influence within the state with other social groups[29] underplay the special claims bureaucrats have to represent the state. Bureaucrats not only administer state policies, but in their individual and collective status they represent and extend the state's legal authority, contributing both to its specialization and legitimization. Differences in the characteristics

of bureaucracies and bureaucracy-state relationships reflect historical variations in state development, civil society, and what Metin
Heper calls the "constitutive system" (political system, minus ruler
and bureaucracy).[30] Such differences also account for the relative autonomy of the state as it varies from one historical case to another.
The modern bureaucracy, even in underdeveloped countries, works
to develop state autonomy while also serving as transmission belt
for particularized interests from the larger civil society.[31] Bureaucrats
serve this autonomy by presenting themselves as uniquely capable
of representing the common interests of the nation-state and its
population.[32] But in fact, bureaucrats—or public administrators—do
not serve the interests of the society; they serve the interests of the
state as distinct from society:

> Public administration is therefore inextricably linked to state
> power. To say that administrators are politically neutral is
> naive. To be neutral with respect to a party or an interest group
> is perfectly reasonable . . . but for the administrator to be neu-
> tral about state power as such is a contradiction in terms. For
> the essential politics of the administrator is the survival, pro-
> longation, and strengthening of the apparatus.[33]

Economic and social policies designed to modernize a nation-
state may indeed serve the specific interests of some groups within
the larger society. First and foremost, however, they serve the interests of the state by expanding the state apparatus. Tax collectors,
extension agents, family planning personnel, teachers, customs
agents, regional development experts, and so on, are public employees, meaning employees of the state. The fact that the state stands
at the juncture of the domestic society/economy and the international system means that there are dual incentives for state authorities to maximize the leverage of the state apparatus.[34]

This bureaucratic phenomenon,[35] both in its historical development and in its contemporary attributes, has had generally
negative consequences for women as a whole, apart from particular
advantages conferred on individuals or groups. The disadvantages result from several interrelated factors. Bureaucratization lies at the
heart of the growing specialization of states in both industrialized
and underdeveloped countries, and this specialization has reinforced
the distinction between the institutions, norms, language, and
rhythms of public and private life. What is true in economic life is
also true in political life: confronted with activities of increasing

size and scope, states have sought to rationalize and routinize roles and activities. "New patterns of bureaucratic intervention developed [in Europe] as officials perceived new problems and new personal opportunities and tried to create ways of collecting information and of handling large, complex tasks."[36] Or in the earlier words of Weber:

> Bureaucratization offers above all the optimum possibility for carrying through the principle of specializing functions according to purely objective considerations. Individual performances are allocated to functionaries who have specialized training and who by constant practice increase their expertise. "Objective" discharge of business primarily means a discharge of business according to *calculable* rules and "without regard for persons" . . . The more complicated and specialized modern culture becomes, the more its external supporting apparatus demands the personally detached and strictly objective *expert*, in lieu of the lord of older social structures who was moved by personal sympathy and favor, by grace and gratitude.[37]

The process of specialization has created a world far from the traditional reality of the household. In underdeveloped societies, the values and habits of the bureaucratized state have little meaning for women, particularly in rural areas: role specialization, economic rationalization, analytical thinking, respect for expertise, efficiency—these may be qualities Westerners largely take for granted, but they are only gradually penetrating many parts of the world. Whether they are intrinsically desirable qualities is debatable; certainly their combined effect has been to alienate women further from economic and political power.

Recognition of this alienation has placed bureaucratization on the feminist agenda in those countries where it has proceeded the furthest—in Western Europe, North America, and Australia, for example. For some, any critique of the modern state must highlight above all the way in which contemporary life reflects the values of bureaucratic order: discipline, linear thought, preoccupation with technique, hierarchy—what Kathy E. Ferguson calls the "bureaucratic discourse."[38] Bureaucratic discourse connects the institutions of bureaucracies and the linguistic justification of these institutions:

> The term "bureaucratization" refers to the invasion of disciplinary technique into both the discursive and the institutional practices of a particular realm of human relations (for example,

production, education, medicine), reshaping both the roles and events available to people, and the language commonly used to describe those roles and events, along bureaucratic lines.[39]

Historically, bureaucracy has contributed both to the distinction between private and public as the realms of work and family became segregated with the expansion of capitalism in the nineteenth century, and more recently to the penetration of private life through consumer advertising, standardization of leisure activities and the like.[40]

Even a position that is less critical of the state and bureaucracies, such as that characterizing liberal democratic feminism, must raise the questions of access and representation. The size and complexity of the bureaucracy renders it largely inaccessible to women because they lack the overall political legitimacy in the civil society or in the dominant political organizations that would permit them as a class or group to insert themselves into the state apparatus, or as individuals (in large numbers) to enjoy profitable careers in the upper echelons of bureaucracy. Without the physical presence of women, state policies will reflect gender concerns only in marginal or short-term fashion. Even though individual women come to represent public affairs in their activities, those activities are insufficient to challenge either the bureaucratic discourse or the fundamental content and priorities of state policies. Strategic, long-term gender interests, defined effectively as private, will always be secondary to the (male) interests of the state.

Bureaucratization of the European state is historically inseparable from the process of state development and, as noted earlier, so are nationalism and militarism. From their inception, states justified and sustained themselves by the mechanisms of war, and with the growth of nationalist conviction, patriotic sentiment was infused with military commitment. Whereas state exigencies provided the coercive order for war-making, nationalism supplied the moral and ethical imperative. There had always been war, but now the war system was integral to the nation-state system. The expansion of the nation-state system beyond Europe similarly occurred largely through military means: even those former colonies that became independent without war felt compelled to establish military institutions that would sustain their independence in a competitive, often hostile, international system. The consequence is the familiar phenomenon of the militarization[41] of politics at both the national and the international levels: the escalation of military expenditures, the glorification of the martial spirit as part of nationalism, the widespread participation of military officers in state affairs on every continent, and so on. The contemporary nation-state, at the conjuncture of international competition and the need to reinforce domestic legitimacy and order, reflects all of these trends.

Militarization, like bureaucratization, affects women negatively both directly and indirectly. As a number of political scientists have stressed, militarization is inseparable from the Western definition of politics.

> War, and the masculine role of warrior-hero, have been central to the conceptualization of politics for the last 2500 years. Moreover, the political community constructed by the ancient warrior-heroes and carried down to us in the writing of political philosophers bears uncomfortable resemblance to a particular type of male community—one whose most extreme form is represented by the military barracks of Sparta, where the male citizens lived well into adulthood. In this community, military capacity, civil personality, and manhood were coterminous.[42]

The consequence of the historical association between politics and military virtue or manhood has been to reinforce the public-private split and to disassociate women from legitimate claims in the public sphere even as, ironically, militarization (like bureaucratization) progressively intrudes on the realm of family and household

Ultimately, the indirect impact of militarization on women takes three forms: it operates through state policies and institutions, state officials, and the definition of politics. The first two are mutually reinforcing in an immediate sense: the impact of military expenditures on the distribution of resources and the setting of social and economic priorities, and the preeminence of military personnel in formulating and executing public policy.[43] The third is related to the other two, but it also has roots in patriarchal societies that have few overt signs of militarism: it is the militarization of culture, a process that places a premium on the hierarchical ordering of personal relationships, sexual exploitation of women, structured or condoned violence, and chauvinism. The militarization of culture reflects a more generally militarized society, a condition stressed fifty years ago by Virginia Woolf when she dissected the links between culture, social institutions, and war, and concluded that business, law, politics, science, and academe were all male institutions, following a military prototype.[44] More recently, Betty Reardon has argued that militarism and sexism are mutually interdependent and reinforcing systems of control as they both reflect partiarchal norms: "The military . . . is the distilled embodiment of patriarchy; the militarization of society is the unchecked manifestation of patriarchy as the *overt* and *explicit* mode of governance."[45]

Militarism has affected women directly through domestic repression, civil strife, and war. The direct participation of women in military institutions and activities constitutes a different kind of link, one which some see as an avenue to be followed by women seeking equitable access to power in the modern state. It has been argued, for example, that the historical nonparticipation of women in military forces has contributed to persistent second class status and delayed the extension of full citizenship rights to women.[46] Historically, this is probably true, for had women participated in wars as men did, their roles in public life would have been undeniable and hence their citizenship attested to. Where military force is an instrument of national liberation or revolution today, women may well share the view of soldiering as the route to citizenship. Here is a Zimbabwean woman speaking to this point in an interview:

> Before, women were not allowed to take a leading role in the community; women were not allowed to speak out publicly; the roles of men and women were clearly defined and the roles of women were subservient. What the struggle has done is that individuals are measured by their effectiveness, by their ability to perform, so that women, a lot of women, have performed very, very well.[47]

The difficulty with this position is that we have virtually no historical examples of states where female participation in armed struggle has permanently reordered a patriarchal hierarchy and eliminated the subordination of women. More frequently, the new order has gradually displaced women from their public roles and the military becomes part of the coercive apparatus of the state. For women in advanced industrialized states, either capitalist or socialist, it seems futile to imagine that female participation in the military might fundamentally alter the system of gender inequality and exploitation in these states or contribute to the demilitarization of politics domestically and internationally.

It is the growing recognition of the interrelationship of the forces that characterize the modern state, plus the realization that gender inequality persists even under conditions of governmental benevolence and improved standards of living that has produced the debate about the implications of the welfare state for women. This issue is addressed in the next section of the chapter.

BENEVOLENCE AND INEQUALITY IN THE WELFARE STATE

The debate about the impact of the welfare state[48] on women is still in its early stages. The timing of the debate reflects the conjuncture of several political forces, including democratic socialism, feminism, and neo-conservatism (liberalism) and is meaningful only in the context of the development of the welfare state in Western industrialized, capitalist nations over the past fifty years. Periodic economic crises, which invariably exact a higher toll (notably in terms of employment) from the young, ethnic, and racial minorities, and particularly women, exacerbate the debate. Many of the questions now raised by feminists about the welfare state go far beyond particular policies to open up an examination of the state itself, as well as to explore the basic sources of gender inequality, the centrality of the family to socioeconomic life, and the efficacy of political participation for women.

The following typology, although oversimplifying positions, presents the central arguments in the debate and illustrates some alternative perspectives present in feminist theory.

Feminist Tradition[49]	*Prostate*	*Antistate*
Liberal Democratic	State guarantees equal opportunity; eliminates discriminatory policies and laws.	State policies constitute excessive intervention in private sphere; need to restore and redefine meaning of family and private life.
Socialist	State leads transformation of society in direction of socialist equality; makes available individual and class socioeconomic benefits.	Welfare policies sustain and reinforce capitalism, and only marginally affect class and gender inequality.
Radical	State protects women in individual cases; fusion of public and private presents new political opportunities for women.	State replicates and forces family patriarchy in the public sphere; state institutions and ideology are male.

One could legitimately argue that some of the suggested positions are more hypothetical or potential than real, or that they do not reflect truly feminist responses. For example, the criticisms made by so-called neo-conservatives (North America) and new liberals (Western Europe) of the welfare state, and some of their policy demands (such as for regulation of pornography) may coincide with feminist concerns but derive from fundamentally different assumptions. Given the diversity of Western feminism, however, it is premature to discard such antistate positions as irrelevant to feminist study of the state. Similarly, "prostate" positions among radical and socialist feminists must be seen as largely conditional on changes in the nature of the state. The following discussion elaborates on the typology, providing some illustrations from recent analysis of the relationship between the state and gender inequality.

At the outset, it should be noted that feminists of virtually every stripe accept certain elements of welfare state policy on the assumption that the immediate transformation or elimination of what virtually all agree is a highly bureaucratized institution is improbable. Thus Kathy Ferguson, whose positions bear testimony to the anarchist tradition in Western political thought, nonetheless argues:

> Many of the most visible and tangible feminist victories have evoked the apparatus of the state to make good on liberal promises of liberty and equality. Liberal-inspired battles for equal opportunity and affirmative action are important for improving the life chances of individual women, and legal reforms in the area of reproductive freedom are crucial for the same reason . . . Entry into the public world, now almost exclusively a bureaucratic world, is necessary to some extent, if for no other reason than to be able to speak against it . . .[50]

The essential differences in the three feminist traditions in the typology derive from divergent assumptions about the origins of gender inequality and consequently the strategies proposed for overcoming it. Insofar as the primary sources of inequality are located outside the family or household realm—either in laws and political institutions or in economic class structures—feminist strategies will typically target changes in the public sphere: legal and institutional reform for liberal democrats, class struggle and worker organizations for socialists. While not eschewing any of these strategies, radical feminists are more likely to give priority to issues of sexuality and to link gender inequality in the private and public spheres. In general, their attitude toward the welfare state is more inclined to be one of ambivalence or hostility, because the central assumption for radical feminists is that the state replicates in the public realm the patriarchal exploitation that is found in the private sphere of family and household. Because the welfare state constitutes simply a twentieth century successor to the nineteenth century bourgeois democratic and patriarchal state, it is argued, its inherent institutionalization of gender inequality has not changed. The institutions and the legitimacy of the state rely on the distinction between private and public. The definitions of the two domains, as well as the policies maintaining the distinction between them are the product of male power and ideology. The state, therefore, is inherently male in gender, and welfare policies replicate this gender construct by biasing men over women, some women over others, and some social institutions (such as marriage and two-parent families) over others.

Nowhere is this bias more evident than in the case of violence against women. Because the laws and ideology of the state are male in origin and substance, domestic violence and rape can be seen only from a generalized male point of view.[51] If a female point of view is occasionally evident, it is not for reasons inherent to the changing nature of the welfare state itself, but rather it is the result of persistent feminist protest. The expanding resources of the welfare state have made it easier to respond to individual cases of male violence than in underdeveloped countries such as India, where violence against women is as widespread; but these resources do not and cannot alter the socioeconomic, political, and psychological conditions that both permit and encourage male violence. Until very recently, for example, domestic violence was viewed exclusively as a private matter and as therefore inappropriate for state intervention.

> That the state can be treated as irrelevant to an understanding of domestic violence is a measure of the power of men to define social reality. . . . The state represents the interests of the dominant group, i.e., men, in confrontations with the subordinate group, i.e. women. Thus it is consistent that in domestic disputes the status of the victim determines the response of that section of the state given the task of controlling violence.[52]

For the same reasons, streets are generally unsafe for women at night, and women do not have entry to public spaces on the same basis as men.

The radical perspective also maintains that the state serves its own interests through policies designed to perpetuate private institutions that by their very nature embody gender inequality: marriage and the family.

> . . . in supporting marriage the state supports a particular, exploitative relationship between men and women in which the wife provides unpaid domestic and sexual services, childbearing and rearing, and wage-earning and contribution to the household income when convenient . . . supposedly in exchange for protection, assured upkeep and some rights to children.[53]

On the issue of marriage and the family, while there are significant differences among radical and socialist feminists on the origin and basic dynamics of family relations, as well as on what might constitute an ideal family, there is a large measure of agreement on the purpose of state policy in terms of maintaining an institution which is typically exploitative in gender terms. Socialist feminists who draw on the Marxist tradition for their analytical categories tend to stress the function of the family in reproducing the labor force essential for maintaining a capitalist mode of production.[54] Beyond this, both the ideology and the social policies of the welfare state serve to perpetuate the fundamental class divisions in society, as well as gender inequality both within the household and also within the public realm. Jennifer Schirmer, drawing on her study of the Danish welfare state, argues that there is inherent contradiction between the social democratic doctrine of egalitarianism and the meritocratic standards of success and self-help which perpetuate a productive system that assumes differential worth of human beings. The assumption of differential worth combined with state policies that reinforce gender roles means that gender relations remain intact. The pervasiveness of laws and policies proclaiming the *intent* of welfare replaces the reality of egalitarianism. The expansion of the state, both in response to social democratic reform and as a concomitant development to increasing corporatism,[55] results in the situation of "incorporatism" which Schirmer sees as the process whereby the state comes to envelop the public-private interactions of everyday life.

> . . . *incorporatism* is a means by which the state both depoliticizes and defines demands and participation. It is difficult

to tell where the state begins and where it ends; that is its nature. It is in fact this *invisibility* or inarticulation which may be precisely the function of the corporate state: to make it appear something it is not; to appear to be concerned with equality, for example, when in fact its priorities lie in sanctioning the power of capital, at whatever cost. . . . It is a form of institutional discrimination that presents women with a double impediment: of having to prove that the market *as well as the state* hinder their attainment of equality.[56]

What is notable about Schirmer's analysis is the tracing of the way in which social welfare measures serve to coopt potential opposition to the state and to further legitimize the state itself by incorporating state influence into private areas of human activity: ". . . its *incorporatism* into women's daily lives makes the state *appear* to be concerned with equality, when in fact its priorities lie in . . . improving the position of women and maintaining them in cosmetically altered, traditional gender roles."[57]

Central to the welfare state's ideology is the assumption of female social and economic dependency, so that state policies are designed to facilitate the dual household and labor force roles that women increasingly undertake, rather than altering the traditional division of labor either at home or in the workplace. In Britain, for example, minimum wage and social security provisions, public housing policies, and supplementary social assistance (such as for daycare) historically bias the "traditional" family of two or three children, father (head of household) working outside the household, mother at home.

> . . . the Welfare State has always been closely connected with the development of the family and has acted to reinforce and support it in significant ways. This it has done by offering various forms of service, both in money and in kind, and also by means of forms of social control and ideology. Thus the Welfare State is not just a set of services, it is also a set of ideas about society, about the family, and—not least important—about women . . . social policy is simply one aspect of the capitalist state . . .[58]

Despite this critique, socialist feminists—like radical feminists—often accept the welfare state not just as currently inevitable but as desirable insofar as its policies ameliorate working conditions, improve standards of living, and provide needed protection for individual women (as in instances of rape). Some go further and argue that the erosion of the public-private distinction under the welfare state provides new opportunities and incentives for women to organize politically and makes social policy part of the controversy over the legitimacy of the state itself.[59] Thus women benefit potentially not only from specific state policies, but may also take advantage of the altered state-society relationship by arguing, in effect, that the private sphere has lost its traditional meaning and so, therefore, have traditional definitions of women's interests, goals and priorities. As Christine Delphy points out (speaking particularly of France), to refuse political action designed to influence state policies leaves the civil society all the more vulnerable to state penetration: "We don't want to be marginalized any more. . . . We don't want to cry in the desert any more . . ."[60]

Delphy rightly stresses the necessary link between the debate on the nature of the state and the debate on the utility of alternative political strategies. Precisely because welfare states have traditions of civil rights, parliamentary democracy, and competitive political parties, liberal democratic feminists, in particular, argue in favor of recognizing the unique *political* advantages available to women in the Western state. Political reforms have undeniably produced major changes in the legal status of women, and twentieth century socioeconomic reforms have protected and benefited women, as well as men and children. The debate among liberal democratic feminists is not about the historical desirability of these reforms; it focuses, rather, on specific policies which should now be pursued in order to eliminate violence against women, sustain female employment and improve pay conditions, and enhance social services available to families, especially where the mother is also working outside the household. Thus the expansion of daycare facilities or (in the United States) pay for "comparable worth" are typical issues on the feminist agenda. At the same time, however, many liberal democratic feminists are increasingly suspicious about the continued extension of state influence in general and the consequent erosion of the distinction between private and public—in part precisely because this threatens the integrity of the family. Welfare state policies are often contradictory or have unintended effects.[61] Moreover, the cumulative effect of the expanding state and the transformation of private into public is to submerge or distort the distinctive (positive) attributes of women. For Elshtain, the contradictions are intrinsic to the development of the state pursuant to nineteenth century liberal

democratic political theories because liberalism did not acknowledge or value the specifically female bases of women's identity:
". . . woman's 'reason' as a public presence couldn't give voice to the
private, social bases of female identity, couldn't allow woman's experience to 'speak to' the public realm."[62] For John Stuart Mill, who
epitomized nineteenth century liberal logic in his *On the Subjection of Women*, this weakness lay in his inability to understand or
accept the psychically bisexual nature of all human beings.[63] Contemporary liberal feminists similarly err by depoliticizing the public
sphere in their talk of roles and functions, which in effect—to take
Elshstain's most telling example—reduces mothering to a role:
"Mothering is *not* a 'role'....Mothering is a complicated, rich, ambivalent, vexing, joyous activity which is biological, natural, social,
symbolic, and emotional."[64]

Economic difficulties, particularly unemployment and persistent budgetary deficits, have increasingly come to dominate political
debates in welfare states over the past fifteen years, and it is clear
that feminist discussion of the nature and policies of the state has
been stimulated by these debates.[65] Political shifts toward self-conscious articulation of conservative/liberal ideologies—in Britain
under Thatcher, the United States under Reagan, Canada under Mul-
roney, or France under Chirac—did not fundamentally undermine
the welfare state. The shifts do, however, challenge feminist assumptions about the resilience of welfare policies and have encouraged
some feminists otherwise inclined to attack the welfare state to rush
to its defense in order to preserve what are viewed as the still significant gains of liberal-democratic capitalism.

CONCLUSION

In view of the unique conditions of the evolution of the Western state, it is logical to wonder how relevant this experience is
for women elsewhere in the world. In fact, however, nation-states
throughout the world have been deeply influenced by Western norms
and practices, including the tradition of appealing to the state for
protection of weak classes and groups. Moreover, the emphasis
which virtually all Third World states now accord to policies of social and economic development suggest that some of the most important effects of state development for Third World women may re-
semble those for Western women even though the pattern of state
development itself it not ruly replicable.

The story of state development throughout the world is the story of elite efforts to maintain and enhance sovereignty in competition with other states. It is also the story of expanding state control over society, with development policies—particularly those of economic modernization—serving as both rationale and as a means of enhanced control. The pattern was set in Western Europe, where the pattern was also set for the distinction between public (political) and private (nonpolitical) spheres. Confined in theory and in practice to the private sphere, the experience of women is largely absent from the story of creating and strengthening the apparatus of the state. Without a legitimate presence in the civil society, women have had no effective base for altering the course of state development. The public-private distinction, while it provides the historic rationale for the exclusion of women from public affairs, is nonetheless increasingly a distortion of reality in welfare states because it obscures the impact which the state, in policy and in ideology, has on women's reproductive and productive activities. The distinction also obscures the support which those activities provide both for the state and for the dominant mode of production.

States depend on authority and coercion for their survival, and both authority and coercion have been enhanced by twentieth century trends of militarism, nationalism, and bureaucratism, with religion adding legitimacy in some instances. Within these broader trends, development policies serve to strengthen the state in several ways. In the most direct sense, they are generally designed to overcome conditions of underdevelopment and the powerlessness that accompanies underdeveloped nation-states in the international system. The policies also directly enhance the administrative appartus of the state—the bureaucracy that takes the lead in designing and implementing policies of economic and social development. And, finally, *insofar as they are successful*, they reinforce the authority and legitimacy of the state. It is this last relationship between development policy and state legitimacy, that offers the greatest potential for bringing women into full citizenship while also altering the nature of politics.

State development has contradictory implications for women. Liberal feminists in Western countries since the nineteenth century have called on the state for protection and for expansion of civil rights for women. The welfare state has generally replaced the family as the chief provider of health care, education, and other services formerly supplied largely by women. Lagging behind has been child care, however, so that women are still almost wholly responsible for social reproduction. What women have gained through specific state policies (policies that have altered the state in turn) they have lost by virtue of the expansion of the state, especially into areas such as sexuality and procreation. Recognition of this fact lies at the heart of antistate feminist critiques. In resource poor states, though, women cannot hope to benefit from liberal feminism in the same manner as Westerners, at least for the forseeable future. The shortage of resources in most Third World countries means that given the prevailing definition of development priorities, women can hope to benefit only marginally from state initiatives. And where it serves the larger (as defined by the state) interests of economic and social development, or where the state itself seems threatened, women's interests simply evaporate from the picture.

The state's commitment to development, nonetheless, does provide a potential wedge for mobilizing women, enhancing female access to the state, and ultimately, transforming politics. States have considerable internal autonomy, but their ability to maintain this autonomy depends on their authority and legitimacy, their ability to sink roots and to reflect forces within society. In underdeveloped states where both state development and class relations are still in flux, there may be more opportunity to build coalitions that depend for their success on mobilizing women. This means asserting the political in the face of the bureaucratic, and also in the midst of the bureaucratic—that is recognizing that command and control from the top in bureaucracies is imperfect and exploiting that imperfection. Strategies for mobilizing women cannot afford to ignore the potential for structural change by altering law, ideology, and the apparatus of the state, for only this offers the possibility of altering state development policies themselves and thereby forcing the state to respond to strategic gender interests. Since I am assuming that development policy contributes to the legitimacy of the state, women must advance the argument that development over which they have no influence is illegitimate, thus raising the question of the fundamental legitimacy of the apparatus that spawned it.

WOMEN AND THE STATE IN EASTERN EUROPE AND THE SOVIET UNION

Sharon Wolchik

In the Soviet Union and Eastern Europe, as elsewhere, women's lives and opportunities have been profoundly influenced by the organization of political power, political values, and policies associated with the state. The impact of these factors has been mediated by the diversity of patterns of social and family organization, popular values (including religious, national, and political traditions, as well as attitudes concerning gender relations), levels of economic development, and other aspects of precommunist conditions. However, although diversity along these dimensions, which predates the communist period, continues to be evident and is reflected by variation in women's roles in individual countries and in rural and urban areas within particular countries, the pattern of change in women's roles is similar throughout the region. There are also many commonalities in the underlying pattern of gender relations assumed or fostered by the state. These similarities, and the ways in which women's status in these countries differs from that of women in other Western, relatively developed countries, reflect to a large degree the impact of a common pattern of political organization, political values, and policy priorities.[1]

The role of the state in shaping gender relations is more immediately evident in the Soviet Union and Eastern Europe than in many other countries. In part, this results from the fact that the political leadership adheres to an ideology that explicitly supports women's equality. But it also reflects the fact that the state has assumed direct responsibility for areas of life, including the economy, culture, social and family life, and leisure, which are traditionally thought to be outside the realm of politics in other political systems. Communist leaders also have affirmed from the very beginning their interest in influencing family relations through the vehicle of family and social policy.

The pages to follow set out some of the distinctive features of the organization of the state and state policies in Eastern Europe and the Soviet Union and explore the impact of these features on gender relations in the region. As they demonstrate, changes in gender relations in the Soviet Union and Eastern Europe have taken place in the context of dramatic political change and efforts to promote large-scale social, economic, and cultural transformation. Men's and women's roles also continue to be influenced by the organization of power as well as by certain unintended consequences of earlier policy initiatives, economic crisis, and, in many cases, either persistent or sporadic political crisis.

THE PRECOMMUNIST LEGACY AND IDEOLOGICAL SUPPORT FOR WOMEN'S EQUALITY

Policy toward women and elite efforts to change gender roles were conditioned in the Soviet Union and Eastern Europe by the legacy of the precommunist period. They also have been influenced to some degree by the support for women's equality found in the official ideology.

Women's roles and gender relations in precommunist Russia and Eastern Europe differed substantially from one country to another and reflected the more general diversity in levels of economic development and urbanization, political organization and heritage, cultural and religious traditions, and forms of family organization and social relations found in the area. There were also signficant differences in urban and rural areas in all countries.[2]

In Russia, the period preceding the Revolution witnessed substantial ferment and discussion of gender relations. Living in the absolutist Tsarist system, which lent the weight of both church and state to bolster men's control over women in the family and society, newly educated women of the intelligentsia joined their brothers in radical political activities in substantial numbers. In debates over the "woman question" and in their personal lives, they protested the circumstances of the majority of Russian women, who remained legally subordinated to their fathers and husbands, as well as to the authoritarian and patriarchal state.[3]

In certain East European countries, including Czechoslovakia and the more urban areas of Poland and Hungary, women's opportunities to receive an education, enter paid employment, and take part in the broader social and political life of their countries were comparable to those of women in the more developed West European countries. Considerable differences persisted in these countries in the lives of rural and urban women, and the ability of women to take advantage of opportunities for education and public activity, as well as their economic status, depended greatly on the socioeconomic status and attitudes of their families. Although gender relations continued to be based on assumed differences in men's and women's natural abilities and callings, the notion of women's rights and the need for some change in gender relations had achieved a certain level of acceptance, if only among the better-educated and better-off segments of the population.[4]

Women's options were far more limited during this period in most areas of the Balkan countries, where religious traditions, general illiteracy, and the influence of the extended family combined to restrict women's activities largely to the family sphere.[5] The situation was most extreme in Albania, where women remained bound in a highly patriarchal, feudal society that granted them virtually no rights as individuals and, in all but the most urban areas of the country, kept them from leaving the privacy of their homes.[6]

In what would become East Germany, women's opportunities to take part in public life or work outside the home were restricted by Nazi ideology (although Nazism's impact on women varied considerably by class), but had been comparable to those of women in the other developed countries of Western Europe in the pre-Nazi period. As the war put increased demands on German industry, work outside the home was presented as part of women's patriotic duty.[7] There were also substantial differences in the opportunities open to women of different classes and in urban and rural areas throughout the region.

The approach political leaders adopted to gender relations was also influenced by Marxism-Leninism's support for women's equality. As numerous analysts have noted,[8] Marx, Engels, Lenin and most other early socialist leaders devoted relatively little attention to women's issues. The flaws in their analyses of gender inequality, including their tendency to subordinate gender issues to class issues and their inadequate appreciation of the importance of reproduction and domestic labor have also been extensively analyzed by Western feminist scholars.[9] Nonetheless, the commitment to women's equality expressed by early Marxist leaders and the Bolsheviks formed the basis of the legal guarantees of equality enshrined in the Soviet and East European constitutions and legal systems. The official analysis of gender relations and the roots of gender inequality also remain firmly based on the analysis of early Marxists, particularly Engels.

As will be discussed in more detail later in this chapter, the impact of the state ideology's commitment to gender equality is to some degree problematic. On the one hand, the existence of a single, officially approved framework for analyzing gender relations restricts debate and discussion to approaches compatible with this framework. In more practical terms, the adoption of gender equality as an official policy goal by the state has preempted much of the work of self-definition of goals and change by men and women themselves and, in some cases, led to rejection of the goal of equality itself.

The differences in women's status noted above and in other conditions during the precommunist period set the stage for later efforts on the part of communist leaders to change women's roles. However, despite continuing diversity in the region and certain features peculiar to particular countries, women's status today is in many respects similar in all of the countries of the region. In addition, the pattern of change in gender roles that has occurred since communist systems were established has been common throughout the region.[10]

In part, these similarities reflect the impact of the official commitment to women's equality discussed above. However, explicit efforts to promote gender equality, although initiated and supported by communist leaders, have had fairly low priority throughout the communist era in all of these countries. Similarly, campaigns to promote gender equality in various areas also have often coincided with efforts to promote other, higher priority goals. As Gail Lapidus has argued in the Soviet case, policies toward women have been determined not so much by an abstract commitment to women's equality (although such a commitment formally exists in these countries) as by larger strategies of economic, political, and social development.[11] At times, policies adopted to pursue these strategies have furthered women's equality. At others, and particularly in certain areas of life, policies adopted primarily to achieve higher priority economic or social goals have had a negative impact on women in these societies. Thus, the similarities in gender relations in the region reflect the fact that, despite the many ways in which the societies they came to rule differed from each other, communist leaders adopted very similar political institutions as well as strategies for economic development and social transformation once they came to power. Many of these similarities also exist in the two countries (Yugoslavia and Albania) that differ most from the Soviet model.

POLITICAL CHANGE AND THE INSTITUTIONAL FRAMEWORK

Efforts to change gender relations in the Soviet Union and Eastern Europe were initiated during a period of radical political change. Soviet, and later, East European leaders, used a number of measures, including social and economic policies as well as institutional changes, to eliminate the power bases of their opponents and reduce the political power of noncommunist groups. They also set up new institutions and political rituals designed to create new allegiances on the part of their populations. As in the policies they adopted in the economic and social spheres, East European leaders borrowed heavily from the Soviet Union and copied many features of the Soviet political institutions which existed at the time. Thus, although there has always been some variation in this respect within the region, and although the way the political systems operate continues to be influenced by the political histories and traditions of the individual countries, the organization of political power in the Soviet Union and the East European countries, with the exception of Yugoslavia, is very similar.

In the Soviet Union and all East European countries including Yugoslavia, the Communist party is the only effective political party, and there is no legal opposition. The party reserves to itself the right to interpret the ideology, set national policy, and control the media. Marxism-Leninism is the official ideology, although the degree to which this belief system influences policymakers or citizens is open to question in many of the countries in the region. Censorship of information also exists in all countries. With the Yugoslav exception, the political systems of all the East European countries are also highly centralized. Finally, in all but the Albanian, Yugoslav, and to a certain degree Romanian, cases, there is a special tie to the Soviet Union that determines the limits of political debate and change in these countries.[12]

By the late 1980s, many aspects of communist state structures and ideologies were being challenged in the Soviet Union and elsewhere in the region, stimulated by Mikhail Gorbachev's efforts to restructure the Soviet economy and change the operation of the political system. Similarly, *glasnost* led to a broadening of debate in many areas of life. However, although the Communist party's monopoly of power and censorship has been contested, this monopoly continues to differentiate communist political systems from others.

The main exception to these regularities occurs in Yugoslavia. Although the Yugoslavs orginally copied Soviet institutions and policies as faithfully as the other East European leaders, since 1948 they have developed an increasingly original brand of socialism that differs considerably in an institutional sense, as well as in the policies adopted, from that found in the other countries in the region. Thus, although the Communist party is still the dominant political force in Yugoslavia and political opposition is officially not allowed, the role of the party (known since 1952 as the League of Communists of Yugoslavia) is quite different from that of the Communist parties in the Soviet Union and the other countries in the region. The political climate also allows much more open and far-ranging debate and discussion. In addition, the Yugoslav political system is decentralized, and the subnational units, particularly the republics, have a good deal of political as well as economic power. This decentralization is also evident in the economic sphere, where workers' self-management exists in the form of workers' councils and enterprise autonomy. A final difference in the political realm is Yugoslavia's nonaligned, independent position in foreign policy.[13]

The degree to which the new state structures and political practices initiated by communist leaders were congruent with precommunist political traditions varied considerably within the region. The clash in values and patterns of participation was greatest in the case of Czechoslovakia, which had a democratic political system in the interwar period and a political culture more supportive of citizen participation than those found elsewhere in the region. In the rest of the region, including the Soviet Union, the new states replaced governments that had been, to one degree or another, authoritarian. Elements of the precommunist political culture continue to have an influence on popular attitudes toward the state and on its operation, however, as illustrated by the differences in the way the political system works in each country.[14]

What does not differ is the extent to which the state was and remains primarily a male preserve. Women played an important role in social, patriotic, national, and charitable organizations in many of these countries in the precommunist period.[15] They were enfranchised in Czechoslovakia, Poland, and Germany in 1919, and, in those countries in which it was legally possible, occasionally served as political leaders. However, in most countries, women's direct role in the exercise of political power was, in practice, quite limited. Women's limited political activism in part reflected the restricted role of all citizens in Tsarist Russia and the fact that, with the exception of Czechoslovakia, the activities of political parties and ordinary citizens were greatly curtailed in the increasingly authoritarian climate between World War I and II in East European states.[16] Popular attitudes concerning women's unfitness for politics and the generally low level of integration of peasants into the larger national political community in many of these countries also limited women's activities in the area.

In the early communist period, communist leaders in the Soviet Union and Eastern Europe tried to overcome this legacy. As part of their efforts to consolidate the new political systems, they attempted to win women's allegiance and urged women to join the party and become involved in politics. As a result, large numbers of women, including peasant and rural women who had had little awareness of the political world, came to take part in the political life of their countries, if only by being exposed to political information or as participants in elite-organized demonstrations and other activities designed to show support for the regime.[17] The personnel changes and political upheaval that accompanied the overthrow of the old state structures in the Soviet Union and Eastern Europe might have been expected to have created new opportunites for women to participate in political leadership as well. However, change in this area has been minimal. In the early communist period, a number of women leaders did in fact emerge in many of these countries. Early women Bolshevik leaders, including Alexandra Kollontai, Inessa Armand, Elena Stasova, Angelica Balabanova, and Nadezhda Krupskaya, had their counterparts in the Eastern European countries, where women such as Maria Švermova in Czechoslovakia, Ana Pauker in Romania, Tsola Draigocheva in Bulgaria, and numerous women partisan leaders in Yugoslavia played an important role in setting up the new regimes and in political life during the period immediately following.[18] As the new political systems were consolidated, however, the direct role of women in the exercise of state power declined. Women continue to play a limited role in the formulation of state politics in these states to this day. Despite their high level of representation in largely symbolic governmental positions, few serve as leaders in the most important political positions, those of the highest ranks of the Communist party.[19]

The features of the communist political systems discussed above structure the policy-making process and determine the options open to women to influence public policy and take part in politics. The dominance of the Communist party means that women, as well as all other citizens, have fewer avenues to participate in politics or become part of the political elite than citizens in democratic political systems. Women who advance to elite positions in these societies are, like their male counterparts, dependent on party backing; given this fact, they appear unlikely to challenge existing views concerning gender roles in a fundamental way or to press women's interests assertively in policy debates. The party's monopoly of power also means that efforts to influence public policy must be channeled through party bodies. Opportunities for political action are somewhat broader in Yugoslavia, but the party remains the most important political arena.

Both the debate on women's conditions and action on women's issues have also been influenced by the fact that these are officially Marxist-Leninist states. Although Marxism-Leninism's commitment to women's equality appears to have been less important than other considerations in determining concrete policy measures that affect women, it does to some extent benefit women, for it has supported certain changes to improve women's status, and it rules out certain policy options that might be considered if they did not so blantantly contradict the ideology. In addition, the fact that there is a single official value system has influenced the terms in which issues related to women, as well as other issues, must be discussed in these societies. In some respects, this framework for discussing women's issues has negative effects for women, for it means that only those solutions, approaches, and analyses compatible with Marxism-Leninism can be considered. And because the ideology does not admit that the interests of social groups will continue to conflict under socialism, and particularly in the past, has tied progress for all groups to the interests of the proletariat as a whole and the advance toward socialism, it typically has not been seen as legitimate to consider the needs of women separately from those of men or of society as a whole. This tendency was reflected in the distrust of feminism and feminist consciousness evident in the early Marxist movements,[20] and is also evident today in debates about women's issues.

Finally, as numerous analysts have noted, the organizational principles of socialist society in Eastern Europe and the Soviet Union mean that women have, in usual political times, very little opportunity to organize independently to define their own interests or to pressure political leaders to take action on issues of concern to them.[21] Women are sometimes able to work through existing groups, including the official women's organizations, to advocate women's interests,[22] but they cannot legally go outside the established structures to set up autonomous groups independent of the political authorities.

Unofficial feminist groups emerged in the Soviet Union, as well as in Poland and Yugoslavia, in the last decade; feminist tendencies have also been evident in East German literature for some time.[23] The number of women involved in these activities, however, has been small in all cases, and mass movements similar to those that appeared in many Western countries have not developed, even in the more relaxed Gorbachev era. With the possible exception of Yugoslavia, where feminist scholars organized as a section of the official sociological association and, in their roles as scholars, journalists, and professionals, publish feminist analyses and draw attention to outstanding inequalities in gender relations,[24] the impact of these groups has been very limited. In the Soviet case the expulsion of several of the most active feminists and continued harassment restrict the activities of those feminists who remain.[25] In Poland and Yugoslavia, where self-identified feminists have been drawn largely from the ranks of younger, well-educated, urban professionals, feminist ideas have found relatively little response among broader groups of women.

STRATEGIES OF ECONOMIC DEVELOPMENT, SOCIAL TRANSFORMATION, AND CULTURAL CHANGE

Gender relations in the Soviet Union and Eastern Europe have also been influenced by the broader strategies of economic development, social transformation, and cultural change adopted by communist leaders. As noted earlier in this chapter, in the early communist period, political leaders attempted to increase women's political awareness and activism. They also, and particularly in the Soviet case, attempted to promote change in popular conceptions of proper roles for men and women and acceptance of a broader definition of possibilities for women to contribute to the new order. But the main emphasis of work among women during this period was related not so much to political as to economic ends, and policies that affected women were determined largely by their relationship to economic goals. This tendency, which became prominent in the Soviet Union in the 1930s, as Stalin consolidated his hold on Soviet society and forced his views concerning the proper way to develop the country on the party, was evident in most of the East European states from the beginning of communist rule.

While there were some variations in individual countries, the basic elements of the development strategy which was adopted were the same throughout the region and included rapid rates of projected growth, a very high rate of investment, and concentration on the development of heavy industry to the neglect of the consumer sector and agriculture. In addition, the plans for economic development also relied on a mass mobilization of all possible labor resources to compensate for scarce capital.[26]

Women were the chief remaining labor reserve and were encouraged to enter paid employment outside the home in all of these countries, although the efforts were less energetic, as well as less effective, in certain countries, such as Poland and Yugoslavia, particularly in the early post-World War II years. As in the Soviet Union, political leaders and activists whose task it was to work among women emphasized the importance of paid employment for women's emancipation and used a variety of financial and moral incentives to encourage women to see themselves as economic producers.[27]

These changes had many positive results for women. Campaigns to eliminate illiteracy and the expansion of educational opportunities opened the way for far greater numbers of women, as well as men, to obtain an education and gain new skills. Similarly, the adoption of ambitious plans for rapid industrialization created a new demand for women workers and employees and undoubtedly helped overcome resistance to women's employment outside the home. In addition, many women, particularly those in rural areas and those in countries that were previously least developed, also experienced improvements in their standards of living. Together with the legal affirmation of women's equality, greater access to education and increased opportunities for paid employment outside the home undoubtedly expanded the range of acceptable roles for women.

There are limits to all of these benefits, however. As in other contexts, modernization in the Soviet Union and Eastern Europe also has had certain costs for women resulting from the destruction of traditional ways of life. In certain areas, industrialization appears to have eliminated some of women's earlier tools of influence without replacing them with forms appropriate to industrial society. Development has also led in many of these countries to the feminization of agriculture, with a corresponding increase in the sexual division of economic functions in rural areas.[28] Equal access to education does not necessarily mean that men and women will end up with the same skills. Nor does mobilization into the labor force automatically lead to equality for women in the area of work (in terms of exercise of power or income), increased influence in politics, or equality in the family. Given the one-sided emphasis on women's economic roles and the lack of change in the division of labor within the home, for many Soviet and East European women entry into paid employment has led not to liberation but, as in other countries, to a double or triple burden.

Much of the continued inequality in men's and women's roles in other areas can be traced to the lack of change in gender roles in the home, which is in turn related to state policies toward the family as well as to broader patterns of cultural and value change. Efforts to promote social and economic change and encourage acceptance of the new political structure were accompanied in the Soviet Union and Eastern Europe by efforts to change values and attitudes. These efforts have, in general, been less successful than the attempt to transform the material aspects of society.[29] As Kenneth Jowitt has noted, the new state leaders did not mount a wholesale attack on all elements of the precommunist value systems.[30] Instead, they selectively sought to change certain values, while retaining or even strengthening others which they felt could be of use in the new order. The elites' approach to women's roles and attitudes toward gender relations was guided by the same principles. Thus, while communist leaders, women's activists, and the mass media sought to encourage acceptance of women's right to an education and employment outside the home and, although to a lesser extent, the notion that women were properly seen as citizens, they did very little to challenge existing patterns of gender relations within the home.

The primary exception to this pattern occurred in the early days of the Soviet state. In the period immediately after the Revolution, numerous policies were enacted to downplay the importance of marriage and the family, and the leadership sanctioned a good deal of experimentation in living arrangements.[31] Efforts to change traditional family roles were particularly great in central Asia, where campaigns to get women to give up the veil, leave their families to get educations, and take part in public meetings were part of a larger attempt to challenge the authority of clan elders and institute the new regime.[32] These efforts were also accompanied by policies designed to provide public substitutes for some of the "unproductive" labor performed by women in the home, including public childcare facilities, communal dining halls and laundries, and cleaning services.[33] Early Soviet leaders also authorized campaigns by women activists and propagandists to encourage men and women to use these facilities, although they committed few public resources to build and expand the facilities required.

With the consolidation of the Stalinist system, policies in regard to the family as well as in the areas of social policy, art, and culture, became more conservative. Rather than being regarded as an outmoded remnant of the old system, the family was now dubbed the main building block of socialist, as well as capitalist, society and policies were implemented to strengthen its role. These measures, which included the institution of fees for divorce and the outlawing of abortion, were supplemented by propaganda campaigns designed to foster family stability.[34] Although the renewed emphasis on the importance of the family was not accompanied by any repudiation of the principle of women's equality, it in fact reinforced unequal gender roles within the family.

In Eastern Europe, where political leaders copied Soviet policies in existence at the time, there was no corresponding period of experimentation in family policy. Following Soviet practice, the family was accepted from the beginning as an essential unit of socialist society. East European leaders did institute certain legal changes that upgraded women's status within the family, in terms of access to divorce as well as to property and inheritance. In addition, they outlawed some of the more abusive practices in this area, such as forced marriage and bride purchase. State authorities also formally recognized women's right to equality in the family as well as in other areas, and affirmed the state's obligation to support women in carrying out their family activities. However, after the enactment of constitutional and legal guarantees, little was actually done in terms of concrete public policies either to support women in these activities or to foster change in the sexual division of labor within the home.

Public propaganda campaigns directed at mobilizing women to enter the labor force emphasized the continued importance of women's maternal functions and the compatibility of women's employment and family life. At the same time that they sought to increase women's confidence in their abilities to take on new roles in the labor force, they also sought to reassure men and women that employment outside the home would not diminish women's special, primarily nurturing, qualities nor induce them to neglect their homes and families.[35] The contribution women made to society by having and raising children was also recognized on symbolic occasions such as International Women's Day. But the actual difficulties women encountered in being both workers and homemakers were seldom acknowledged by political leaders or addressed by public policies.

In the early communist period, leaders of the women's organizations and political leaders gave some attention to the practical problems women workers faced in running their households. As in the Soviet case, however, these efforts were not accompanied by the commitment of adequate state resources. Particularly after the early 1950s, when East European leaders, following the Soviet example, declared that women's equality had been achieved and disbanded the mass women's organizations, women were urged to rely on good organization, will, self-help, and volunteer communal activities to remedy their problems.[36] To the extent that the state played a role in this area, it focused on the provision of public childcare facilities and social welfare policies, such as child allowances and maternity leave, designed to ensure a minimum standard of living and family stability.

In sum, with the exception of the early communist period in the Soviet Union, political leaders in the Soviet Union and Eastern Europe clearly anticipated that women would continue to perform their old roles in the household as well as assuming new roles in the economy and public life. The importance of this assumption, which was reflected in what Lapidus has termed an assimilationist strategy of sex role changes,[37] to the larger strategies of social and economic development that were adopted is difficult to overestimate, for it enabled the new leaders to greatly increase the labor force without a commensurate increase in public expenditures for services or household durables. Their ability to rely on gender differences in the area of domestic labor and on those elements of the precommunist value system that legitimated inequalities in this area as natural and acceptable also allowed communist officials to diffuse the male opposition that might have developed had men been required to share an equal amount of the burden of both working and running a household under the new circumstances.

Gender relations within the family, then, have been affected by the state and state policies in Eastern Europe and the Soviet Union. The outlawing of the most obvious abuses of women in the family, the granting of legal equality in family matters to women, and, perhaps most important, the effects of modernization and urbanization have led, particularly in urban areas, to what Soviet and East European analysts describe as a move away from strictly patriarchal toward more egalitarian relations within the family.[38] Despite these changes, and in contradiction to the support for equality in this area expressed by both men and women in survey research, the actual division of labor within the home remains markedly unequal.[39] Tendencies toward greater egalitarianism within the home have also been counteracted by the policy emphases noted above, which presume that, whatever roles they assume outside the home, women will somehow manage to perform most of the labor done in the home.

PRONATALISM: THE RENEWED IMPORTANCE OF MOTHERHOOD

Policies that affected women and the approach to women's issues that prevailed in the Soviet Union and Eastern Europe through the 1950s were based on the assumption that women would continue to contribute to the building of socialism by bearing and raising children, as well as by working outside the home. But, with few exceptions, women's maternal and domestic roles were not emphasized to any great degree. Beginning in the mid-1960s, however, policymakers in many of these states have increasingly emphasized women's reproductive roles.

Change in the approach to women's roles came about largely as the result of the unintended consequences of earlier state policies. In this area as in others, the strategies of economic development and social transformation adopted have led to a number of unforeseen results.[40] One of these with particular implication for gender relations was the impact of the development strategy on the demographic situation.

Beginning in the early 1960s, many of the East European countries began to experience declines in their birthrates. To some extent, these decreases parallel the pattern that occurred in many Western countries as they became more industrialized. However, in many East European countries, the drop in the rate of natural increase also reflected the particular features of the development strategy chosen, including high rates of investment in heavy industry to the neglect of the consumer sector, housing shortages, the high cost of raising children, and the high employment rates of women in the main childbearing ages.[41] The decline in the birthrate has been of greatest concern to policymakers in Czechoslovakia, Hungary, Romania and the German Democratic Republic, but political leaders in Poland and Bulgaria also have been alarmed by population trends since the 1960s. In the Soviet Union, policymakers have been concerned about regional differences in the birthrate, and, in particular the decline among the European Russian population.[42] Only in Albania, where the rate of natural increase and levels of population growth are still the highest in Europe, despite a marked decrease in the birthrate from the mid-1950s to the late 1970s, are trends different in this respect.[43]

Fearful of potential labor force shortages and other negative results of low birthrates, including aging of the population and, in Czechoslovakia and the Soviet Union, a potential upsetting of the ethnic balance, political leaders in a number of the East European states adopted aggressively pronatalist programs.[44] Pronatalist measures were adopted earlier and more extensively in Eastern Europe than in the Soviet Union, where the regional imbalance in rates of reproduction, as well as more visible opposition to such measures by certain specialists and professionals, led to a reluctance to move definitively in this direction. However, the Soviets have also adopted a number of pronatalist policies in the recent past.[45] Policies to increase the birthrate have been accompanied in many cases by a shift in emphasis in the elites' orientation toward women's roles and issues. With the exception of Albania, where no pronatalist program has been adopted, policies toward women are now determined largely by reference to their relationship to the demographic situation. The earlier emphasis on women's roles as economic resources has thus given way to renewed focus on the importance of women's roles in reproduction.

In many countries, investigation of the causes of the birthrate problem also led to a reopening of discussion, at least at the elite level, of women's issues after over a decade of official silence concerning women's problems. As a result, leaders of the official women's organizations and, occasionally, party leaders, now describe women's situations more accurately and acknowledge remaining inequalities more openly than in the past. Social scientists and other specialists and professionals now also discuss and do research on a broader variety of issues related to women's status and gender inequalities.

In some respects this new orientation has been beneficial for women, for it recognizes the contribution women make to society by bearing and raising children. In those countries in which this recognition has been accompanied by extensions of maternity leave and payments to women who stay home to care for small children, it also has been of help in a more practical sense, for it relieves women who choose to take advantage of such leaves of the need to juggle the competing demands of work and family while their children are infants. However, while these measures may aid certain women in coping with the demands they face in the short run, their impact on women's equality is problematic. Because the effect of extended maternity leave and mothers' allowances is to remove young women from the labor force for several years, such policies reinforce old attitudes about the appropriateness of separate roles for men and women and perpetuate the unequal division of labor within the home. They also reinforce the notion that women are first and foremost mothers and thus impede women's advancement in other areas of life.

The impact of pronatalism is compounded in many of these countries by renewed emphasis on the part of educators and psychologists on the desirability of gender differences in traits and characteristics. Reacting against what they see as an excessive blurring of gender distinctions, Soviet educators in the last decade and a half have begun calling for greater attention to developing nurturing, "feminine" qualities in young girls, and "manly" attributes, such as bravery, stamina, and persistence in little boys.[46] Admonitions to women in advice columns, marriage manuals, and other popular materials to remain "soft" and "tender", as well as the growing, and it appears, officially sanctioned interest in fashion and the other outward trappings of femininity are further manifestations of these attitudes.

POPULAR RESPONSE TO THE STATE'S SPONSORSHIP OF GENDER EQUALITY

To some extent, the impact on women of the uneven pattern of change in gender roles evident in the Soviet Union and East European countries has been similar to that experienced by women in other states. Women's lack of interest in increasing qualifications or accepting leadership positions at work, lower levels of political participation, fatigue, and family stress are some of the commonly reported consequences of the current constellation of gender roles in these societies. Evident in survey research, letters to the women's and broader circulation press, conversations with ordinary women, and the remarks of outside observers, the daily manifestations of these strains are perhaps best captured in literature, including the poignant novel "A Week Like Any Other" by Natalia Baranskaya, which describes the harried life of a young mother and technician as she tries to meet her various daily obligations.[47]

In addition to these effects, also evident in other countries, the uneven pattern of changes in women's roles and the state's appropriation of gender equality as a goal have additional consequences in Eastern Europe and the Soviet Union. Coupled with the difficulties of running a household on a daily basis, recurrent economic difficulties, and, in some cases, broader systemic crises, the contrast between the regime's proclaimed goal of equality and the reality that women face in their daily lives has decreased interest in women's equality as a goal. Thus, while there is ample evidence that Soviet and East European women are aware of continued inequalities and dissatisfied with many aspects of current gender relations, few have any interest in working to change the situation, either by pressuring government leaders to use public resources to alleviate some of the strains they face or by rethinking the division of labor within the home and the patterns of organization of public and private life that result in women's continued exclusion from decision-making responsibilities in these societies.

As noted earlier, the development of feminist movements in Eastern Europe and the Soviet Union has been inhibited by the organizational principles and political values of these societies. The monopoly of power and access to the political arena by the Communist party, and also an ideology that, with the Yugoslav exception, has until recently denied the existence of conflict in socialist society and therefore the need for the interests of particular groups to be considered separately from those of society as a whole, inhibited independent organization or pressure group activity by all citizens. The impact of these factors and the distrust of separate organizations for women was evident in the fate of feminists in the early Marxist movement, the dissolution of the women's sections of the Communist party in the Soviet Union in the 1930s, and the degrading of the role of the mass women's organizations elsewhere in Eastern Europe in the 1950s.[48] It also has been illustrated more recently by the "normalization" of the women's organizations in Prague after the end of the Czechoslovak reform movement in 1968 and by the expulsion of the most active Soviet feminists in the early 1980s.[49]

However, organizational and ideological limitations are not the only explanations for the lack of the development of feminist movements in these countries. Another factor, which may well be more critical, is the lack of interest in or outright rejection of women's equality as a goal by many women in these countries. Attitudes in this regard are difficult to judge, and, as the information we have suggests, somewhat ambivalent. They also vary according to age, occupation, and educational levels as well as the aspect of life being considered. Large groups of women in many of these societies appear to support certain elements of women's equality, including the right to work in particular. Many women and men also appear to accept the notion that there should be equality in the family, at least on a theoretical level. There is, in addition, ample evidence that the ability to obtain a higher education, hold jobs, and, whether by choice or necessity, lead lives independent of their families, has had an impact on women's sense of themselves and self-worth in these societies.[50] However, faced with the daily contradictions between proclaimed goals and reality, many men and women appear to favor a return to earlier patterns of gender relations and behavior, at least in certain areas. Evident in the continued tendency of many Soviet and East Europeans to define women primarily in terms of their maternal and domestic roles, these attitudes are also reflected in the widespread popularity of pronatalist incentives for childbearing and in the emphasis placed on the need to strengthen the family by officials and dissidents alike. Leaders of the women's organizations in Czechoslovakia in the late 1960s, for example, called on political leaders to recognize the importance of women's maternal roles and adopted a differentiated approach to the needs of various groups of women.[51] A similar approach has characterized the position of Charter 77, the main dissidents' group in Czechoslovakia, to women's issues. Although the Charter has not given much explicit attention to women's issues, it does continue to affirm the principle of women's equality. Other dissident groups, however, have raised questions about efforts to reduce gender differences because such efforts are perceived as a threat to family stability. In Poland, a similar preoccupation with safeguarding the traditional family was evident in Solidarity's activities in the early 1980s. Still other opponents of the current regimes, such as Czech dissident writer Eva Kanturkova, approach the issue from a different perspective. They call on women to reject what they see as a regime-directed emphasis on career and political activism, in order to retreat from the workplace and find patterns of existence more specifically suited to women.[52]

THE IMPACT OF ECONOMIC AND POLITICAL CRISIS

Attitudes toward gender roles and the approach of Soviet and East European leaders to policies that affect women have been influenced in the recent past by the persistent economic crisis that has existed throughout the region. Due in part to the chronic problems of centrally planned economies but also to the unanticipated impact of world economic trends, including high energy prices and economic recession in the West in the 1970s, the East European countries entered a period of economic retrenchment and austerity in the 1980s.[53] Concerned with saving scarce raw materials and conserving energy, reluctant or unable to turn any longer to the West for technology and loans, leaders in Eastern Europe adopted economic plans designed to make more efficient use of domestic resources. The austerity measures adopted in the mid-1980s were followed by Gosbachev's efforts to promote *perestroika*, or the restructuring of the economy in the Soviet Union and elsewhere in the region.

The era of austerity as well as the renewed discussion of the need for more radical economic and political change that accompanied *perestroika*, had a number of additional implications for women and policies toward women in these societies. Coupled with the poor economic performance that preceded them, the austerity measures led, in practical terms, to greater hardship in daily life: fewer consumer goods, shortages of food and basic supplies, longer lines, and fewer services. Since it is still women who are primarily responsible for running the household and caring for the children, they undoubtedly feel these changes more on a daily basis. In addition, in several countries, the austerity programs have been accompanied by a decrease in spending on social services, as well as a reduction in the number of retail outlets.

Ironically, it is likely that issues typically regarded as women's issues, such as food supplies and the availability of consumer goods, will be among the most important political issus of the next decade in the Soviet Union and Eastern Europe. But in the current economic and political climate there is little evidence that political leaders will pay particular attention to issues specifically related to gender equality. Preoccupied with economic matters, leadership change and, in many East European countries, with the need to find a new formula to ensure political stability, it appears unlikely that Soviet and East European leaders will initiate or even encourage any concerted attack on the remaining sources of women's inequality in these societies.

Economic crisis has also tended to deflect popular attention from issues related to gender equality. In part, this has occurred because difficult economic conditions have increased the importance of the family to individuals, in practical as well as emotional terms. In countries such as Poland and Romania, where the problems of running a household on a daily basis have taken on such large dimensions, dissidents and ordinary citizens, like political leaders, generally see gender equality as a low level concern.

These factors have both direct and indirect impacts on gender relations and gender equality. As Renata Siemieńska has argued, the Polish crisis of the 1980s had a direct and immediate negative effect on women's role in political leadership in Poland. Although a woman was chosen for the Politburo, the top party decision-making body, during the Solidarity period, women's representation on the central committee of the party was lower than it has been for most of the post-World War II era.[54]

There was also little direct action on women's issues during the 1980s as both political leaders and the general population focused on the broader economic and political situation. To the extent that Solidarity and other activists focused on gender issues, they tended to reinforce rather than challenge traditional conceptions of gender roles. The demands of Solidarity that dealt with women's situation, for example, such as the call for better childcare facilities for children of working mothers, more adequate housing, and extended maternity leave, were motivated more by the concern to facilitate women's roles and strengthen family life than by a concern for women's equality.[55]

The process of change initiated in the Soviet Union by Gorbachev similarly has had little impact on gender inequality to date. Despite Gorbachev's reference to the need to make better use of women's talents, the broadening of the terms of public debate as the result of *glasnost* had not led to any significant challenges to the prevailing analysis of or approach to women's issues. If the experience of the East Europeans during periods of change is any guide, *glasnost* may in fact give rise to the more open airing of traditional views concerning women, views which could not be openly expressed earlier. Some of the other changes being contemplated, particularly in the economic sphere, may also work to women's disadvantage, at least in the short run. While improved economic performance would benefit women as well as men, for example, economic reform could also have negative consequences for some women if planners and economists come to question the full employment of women with small children from the perspective of economic efficiency.[56] Preoccupied with consolidating its power and the debate over the extent and nature of needed change in the economic and political realms, the Gorbachev leadership appears no more likely than its predecessors to give serious attention to gender issues.

CONCLUSION

As the preceding pages have illustrated, the patterns of political organization, political values, and policy choices associated with the state in the Soviet Union and Eastern Europe have influenced gender relations directly and indirectly. In certain areas, state policies have resulted in a redefinition of possibilities for women; in others, traditional conceptions of different roles for men and women persist or have been strengthened by the consequences of such policies.

The result of the interaction of policies specifically designed to foster women's equality, policies in other areas that affect women, and underlying patterns of social and family behavior, gender relations in the Soviet Union and Eastern Europe reflect the mixed impact and unintended consequences that characterize policies in these states. They also reflect the tendency of political leaders to view women for state purposes. In the early period of communist rule, women's roles as economic resources were emphasized. More recently, policies toward women have been influenced by the unintended consequences of earlier development strategies, including declining birthrates and recurrent economic and political crisis.

What is common to both periods is the appropriation of the goal of women's equality by the state and the limitations that political organization and state policies set on any feminist action to challenge prevailing conceptions of appropriate gender roles. Together with the impact of economic and political crises, these factors have led to a coincidence in the views of leaders and many segments of the population in support of reemphasizing maternal roles and strengthening the traditional division of labor within the home.

The reemphasis on traditional female roles in the home and the importance given to the family itself as a social unit illustrate once again the extent to which gender inequality has been and remains one of the props of the socialist state. The official commitment to gender equality remains intact and voices calling for more attention to women's issues continue to be heard occasionally in Eastern Europe and the Soviet Union. But powerful organizational, as well as more immediate economic and political factors, militate against the adoption of any concerted effort by party or state officials to eliminate remaining gender inequalities, and against the development of feminist challenges to prevailing patterns of gender relations. In these circumstances, the uneven pattern of change in gender roles that characterizes these societies is likely to persist.

4

THE STATE AND GENDER IN COLONIAL AFRICA

*Kathleen Staudt**

The state, recently exhumed from its conceptual origins in political science and political economy, represents a tool by which to analyze the social construction and institutionalization of gender relations. Feminist theorists have remarked that state-created gender distinctions, between a so-called private world in which women are lodged and the public world of men, are mystifying because we have not seen those distinctions set in motion.[1] With a focus on the discourse of those men who gave form to a transplanted version of the European state in colonial Africa, we can demystify that process.

In this chapter, particular attention is given to the historical record of missionaries, colonial officials, and local agents in the establishment and consolidation of colonial rule. Their discourse represents a time-specific gender ideology which influenced laws, public policies, and economic opportunities or constraints for women and men. In this gendered approach, I examine state officials, their allies, and the incentives they tried to create to stimulate more accumulation among men. While women were central to the incentive structure, they did not fully cooperate.

It would be a mistake to reify the state and its impact on extraordinarily diverse societies, which vary in terms of marital exchange, property transmission, and indigenous political structure. Moreover, states in Africa are relatively weak, compared to those in other parts of the world. However, it would be similarly mistaken to ignore the homogenizing effects of states as they tug at distinctive groupings within their boundaries. To be sure, that tugging process may take centuries as different peoples are differentially "integrated"—or perhaps more appropriately, "captured"—under the state umbrella. The process has only just begun in Africa.

"How does male power become state power?"[2] Outside of analyses about pristine societies, few answers exist. Yet these analyses do provide insight into how men came to be defined in the public world and women in the private. In Inca society, ideological changes accompanied empire expansion such that men symbolized the conqueror and women, the conquered. In ancient Sumer, a combination of chronic warfare, the growth of private property, and a religious-managerial class which transformed ideology to legitimate those changes destroyed kin-based control over resources and made relatively autonomous women dependent upon men. Similarly, a combination of "male specialization in warfare, predatory conquest, a state bureaucracy based on patrilineal nobility supported by an ideology of male dominance, and differential access of men and women to its benefits" worked to diminish women's power in the growing Aztec empire, a process that took more than five centuries.[3] Scanty as those documents and ruins must be to reconstruct such changes, it is surprising that we do not have more detailed studies of the dynamics by which the state constructs gender reality in the contemporary human laboratory.

However tantalizing his title, Engels tells us very little about *women and the state* in his classic study.[4] It took Karen Sacks to insert, for Engels, the *political* connection between women's subordination in class-based societies and the state. She argues that social, or public, labor in productive groups larger than or separate from the household, makes one an adult in a society's eyes. If women are excluded from such labor, or their performance in it denigrated, a basis exists for denying their adulthood. As states form and rulers need surpluses to maintain those states, they recruit men to participate in large-scale social labor, such as corvée public works, conscription, or collective labor. Men are the recruits because they are more mobile and can be more intensely exploited, given women's role in reproduction. Meanwhile, foundations are laid for denying adulthood to women and for defining them as wards of men. Both kin groups and women are key losers in the process of state formation, with states destroying the possibility of sisterly relations among women.[5]

Why did men submit to these changes? Men lost autonomy in kin corporations; surplus was extracted from their public labor. Heidi Hartmann argues that "the ascending rulers literally made men the heads of their families in exchange for the men's ceding some of their tribal resources to new rulers."[6] Men also acquired political accountability and, importantly, responsibility for the base family units of the social structure. Responsible men are, after all, better subordinated to the system, says Sherry Ortner.[7] Men are engulfed in state hierarchy, albeit differently from women.

Insightful as these anthropological analyses are, they are based on ethnographies completed when gender analysis was not central (or even peripheral) to research. More importantly, they omit the key turning point of colonialism. Often fueled by economic determinist models, analyses that deal with colonialism focus on the modes, means, and/or relations of production; the state as instrumental to forging or mediating these relations does not appear to matter.[8] All societies are now, thanks mainly to colonialism, incorporated into states, an entity left largely intact as nationalist "founding fathers" administered their countries thereafter. Rayna Rapp calls for an examination of state formation and gender relations in the "bloody laboratory of colonial penetration," which differs from pristine states, but she cautions that each country has its own history as does each colonizer.[9] With a focus on the colonial period, we can begin to understand the gendered quality of state formation at a time of heightened accumulation on a world scale.

The framework for this chapter examines the state construction of gender relations and the ways that men and women further refined and molded that reality during the colonial era. States facilitated the accumulation process in gender-specific ways. In Africa, the transplanted European officials and missionaries attempted to streamline societies into stable, accumulation-oriented, bridewealth systems in which men had the upper hand.[10] Colonialism's bloody laboratory provides a relatively recent, telescoped arena in which to examine the mechanics by which these foundations were laid and is thereby suggestive of similar processes elsewhere. Unlike analyses of pristine societies, colonial actions occurred in the context of capitalist accumulation on an international scale. Not addressed is whether the colonial model altered or merely aggravated gender subordination in those societies with which it collided. Once implanted, however, people accommodated themselves to the model in differing degrees, depending on their class and systems of land transmission among other factors.

Still, the colonial model of capitalist accumulation was relatively ineffective. While women's labor underwrote male and capital accumulation, accumulation among potentially more productive women was stifled. Colonial Africa laid the ideological foundation for male preferential policies which contributed to Africa's development crisis.

THE COLONIAL STATE

The colonial experience, which Bruce Berman calls "one of the most consequential efforts to modify or create entire social structures,"[11] left enduring legacies upon the African continent. Diverse European states, including Britain, France, Germany, Belgium, Portugal, Spain, and Italy, clutched at as much of the continent as they could manage. Much has been made of the differences in colonial rule, particularly between Britain and France, who in leaving behind a great deal of writing on the supposed distinctiveness of their imperial experiences, exaggerated differences between themselves. Colonies shared a great deal regardless of the source of European control: dependency on a distant metropolis, authority exercised by outsiders who knew little about the colony, and the prevalence for metropolitan considerations to overwhelm local needs.[12] So obvious that historians do not state it, European state models shared male hegemony as well.

At least on paper, British Indirect Rule contrasted markedly with French Direct Rule. As elaborated by Lord Lugard in his classic, *The Dual Mandate in British Tropical Africa*, colonialism should tamper little with indigenous structures, but rely instead on local authorities and customs amidst evolutionary guidance toward "civilization." The French Assimilationist and later Associational models (the latter moving France toward Indirect Rule practice) held out the possibility of French rights and citizenship to those who assimilated French culture in colonies which were integrated into the French parliament and bureaucracy. Nevertheless, only a minute fraction of Africans acquired citizenship status, and colonial officials relied on local authorities to implement their policies. For both Britain and France, conflict resolution and revenue collection occurred in a prefectural-style bureaucracy, manned by what A. H. M. Kirk-Greene calls a "thin white line" of officials dependent upon local agents.[13] On superficial glance, the French cultural mode, toward which upwardly mobile Africans were to aspire, might have appeared to deepen French ideological inroads, but the heavy influence of missionaries in the British-controlled areas, in which more Africans lived, had similar ideological effects. "British missionary theory, insofar as it believed that the reconstruction of African society should accompany the spiritual rebirth of individual Africans, represented a religious equivalent of the French imperial theory of assimilation."[14]

Yet France and Britain did have different recruitment and training programs for their overseas officers. In the earliest days of colonial rule, local recruitment attracted a motley crew of adventurers and nonconformists. "No matter how inept or depraved," French Equatorial Africa in particular became a "human refuse bin for personnel discarded by other colonies in the years before World War I."[15] France established the École Coloniale in 1888, with its courses in ethnography, to train officials for Africa. Before 1914, however, less than a fifth of its officials passed through the course, and most recruits were poorly educated, with the majority lacking secondary education.[16] Later, as recruitment became more systematic, candidates were selected by examination. Whatever their class background, they were proud of French language and culture, but averse neither to "mingling with the natives," nor "haggling in the market," much to the dismay of those who applauded British procedure.[17]

Britain, in great contrast, attracted recruits from public schools and the Oxbridge establishments, who were cut from the same mold as governing administrators in Britain itself. Recruitment was based on finding "the right sort of gentleman" with proper background and character. Great care was given to reference letters, family background, educational institutions attended, and the interview process where notes were made on poise, stature, steadiness of eye gaze, and such other seemingly obvious signs of upbringing. The British public schools drew from "the privileged—but not too privileged" to provide intensive, sex-segregated formative training, thought to inculcate responsibility, inner strength, leadership, obedience, and chivalry. As Robert Huessler, chief historian of the recruitment process concludes: "The life for which the public school is preparation is to be male-dominated and authoritarian."[18] Helen Callaway, anthropologist of imperial "culture," analyzes how "The colonial service in Nigeria considered itself to be a men's institution, doing a job requiring 'masculine' capacities." As such it was another manifestation of "separate sex arrangements" of the British middle class.[19]

Whatever differences selection methods and training produced, the commonality these men shared, above and beyond European culture, was the sense of racial superiority—a justification for empire itself. While missionaries professed an egalitarian message of salvation for all, their knowledge of African society was scant (though more extensive than that of usually monolingual officials) and they often held a profound disgust for "heathen ways."[20] Even early academics of colonialism shared the prevailing racism, as did Stephen Roberts, who bemoaned the depopulated French Equatorial Africa. "The population in general was miserably scant: the bulk of them were animal-like rather than human in their characteristics."[21] To these men, male and female alike were subhuman, for in the colonizers' implicit civilizing mission, clear ideas existed of civilized male and female behavior. Among these were the legitimacy of male rule and male representation of women; the requisites of economic development, including greater male productivity; and the importance of sexual "morality" for general social stability. Officials, missionaries, and their local agents imprinted an ideology upon family laws, economic and education policies, and a European-style boundary drawn between public and private spheres, all mechanics by which male interests were consolidated into the state.

In the initial years of colonial state formation, officials expressed some benevolent concern for women, particularly in the matters of marital free choice and of burdensome female work. As state consolidation proceeded, however, officials' conceptions about raising women's status meant proper marriage—even reinforced with brideprice where no such custom existed— and an end to "immorality" which they judged as cheapening women. Indeed, officials frequently expressed concern that women were "too free," or as one said, "not as disciplined as young English girls of today."[22]

A glimpse of administrators' attitudes from travelogs and memoirs further elaborates these views, however rare the mention of women. Sir Stewart Symes remembered conversations with only two women in his early 1930s Tanganyika tour of duty. Symes had one conversation with a nurse, "a tall, upstanding, black matron with a generous bosom," while the other was with a "lady of the hut" "almost as naked as she had been borne." Sir Charles Dundas remarked not once, but twice, in his memoirs about a Kikuyu woman carrying firewood weighed in at 384 pounds. He also noted women's heavy field work and men's reluctance to work or serve as porters. Sir Philip Mitchell, in an early 1920s trip through a Hima village, seemed astonished with women chiefs, one of whom he said had a "hen-pecked husband."[23]

The colonial state laid the foundation for societies to conform with its cultural notions of appropriate gender relations in industrializing class society, in which men are breadwinners, women enable and stimulate male workforce productivity through home labor (which in Africa includes food production, water and fuel collection) and consumer demand, as well as serve as a low-skill reserve labor force. While Victorian ideas inspired these notions, they were reproduced across generations well beyond that era. Colonial officials' initial efforts were directed toward men and men's interpretation of indigenous realities, when the latter served colonial interests. Female political voice lost whatever institutional character it had in some societies, and women responded and resisted informally and spontaneously to this new version of male order, as is later developed. Colonialism thus set the stage for state structures manned to solidify female subordination.

MISSIONARIES AND THE STATE

Forerunners of European intrusion, Christian missionaries made their presence felt in rural Africa as much as forty years before the feeblest of colonial state institutions were established. While missionaries shared their Christianity, differences existed among them by denomination, level of home-country funding, and sexual behavior, both in terms of the presence of female missionaries and of "model family" mission couples.[24] Yet state-mission cooperation was fruitful to the growth of both. Missionaries were advisors to and intermediaries with the colonial government. They interpreted African society to officials, as many had acquired bilingual capability. Missionaries were the "eyes and ears" of the colonial government in rural areas.[25] Common also to both was the Victorian ideology of dichotomized gender behavior. Christian missions, as custodians of morality extending into all areas of life, considered family life the legitimate object of social intervention. Definitional control over Christian marriage was part of their power, and a Christian marriage was monogamous and lifelong.[26]

The common indigenous practice of polygyny permitted increased male prestige, additional labor for men to expand land under cultivation for accumulation and exchange purposes, and knots to tie together diverse kinship groups. Missionaries viewed the institution as un-Christian, lustful, and degrading to women even though the Old Testament, Africans noticed, contained numerous accounts of polygynous men whom the Deity favored. Divorce, an essential ingredient in matrilineal society, permits both women and their (usually) male kin to exert power. Missionaries viewed this, too, as un-Christian and paradoxically, given the seeming concern over female degradation, would have maximum authority to be invested in the husband alone. Still, in the early colonial period, many marriages remained in customary form outside the law.[27]

Missionaries worked to infuse Christian principles into the new family law. Myriad complexities then emerged, with on-the-spot church policy adaptation. Suppose a polygynist were baptized, tired of some wives, and then sought to discard those who were termed "surplus wives": who remained his official wife? Suppose a Christian wife's husband sought more wives, should she avoid sexual intercourse? Here, mission-state cooperation was somewhat tenuous, as too quick a conversion to European ways, officials worried, would destabilize society or undermine traditional rulers on whom they depended.[28] Still, as civil marriage law gradually evolved, its form resembled Christian marriage: monogamous, with men in authority, and state-defined grounds for divorce. Only that latter component—divorce—made missionaries shudder.

The earliest mission stations were self-sufficient, with compounds surrounded by fields on which converts worked. Often outcasts, slaves, or women escaping bad marriages, the converts' very separation from other people increased their stake and commitment to this new world view. Unless cooperation was advantageous, or the skills missionaries had to offer were evident, mainstream Africans were reluctant to forgo crucial elements of their own social fabric to adopt European ways. Turn-of-the-century mission schools, for example, had vacant spots because parents were reluctant to release labor or even insisted on compensation for releasing a child. Culture is deep-seated, and missionaries necessarily accommodated themselves to aspects of African culture that did not contradict their fundamental visions of Christian life. Mission historian Roland Oliver, for example, reports that lone men, after serving a probation period on mission stations, were "bought" a wife by the missions and then settled among the married pupils.[29]

Missionaries were aware that men's conversion required some compensation for them to abandon privileged traditions that missions abhored, such as polygyny. According to Oliver:

> If the African Christian was to abandon his place on the ladders of economic prosperity and social prestige by practicing monogamy, he must be compensated by learning a trade or new methods of agriculture which would open the way to new ambitions.[30]

MEN: THE INITIAL TARGET

Missionaries and colonial officials made their firmest ideological alliance to stimulate more work from men. Agricultural and industrial education programs, along the vocational lines recommended by visiting Phelps-Stokes Commissions, were intended to remedy the "natural laziness" so many missionary and colonial accounts describe.[31] For missionaries, overburdened women would be free to devote themselves to their families once their husbands shared burdens more fully. Missionaries tried to introduce "new agricultural methods to the extent of making it possible for their converts to lead truly Christian lives . . . in which the husband did his fair share of the work."[32] In Northern Rhodesia, Marcia Wright describes how the Jesuits, soon after their establishment in 1905, promoted ploughing among men, lending equipment to influentials who would set an example.[33]

The state had an interest in inducing men to take a greater responsibility for household maintenance with more labor inputs, tax payments, and ultimately, greater contributions to the accumulation process. In short, colonial officials' ideology of economic growth required greater male productivity. Yet administrators had a more immediate, practical concern. As colonies were self-supporting, necessary revenue could be generated with a larger wage labor force and more cash crop agriculture. Numerous studies analyze how agricultural agents pressed men into cash crop production.[34] Lord Lugard, for example, whose thinking and writing was disseminated throughout British colonial Africa, said that "since men alone tend oxen in Africa, the result, as I have elsewhere said, will be to replace female labour in the fields to a large extent."[35] Later, a similarly influential Lord Hailey wrote in his monumental description of British dependencies that "it is difficult converting people to agricultural practices where established custom regards it as proper for wom-en."[36] Policies were thereby established to pressure men to enter the wage economy through taxation (and sometimes compulsion via the euphemistically described "labour policy"), to train men for a com-mercial economy and civil service, to put property in men's names through land reform, and to subsidize men's farming through credit and extension services.

Bridewealth, if not already present, was encouraged for the ways it facilitated commercialization and colonial state stability goals. Bridewealth builds on the widespread indigenous tradition that people are resources to be accumulated. In times of scarce labor, women and their offspring provided a convenient source of labor, one that would be stabilized and cemented by marriage ties. Moreover, the higher the bridewealth, the greater the power to husbands and the more thorough their control over women and children.[37] Colo-nial officials encouraged bridewealth exchange both to enhance sta-bility through curbing women's freedom and to stimulate the accumulation process.[38] Some missionaries, initially uncomfortable with the seeming commercialization of marriage that bridewealth exchange entails, later became convinced that it strengthened the marriage bond. Missionaries' main concern was that bridewealth not be so excessive as to discourage marriage.[39] Union Minière, in the Belgian Congo, even contributed toward bridewealth in its labor stabilization policy.[40]

POLICIES OF OPPORTUNITY AND CONTROL

A particular division of labor was sought in training and employment policies. Turn-of-the-century Johannesburg, South Africa, with its shortages in cheap mine and domestic labor, saw cooperation between the British Colonial Service and women's emig-ration associations to recruit what were termed surplus British female domestics to replace "houseboys."[41] African women were later sought, as they were thought to be naturally more suited to domestic labor as well as cheaper than men. Also aware of the prob-lem, the Church of England Mission trained "native girls" in house-work, cooking, and laundry work to replace male domestics needed for mine labor.[42]

In the work and training spheres, church and state worked to-gether. Yet missionaries were wary of what they perceived to be a growing materialism that would detract from spiritual concerns.

Even as missionaries became a veritable thorn in the side of the state, more so after World War I with their criticism of compulsory labor, taxation increases without benefit or representation, and land alienation,[43] their commitment to a vision of a hierarchical, husband-wife (albeit educated wife) relationship remained.

Without missions, few educational and health services would have been established in early colonial years. Missionaries also sought to educate the future class of leaders. In schools infused with Christian principles, the educated would imbibe values important to their future policy making. Early colonial governments put little or no energy into public education, and even less for girls' education, but the British gradually began to subsidize and regulate mission education. Indeed, churches were heavily dependent on per capita state subsidies, from which more money was obtained than from home sources. As "salaried agents" of the state, however, teachers embodied the linkage of church and state in people's minds.[44] France, wracked by anticlerical sentiment at the turn of the century, ordered the secularization of some mission schools. Thereafter schools—few as they were—were government run; France provided no subsidies or regulation of the mission "bush" schools.[45] In these early schools, the connections between ascendant classes and bourgeois family forms were established.

Besides more work from men and greater marital stability, missions and colonial officials shared interests in reducing what was viewed as sexual laxity; morality and Christian family went hand in hand. Missionaries even argued in statist terms. The Anglican Bishop in Uganda stated that "the true foundation of any nation is true and permanent marriage, and without that a nation cannot survive."[46] "Moral" women, trained in domestic skills, would provide Christian family foundations for a stable society with a productive male work force. The initial volumes of the *International Review of Missions*, a quarterly journal begun in 1912, contained descriptions of special work among women and a regular section which was called "The Ideal of Womanhood as a Factor in Missionary Work." Numerous examples of programs can be found to make women "civilized helpmates," or "purer wives and better mothers," and to teach domestic science including its late Victorian adjuncts of needlework, sewing, and knitting. These home and marriage training programs provided resilient models for later governmental development efforts.

In Uganda, missionaries concerned with declining moral standards supported legislation to hinder adultery. The Synod adopted a resolution in 1919 to restrict female movement from subcounty administrative units without a permit. The Lukiko local council, on which Christian chiefs sat, passed laws to restrict married women's movements (vesting control in husbands' hands) and to abolish women's traditional right to return to parents upon marital separation. Elsewhere, urban women without certificates of registered marriage were repatriated to rural areas. In Sefwi Wiawso, Ghana, the Free Women's Marriage Proclamation of 1929 had women traders and alleged prostitutes jailed until a man claimed them.[47]

Descriptions of schools and curriculum in both British and French colonial Africa, whether secular or mission, denote special household training for girls for whom schools were belatedly available compared to boys. Girls received education later than boys due partly to missionary views that teachers of the opposite sex were unseemly. Women missionaries and wives of missionaries arrived later than the men. The women were neither present in the same numbers nor exercised the same authority as their male counterparts.[48] Yet missionaries worried about women's "backwardness" compared with men for lack of suitable Christian wives for converts. Still, male dominance of mission policy precluded altering male preference or providing equal access for girls. Too much education, missionaries feared, would teach a woman to despise manual labor, "unfitting her for her future life and usefulness as a married women."[49]

In the post–World War I period, missions experienced a decline in their contributions from home, but the number of Christians increased fivefold. Increasing numbers of African catechists spread the religious message; some broke away from missions to form independent churches. The hunger for education, satisfied largely through missions, also increased the spread of Christianity.[50] Gender ideology spread accordingly.

WOMEN IN "SOCIAL" POLICY

By the early 1940s, the colonial state increased attention to social policy as a result of changes in the international arena, the growth of African nationalism, British Colonial Development and Welfare Act funding, and expansion of the European state itself. "Mass education" and "community development" became the buzzwords of the time, and new journals with this developmental ideology disseminated social program models. Although gender titled Women Education Officers and Nursing Sisters were recruited in specialized branches of the British Colonial Service, only in 1944 did women get administrative posts.[51]

A focus both on the "masses" and on "communities" necessarily integrated women more fully into administrative activity, on somewhat different, but still familiar domestic terms. Some, like the Ugandan school described below, even taught women English.

> They need to know enough to be able to follow printed instructions in books on domestic subjects: to use a recipe, to act on instructions about laundry, to make cushions, curtain covers, etc., to use paper patterns and to understand simple books on childcare. . . . [In addition, English enables them] to make contact in the simple level of domestic interests with English women whom they meet.[52]

These bourgeois housewife notions did not mesh well with women's continuing subsistence work in agriculture, now extended with heavy male outmigration for wage labor. Only a privileged few in the ascendant classes could join ideology and practice.

Women were also viewed as consumers who motivate men. A colonial official in Kenya described a deliberate policy "to create female competition and jealousy" to spur men's productivity.

> She must be educated to want a better home, better furnishings, better food, better water supplies, etc. and if she wants them she will want them for her children. In short, the sustained effort from the male will only come when the woman is educated to the stage when her wants are never satisfied.[53]

Overlaying all this, the colonial state forged a public sphere, elevated from the lineage, clan, and/or ethnic identity to the level of the state, that was one and the same, a male sphere. This new public sphere made marriage and divorce, and thus control over surplus accumulation and labor, a public matter, administered by men, for what was often formerly a family matter. Quarrels were now transformed into legal cases. British-appointed chiefs under Indirect Rule, some of whom had no real indigenous authority, were now colonial agents, anxious to enlarge their jurisdiction and able to justify this intrusion through their knowledge and application of customary law. They formed a ready alliance with colonial officials and missionaries who worried about morality, and marital and social instability.[54]

REACTION AND CONSOLIDATION

Attention to the overarching conception of the state, particularly the colonial state diffused as it was by force, should not divert analysts from attempting to understand the ways in which indigenous peoples received, maneuvered, and accommodated themselves to the new institutions in which they were ensnarled. Intricate patterns of domination and subordination—themselves constantly undergoing change—fed into colonial state formation. Laws, economic opportunities, and ideologies are all means by which people seek leverage in dynamic historical circumstances.

Struggles are often mediated through law. Who defines and who controls that law are therefore crucial questions. European states transferred legal systems, by definition part of a public sphere. In British colonial Africa, under the principles of Indirect Rule, colonial officials sought to handle conflict through the application of customary law, with justice meted out—once knowledgeable persons were discovered—through native courts. A fluid complex of indigenous legal systems, where conflicts were resolved through negotiation, ordeal, and/or compensation, was molded and ultimately warped by incorporation into the contrasting, precedent-seeking and setting putative nature of British law. To discover the principles of customary law, colonial authorities went to men Martin Chanock called "adversely affected" by changes in an "irrevocably altered" setting from precolonial times. The upheavals of the latter half of the nineteenth century and of the early colonial period threatened gender controls. Horrified at women's conditions, as Parpart terms it, the British briefly provided women with opportunities to litigate and courts were swamped with women seeking divorce. Women flocked to urban areas, capitalizing both on their economic skills and their scarcity in relationships with men.[55]

"A blend of tradition and wishful thinking," customary law, was created and transformed through male elders as they responded to the contemporary threats posed by temporarily loosened control over women. Men referred to a mythical Golden Age when women were obedient to men, adultery was penalized by torture and death, and marriage was of lifelong duration.[56] Martin Chanock, writing on case law in Northern Rhodesia and Nyasaland, shows how customary law—the most effective means by which men exerted power in native courts under colonialism—was contrived and used to reestablish control over women in what he calls an alliance between African men and colonial rulers. Marcia Wright, too, analyzing cases in a magistrate's court in a nearby area around the turn of the century, found "no issue more sensitive than the control of women," as changed economic opportunities opened new alternatives and demand for women.[57] Select women attempted to play one legal system off the other, in the legalistic pluralism of state formation. As state control was consolidated in the 1930s, the period Jean Hay analyzes in western Kenya, societies in which neither men nor women owned land were transformed into societies in which land ownership became a male right. She attributes this to "conservative backlash from Luo men, and from male elders in particular, and their desires to re-establish control over women." Before 1945, a combination of land surplus and labor shortage eased women's ability to negotiate for themselves, to evade lineage controls over how they disposed of their goods, or to return to their homesteads of birth if marriages proved unsatisfactory.[58]

Initially, many more men than women submitted to the colonial state, a result of force, resignation, and rational calculations of rewards. As Berman relates on participation in the rewards of education, employment, public works, and profit from the surpluses of production, "it is clear, nevertheless, that the demands of the rulers for obedience also contained a promise of African participation in the benefits of a controlled process of change towards a new and superior social order based on European forms."[59] That this order was to be male-controlled was also clear.

Ideology is even more encompassing than law as a means of mediating struggle. New belief systems, such as Christianity, offered new opportunities that were laid with snares. Christianity held forth the prospects of a new social order to some, or at least an escape from the worst binds of the old. In Cameroon, the Catholic mission served as a sanctuary for women escaping unacceptable marriages. Besides allegiance to the church, a woman in such sanctuary underwent training for Christian marriage, and suitors approached the priest rather than her father to tie the knot.[60] Women, too, "invented traditions," to paraphrase Hobsbawn and Ranger. In Malawi, Anglican women created the Mothers' Union which they used to restore some of their former powers and to counterbalance the sudden ascendance of male power in the late nineteenth century.[61] Frank Salamone, drawing heavily on the work of Victor Uchendu, discusses how Igbo men in Nigeria tried to use Christian ideology to reinforce male dominance in a culture where the gap between male dominance ideals and actual practice was always great. He says that "old weapons" for controlling sexual freedom no longer work and men use new ideological weapons, especially Roman Catholicism, to serve traditional cultural ideals.[62] Christian marriage turns into a "community property" ideology, argues Regina Oboler. Whatever the good intention of the philosophy that family life is corporate, harmonious, and without separate economic interests, when implanted upon societies that respected separate female property, "various categories of property are merged," and "the husband assumes the dominant role in controlling everything." Young westernized Christian Nandi took this position.[63]

WOMEN'S WITHDRAWAL STRATEGIES

On the whole, women rejected and/or withdrew from the redefined political order to the greatest extent possible. Later, as male control became institutionalized, as women became as divided as men, and as the political agenda and participation rights extended somewhat to include women's issues in selected social policies, female activists used the political process with varying degrees of effectiveness. In so doing, they voiced concerns compatible with state gender distinctions. In the meantime, though, the political agenda was being established by colonial officials and the ascendant male class.

During the early half of colonial rule, women's indigenous political authority was invisible, except in periods of crisis. A famous incident associated with colonial misconceptions about women's power was what women called the Aba "women's war" in depression era Nigeria. In response to rumors that native authorities would impose new taxes, women utilized their traditional political institutions, *mikiri* (meetings), to mobilize women. In 1929, women mobilized against native authorities in what were termed "mobs," "operating in a state of frenzy," stamping, making noise, and destroying offenders' huts. Those protests were not isolated; historians of women's politics in southern Nigeria document women's constant and continuing activity against state-imposed produce prices, water fees, produce inspection, taxes on women, and the loss of communal land.[64]

The taxation of married women was vigorously opposed on more than economic grounds. A. E. Afigbo cites activist Enyidia of Oloko, Nigeria, testifying after the women's war:

what have we women done to warrant our being taxed? We women are like trees which bear fruit. You should tell us the reason why women who bear seeds should be counted.

At stake here was more than economic extraction, but the invasion of and potential threat to fertility and life itself. As Afigbo explains, "just as one cannot, in the interests of human beings, joke with the survival of fruit-bearing trees, one could not play with the fate of women." In the view of these people, female reproduction should be outside the folly of colonial order.[65] Reproduction was perceived as larger than, rather than subsumed in, the state. Still, states aim to envelop women and reproduction on men's terms.

Class differences among women began to be important in characterizations of women's politics.[66] Nina Mba's careful documentation of women's politics in Nigeria reveals both the changing character of women's demands and the increasing divisions among them as they were *differentially incorporated into the state.* Women's unions, some of which were affiliated with international women's organizations, articulated goals compatible with state-drawn public-private boundaries. Such goals included more political representation for women and equal education with men. Occasionally, women went so far as to seek state legitimation for reallocating household obligations which in most of Africa fall heavily on women. In her protest of water rates, Mrs. Kuti wrote that this "should be the responsibility of husbands on behalf of their homes." Market women struggled to retain their regulatory functions, usurped by the local administration.[67] In Zambia, "women could not sue men for adultery and polygamy," (as men could to obtain divorces from women).[68] Therefore, women complained of neglect and assault, using the moral values of the authorities to win cases. In 1913, South African middle class married women—"who prided themselves on being 'respectable,' their lives modelled on church ideals and mission education"—fought pass laws and endured jail "for their right to remain at homes as housewives." With this domestic ideology, women were thereby able to exercise independence from state labor control laws.[69]

Although state construction of gender ideology aims to obscure male-female conflict, women do not forget their distinct interests. These interests vary by class. As Jane Parpart concludes:

And like class struggles gender struggles were mediated by political, economic and ideological factors. Poor women fought different battles, for different rewards than women in the middle class. Poor women were more interested in autonomy, as they had less to gain from marriage, whereas elite wives had more to gain within marriage . . .

Wealthy Tonga women assert matrilineal prerogatives, representing lingering resistance to encroaching male control. Of course, strategies like these take place within the context of a male-ordered state.[70]

In pursuing their interests, many women simply ignore or evade restrictions. By the 1950s, for example, repatriated Zambian women returned to towns in such numbers that colonial courts simply abandoned this control policy. Women elope or join informal liaisons, avoiding the control implicit in bridewealth or government certified marriage. Kisangani market women operate in a "second economy" to avoid the state's attempt to authorize male control over their economic transactions.[71]

Nationalist movements focused on the struggle for independence, rather than on class or gender interests. Women participated in nationalist movements, the outcomes of which were, however, grounded in a continuation of the modern state and its gender baggage. Elsewhere, I have analyzed implications for women's politics in the postcolonial era.[72]

Some African states have established Women's Bureaus or Women's Ministries, structures that support a new type of gender ideology that recognizes women's public labor and expands the political agenda. Typically, governments respond largely in terms of welfare, now nearly etched in stone with decades of policy and program precedents, or let programs shrivel for lack of budgetary commitment. Bureau advocates face a bureaucratic elite which has absorbed and internalized the notion of women as domestic helpmates. As James Brain concludes in an analysis for women in seemingly progressive Ujamaa villages of Tanzania:

> the sentiments of relatively uneducated and unsophisticated men settlers were far more in accord with the views of President Nyerere regarding justice for women than were those of the ruling elite, who in rejecting colonial rule have nevertheless retained attitudes about appropriate sex roles not very different from those found in bourgeois Victorian England.[73]

Daivd Hirschmann's interviews with Malawian bureaucrats reveal their denigration, compartmentalization, and trivialization of matters dealing with women's work. According to a senior official he interviewed:

> Men's superiority here is customary—also it's Christian—it's in the Bible. We expect our wives to respect us and despite the talk of equality, we must lead—we can compromise a bit, but we must lead.[74]

Officials' values have obvious implications for decisions about the distribution of public resources.

Contemporary African states have been widely characterized as arbitrary, personalistic, corrupt, and ineffective. The optimism of the postindependence decade has given way to profound pessimism about prospects for development, however defined. Africa's current development crisis has its legacy in authoritarian colonialism. Crawford Young eloquently describes the "ephemeral. . .graft of cuttings of parliamentary democracy upon the robust trunk of colonial autocracy."[75] Male opportunism needs to be added to this grim list of adjectives about the heavy-handed state. As near consensus approaches about the decay of the African state, will the state's major success story be its firm foundation of male hegemony, a "normal" transcendent feature of state systems? Or will women be able to withdraw even further from the state, weakening it more? And will that withdrawal be alone or in solidarity with other women?

CONCLUSIONS AND IMPLICATIONS

The process by which states draw particular lines between public and private and thereby gender relations are not so mystifying after all, once linkages are set forth. Colonial officials shared, with missionaries, an interest in increased male accumulation behavior and morality in order to transform the economy yet generate social stability. They worked with local officials on whom they depended to establish a foundation in which female sexuality and labor would be controlled under the dual authority of husbands and male state authorities. Their gender ideology gradually affected educational institutions, law, and policy, thus making its way into people's consciousness and political participants' agendas. In response, men and women used laws, ideologies, and economic opportunities to counteract and/or consolidate their positions.

However heavy the ideological, legal, and policy grid, women are not fully integrated into or captured by these social constructions.[76] Besides, women were enveloped into states with various levers available to protect their interests. As Thomas Callaghy puts it, the African state is a "Leviathan, but a lame one."[77] After all, state formation and consolidation have been in place for less than a century. Women's resistance to or even withdrawal from the state is a pattern which more men are now imitating. Citizen "disengagement" has replaced "national integration," in Africanists' conceptions of state-society relations.[78] At the same time, state renewal may have the effect of "integrating" women more fully, as officials begin to realize the economic possibilities of stimulating rather than stifling accumulation behavior among more women. But what voice will women have in this process and will it be on their terms? Otherwise, "capture" becomes the more appropriate term.

WOMEN AND THE STATE IN ISLAMIC WEST AFRICA

Barbara Callaway
Lucy Creevey

This essay seeks to explore in a preliminary way the relationship between women and the state in countries which are predominantly
Islamic in West Africa. The focus is on whether, owing to religious
beliefs, there is common treatment of women in predominately Islamic states and, if so, what the basic characteristics are of such
treatment. The two nations chosen in which to examine this question are Senegal and Nigeria. In both countries, Muslims are either
a majority or the major minority component of the population. In
Nigeria, 42 percent of the total population is Muslim, but in the
most populous northern state of Kano, 98 percent are Muslim. In
Senegal, more than 90 percent of the population is Muslim with the
largest percentages of non-Muslims located in the Dakar area and in
the southern Casamance. Neither state is officially an Islamic state
governed by purely Islamic law. There are no officially Islamic states
in West Africa other than Mauritania which, by the nature of the

ethnicity of its population and culture, may be more truly grouped among North African states rather than West African. This chapter explores the question of how two states with large Muslim populations relate to women. Both states abide by secular law, but one has an overwhelming Muslim population and most government officials are Muslim (Senegal), while Muslims are only a simple majority in the other. In that country (Nigeria), the most populous area, Kano State, is controlled by fundamentalist Islamic leaders. How are women treated in that state as opposed to other Muslim women in Nigeria and Muslim women in Senegal?

The teachings of Islam about women have been the subject of much comment, especially since the political takeover in Iran by Ayatollah Khoumeni in 1979. In Iran, in the eighty years before the takeover, women had gradually won the right to pursue education, to vote, not to wear the veil, obtain free abortion, to have a monogamous marriage, and the right to maintenance after divorce. The Khoumeni reversal was dramatic and extreme. As one analyst, Haleh Afshar, has written:

> The Islamic Republic in Iran has created two classes of citizen; the male who benefits from the provisions of Islamic law and justice and the female who does not. With the sole exception of the right to vote, Iranian women are in all other respects formally recognized as second class citizens who have no place in the public arena and no security in the domestic sphere.[1]

Among examples cited by Afshar are the reimposition of the veil, the encouragement of young polygamous marriages, the reassertion of the husband's right to custody of children after divorce, unilateral divorce by his decree, and no obligation on the part of a husband to maintain his divorced wife (wives).[2]

Reaction in the West against this treatment of women in Iran has parallelled the burgeoning interest in the situation of women vis-à-vis the state in developing countries in general. Increasingly, Western feminists are trying to make contact with women in Africa, Asia, and Latin America. Efforts have been made to make more widely available some of their writings and to let them speak for themselves rather than imposing American or other Western views. As a result, numerous books and articles by women of various nations (and some men) have been published in the last six years focusing on Third World women. A subset of those books focus specifically on the plight of women in Islamic countries.[3]

Islam has drawn extremely close attention by those with an interest in the status of women because of the totalistic nature of the religion. Islam does not distinguish between sacred and secular spheres, and does legislate the behavior patterns of men and women in daily life. Even before the Ayatollah Khoumeni's accession to power, numerous studies were written which pointed out the particularly restrictive features of Islamic law and society in regard to women.[4]

This brief study, then, is set against a background of writings on Islam and on women subject to Islamic law which is, in general, critical and negative about the impact of this major religion on the status of women. Yet, despite striking evidence in some West African Muslim dominated states of official denigration of women, two questions will be raised here which, rather than contributing to a total condemnation of Islam, may lead to a greater understanding of the circumstances in which Islam is used to the disadvantage of women. These questions are: How is the impact of the *state* on women to be distinguished from that of *religion* in a state, even in a self-identified religious state? Second, to what extent is the developmental status of a society determinant of, or determined by, the character of religion? Ultimately, the authors, who are not Muslim, cannot presume to judge a religion which is not theirs; they cannot have the inside understanding of that faith to justify this judgment. They can, as concerned feminists, however, bear witness to the evidence of how women live and what they say they feel. And they can draw conclusions as to what factors appear to be the most significant in establishing the present and probably future situation for women in Muslim dominated states in West Africa.

CHARACTERISTICS OF ISLAM

Islam regulates all aspects of human life. As such, Islam, like Hinduism, is what Donald E. Smith has called an organic religion, as opposed to Christianity or Buddhism, which separate society from religious organization/bureaucracy and which are able to distinguish the sacred from the secular.[5] Islam prescribes a set of beliefs, a way of worship, an integrated system of criminal and civil law, an economic, and a political system. It sets out the way to run the family, prescribes for inheritance and divorce, dress, etiquette, food and personal hygiene, and the relationship between the sexes. The family is believed to be the center of the Islamic social order and, thus, Islamic law especially addresses itself to this topic. Approximately one third of the *akham* (legal injunctions of the *Qu'ran*) relate to the family and its proper regulation.[6]

Believed by Muslims to be the last of the line of prophets from Abraham through Moses and Jesus Christ, Muhammad is above reproach and cannot be criticized or portrayed. The *Qu'ran* in its entirety is the word of God spoken to Muhammad by the angel Gabriel and then recited by the Prophet to his followers. The *Qu'ran* is more than a book of teachings, it is sacred in its own right. Until this century, the *Qu'ran* could not be translated into other languages, and translations are only acceptable today if the Arabic text is printed along side of them. Hence, the *Qu'ran* has been preserved in its pure Arabic form as originally transcribed.

The writing of the *Qu'ran* in the form of 114 *suras* (chapters) was completed under the third successor to Muhammad, twelve years after his death. The teachings of the Muslim holy book include legislation for political leaders and rules for family behavior. Unlike Jesus Christ, but like major leaders of Hinduism and Buddhism, Muhammad was seen as a soldier, a ruler, and a family man as well as a prophet. His behavior and teaching in these worldly spheres is as carefully studied as in the explicitly religious domain. This background and basis of Islam have particularly important implications for women, whose "place" in the scheme of things is carefully described in many of the holy writings, still held to be sacred in the form in which they were written over 1,300 years ago.

After Muhammad's death in A.D. 632, his successors sought more detailed explanations and justifications for religion and daily life. They found this in the recollections of Muhammad's chosen companions, relatives, and early followers. The authority was of two kinds: what Muhammad said (the *hadith* or traditions) and what he did. Together, the two comprise the *sunna*—literally "the trodden path." The *sunna* began to be committed to writing fifty years after the death of the Prophet and provide the prophetic sanctions for the detailed legislation which characterizes Islamic government.

Islam is a religion of laws. The judicial system is based on the *ijma*, or the consensus of the learned Islamic community, and is established through the development of *qiyas* or deductive analogy. Central importance is given to the community and its majority, the *umma*. In Islam, there is nothing resembling the institutional church; its corporate functions belong to the *umma*. In large measure, the essence of Islam is a legal creed, a creed which cannot be changed but is interpreted by men learned in Islamic doctrine, the *ulema* or religious lawyers. These jurists, in the early years, varied in their interpretations of the law and thus gave rise to four major schools of Islamic law: Hannifi, Shafi, Maliki and Hanbali.

Together, the *Qu'ran*, the *hadith*, and the *sunna* form the entire corpus of Islamic law or the *Sharia*. The *Sharia* needed codification and this was accomplished by panels of jurists between A.D. 767–855. Thus, by the middle of the ninth century, the total legal entity known as the *Sharia* was established and, in principle, "the gates of ijtihad were closed"; that is, independent judgment was henceforth prohibited as laws described all that men (and women) could and should do. Only deeper and more literal understanding of the words recorded was to be permitted thereafter.

In Islam, religious beliefs and teachings are closely interlinked with teachings about society, policy, economics, and the family. This totalistic system has been central to Islam. In the West, in contrast, there was a decline of European notions of sacral government in the seventeenth century, which led to the formulation of secular ideologies to take over the legitimizing functions of religions. Theories of social contract, representative government, or other variations on the basic idea of democracy were most prominent, but there were also secular versions of authoritarianism. Thus, liberalism stressed individual freedom in matters of religion; revolutionary nationalism emphasized the sovereignty and integrity of the modern nation-state; and Marxism attacked the reactionary core of religion in society.

Christianity in its changing forms has coexisted, sometimes uneasily, with the secular ideologies which arose in Europe and spread throughout the nominally Christian countries of the world. Islam, unable by virtue of its structure and beliefs to retreat easily into the sanctuary of the church (as opposed to the secular world), often has been opposed to ideologies which threaten its dominance in the state and society. The secularization of Islam is the more problematic because the laws have been held to be immutable, preserved in the form they were written in premedieval Arab society.

ISLAM AND THE POSITION OF WOMEN

Because the *Qu'ran* focuses so much of its content on the family, its regulations are quite explicit about the role and place of women in society. Originally, the intent of these laws was to improve the position of women.[7] Before Islam, under tribal law in

Arabia, women had virtually no legal status. Various provisions of the *Qu'ran* markedly improved the situation giving them the right to their bride price, rights of inheritance and some protection in the event of the husband wishing a divorce. The *Qu'ran* enjoined that women be treated fairly and equitably. But the specific provisions of the *Qu'ran* were then interpreted and made more concrete in the body of Islamic laws and jurisprudence in the context of the existing traditions and customs of a given society. As Coulson and Hinchcliffe have written:

> The modicum of explicit Qu'ranic legal rulings on the status of women were naturally observed, but outside this the tendency was to interpret the Qu'ranic provisions in the light of the prevailing standards of the tribal law. . . . The result was that the Qu'ranic provisions concerning women's status and position in the family were dissipated and largely lost. Islamic law continued to reflect the patriarchal and patrilineal nature of society based on the male agnatic tie. Within the scheme of family law which developed in this way, woman, whether as daughter, wife or mother, occupied an inferior position.[8]

The general thrust of the references to women in the *Sharia* is that women are dependent on men and are fulfilled only through subordination to them. Although the roles of wives and husbands are viewed as complementary rather than "unequal", it is quite clear that relationships within the family are hierarchical and patriarchal in nature. The role of women is complementary to that of men, but it is not equal in any literal sense of the word. Even the *Qu'ran* states "women have the same rights in relation to their husbands as is expected in all decency from them, but men stand a step above them. God is mighty and wise" (*Qu'ran* 2:229).

Islamic teachers emphasize that a woman's primary concern is the family and within it she has both rights and duties. The obligations of a woman within the family are related to stages in the development of her life cycle with primary responsibility occurring during the childbearing years and lessening with the passing of this stage. Under traditional Muslim law, girls may be married when they reach puberty, which the law holds to be from age nine onwards and believes to have occurred conclusively by age fifteen.[9] Until her childbearing years draw to a close, a woman is under the care and authority of the men in her life. A marriage guardian traditionally would ensure that her marriage is properly arranged and the appropriate bride wealth or dowry set. The duty of a married woman is to be chaste, modest, and obedient to her husband. The *Qu'ran* says:

> Men are guardians over women because Allah has made some of them excel others, and because they (men) spend of their wealth. So virtuous women are those who are obedient . . . And as for those on whose part you fear disobedience, admonish them and leave them alone in their beds and chastise them. Then, if they obey you, seek not a way against them. Surely Allah is High, Great. (*Qu'ran* 4:35)

The obligations of both men and women in marriage are carefully spelled out in the *Qu'ran*. Men are expected to support their wives, although wives are not expected to support their husbands even if they become ill or incapacitated. Wives, however, are expected to be obedient to their husbands and may forfeit their support if they disobey.

The *Qu'ran* states that a man must marry only as many wives (up to four) as he can treat fairly and equitably (*Qu'ran* 4:4). Under no circumstances, however, may a woman marry more than one husband, although she may remarry at the death of her husband or when she is divorced. She does also have a specified right to her own inheritance and that which she earns for herself (*Qu'ran* 4:5, 8, 12).

A husband may divorce his wife, although he is enjoined to do so only for serious cause. A wife may be granted a divorce only by a court and then is required to show that her husband did not meet a specific obligation to her (such as providing support). Upon divorce women retain the right to their children only as infants and very young children—according to one school of law a two-year old boy and a seven-year old girl pass automatically into the care of their father or an agnatic male relative.[10]

Although the *Qu'ran* protects a woman's right to her inheritance, she receives only one half of what her brother inherits (*Qu'ran* 4:12). Moreover, her testimony in court is considered to be one half the value of a man's (*Qu'ran* 2:283).

Seclusion, by which a woman is either not allowed to go out of her house in public (except before she reaches puberty and after the age of childbearing passes) is not prescribed in the *Qu'ran*. Nor is the wearing of a veil to keep a woman's face (her "charms") from the eyes of a stranger. But the *Qu'ran* does admonish women to hide their beauties and keep them for the eyes of their husbands only (*Qu'ran* 24:32). There is no such advice given to men.

Muslim scholars maintain that the *Qu'ran* explicitly demands the same standard for men and women and thus they are equal before God. "And whosoever does a righteous deed, be they male or female, and is a believer, we shall assuredly give them a goodly life to live: and we shall certainly reward them according to the best of what they did" (*Qu'ran* 16:97). But the preceding paragraphs on the teachings of Islam in regard to women show the problems with asserting that men and women are equally valued by Islam. It is true that the *Qu'ran* does not say that women are worth less than men to Allah. It does not prohibit women from taking paid employment. It does not proscribe them from public office nor enjoin them from seeking education. It is also the case that certain property rights are protected and certain marital obligations assured for their well-being. As is shown here, however, the *Qu'ran* at length and in detail spells out a system of domestic law in which the wife is protected, cared for, guarded, and controlled by her male relatives. A woman's life, according to the *Qu'ran*, is centered in the family, while a man is seen as having the public wage earning and family support role and, along with it, the responsibility and authority of the family head. In an Islamic state, or a state living according to Islamic law, these inequities have the status of civil law.

WOMEN, ISLAM, AND THE STATE IN SENEGAL

Islam was spread into the area of present day Senegal during the eighteenth and nineteenth centuries. The missionaries of Islam were from brotherhoods or *tariqas* based in North Africa.[11] These *sufi* orders were tightly organized and hierarchal from the *Shaykh* at the top, through the *khalif* (leader of an individual regional branch) to the *taalibe* or individual members. The *sufi* orders were somewhat less orthodox than those of Saudi Arabia itself and made the teachings of Islam more intelligible to the average uneducated lay people who received the religion. This leavening was accomplished by greater emphasis on magic, mysticism, and on the power of the *sufi* brotherhood's leaders to intercede on behalf of followers who were blindly obedient to their commands and teachings.[12]

Islam did not become the dominant religion in the Senegal area until the end of the latter era. Thus, it coincided with the takeover of the region by the French colonialists who were spreading out into the hinterland from their bases in St.-Louis and Dakar, the two principal trading posts on the coast. In the early years of the nineteenth century, Islam had been resisted by the leaders of the precolonial kingdoms among the two dominant ethnic groups in the region, the Wolof and the Tukulor. By the end of the century, virtually all of the population of these two ethnic groups (the largest in Senegal) had been converted. Islam, in its popular brotherhood form, had taken on a social and political role in the process of transformation of the society. In the first place, the brotherhoods acted as opponents to colonial domination. It was Muslim leaders who led periodic revolts, often called holy wars, which were the major political obstacle faced by the French in their conquest and pacification of this area.[13]

In addition, the brotherhoods in their earliest stages offered a kind of social mobility to the people that had not been present in the earlier society. In pre-Islamic times, the Wolof and Tukulor were characterized by distinct social classes headed by an aristocracy ruling over a lower class or caste group of *griots* (singers), blacksmiths, and others commonly grouped together as slaves who served the needs of the aristocracy. The arrival of the French undermined the traditional social order and weakened the power of those in control. In the period of social ferment which ensued, the advent of the brotherhoods gave a chance for former slaves to disobey their masters (by giving their loyalty and obedience to a Muslim leader of their choice) and even for a lower caste male to rise to the position of a religious leader himself.

Whatever their initial role in social reform of society, however, the brotherhoods quickly became assimilated into the new establishment. With a few exceptions, it was members of former aristocratic families who became leaders of the *tariqas*. In essence, the preexistent social order, with some modifications and some changes in names and faces of those in power, was absorbed in the Senegalese chapters of the Muslim brotherhoods. The initial brotherhood effort to dislodge the French was quickly dispelled. Once French political control was assured, several years before the First World War, the French had begun to ally themselves with the brotherhood leaders. They practiced a form of divide and conquer, pitting some leaders against others, but basically using the Muslim brotherhood heads as their intermediary through whom they reached and controlled the rural population of the country.

This pattern of sacred and secular cooperation persisted after the colonial period when Senegal became independent from France in 1960. Even though ruled until 1981 by a democratic regime headed by a Catholic president, Leopold Sedar Senghor, politics in Senegal were dominated by a group of government politicians who carefully courted the major Muslim leaders in the countryside to ensure their support and their help in organizing the rural population. In return for their support, politicians gave major Muslim leaders gifts of money and pressed very softly on social reforms of which the religious leaders disapproved.[14]

In 1981, Senghor's protégé, Abdou Diouf, became president. Although a Muslim, he is described primarily as a "technocrat"; and soon after his accession to power he appeared to be pressing for much more strigent social and economic reforms than had his Christian predecessor.[15] His actions had strong repercussions among the Muslim leaders. Carefully groomed by his predecessor, he was already a familiar figure in the exchanges with the major powers within the brotherhoods. Diouf's successes and failures in winning the approval of Abdou Lahat, *khalif* of the powerful Muridiyya, caused open comment among observers in Senegal. His deep and personal relationship to Abdul Aziz Sy, leader of the larger but less political Tidjani order, despite his reform politics, was widely known.

Interestingly, along with the push for secular reforms which potentially could undercut the political and economic power of the *marabouts,* and which would benefit women, Diouf's government is also associated with a deepening of Islamic consciousness in Senegal. In the colonial period there had not been a large class of Muslim teachers and scholars in the urban areas in Senegal as there had been in North Africa and Nigeria. There were thousands of *marabouts* (Muslim leaders) in the rural areas, but few of these had a large following and only a few were hightly educated men (such as Al Hajii Shaykh Ibrahima Niasse, whose writings were known throughout West and North Africa). Qu'ranic schools taught a smattering of Islam to young followers who could not read or write in Arabic, and who learned Qu'ranic verses by rote with little understanding of what they were about. In contrast, by the mid 1980s, many Senegalese had been educated in the Middle East and North Africa. Other university students in Senegal were turning from Marxism to Islam. Aid from the Middle East had helped in the construction of mosques, and there was a flowering of Islamic religious and cultural associations. Many Islamic holidays were now recognized either along with, or instead of, the Christian holidays acknowledged by the French. Qu'ranic schools proliferated in the countryside, many of which offer much more detailed teaching of the *Qu'ran* than was available to all but a tiny few in the past.[16]

As in the first years of the establishment of Islam in Senegal, the new wave of interest had political and social implications. Weighted with long ties to the French, with a powerful implied criticism of the culture and customs which had predated colonialism, the Senegalese turned to Islam for an affirmation of their national identity apart from France and from the West. As Sheldon Gellar wrote in 1982:

> Today, Islam is once again on the move in Senegal, challenging the alleged superiority of the Western values held by the secularized Senegalese elite now in power. Islam could very well become the new rallying point for Senegalese political and cultural nationalism, as it was during the nineteeth century. Indeed there are some signs that Diouf and the new generation of Senegalese assuming power in the early 1980's are 're-Islamizing' their value systems and lifestyles.[17]

In pre-Islamic Senegal, which was a subsistence agricultural society with some trade to the outside world (primarily across the Sahara to North Africa), women had an acknowledged place in the sedentary ethnic groups. True, the society of the Wolof and Tukulor was patrilineal and patriarchal, and men were the kings of Baol and Cayor (two of the Wolof kingdoms in the precolonial period). Men allocated the land, hired labor, or bought slaves to work for them. But, custom and tradition also dictated that women had certain rights. Following a pattern of polygamous societies in this area, women were entitled to use the land, were allowed to keep the fruits of their labor in their own plots, and they were paid in cash or kind for the work they did in the family fields controlled by their husbands as heads of family. They had, thus, a certain measure of independence. Should they be fortunate enough to grow a surplus, they would be allowed to sell what they produced and use the proceeds for whatever they wished.[18]

As in Islamic societies, in the pre-Islamic animist kingdoms of the Wolof and Tukulor, men were allowed to marry many wives (by agreement among families, and limited by financial means). Women could marry one man, although in the event of death or divorce, they could remarry. In regard to inheritance, the pre-Islamic picture of rights for women is not clear. Men, however, were the major designates of both political power and family possessions. Women could pass their own personal possessions on to their daughters, but their dowry would not revert to their relatives if they predeceased their husbands, who would retain it. Land was given for usufruct only and was not disposable, although the use rights remained in the family and were passed on by the male to his male children.

Of course, the description above cannot delineate clearly what women could and did do before ideas associated with Islam had infiltrated the region. All of the written observations of Wolof and Tukulor society derive from a period after Islam had already begun to influence the thinking and customs of the people in the Senegal area.[19] Thus, depictions in anthropological studies of the Wolof are a mixture of what existed before the introduction of Islam and what has been derived from the superimposition of Islamic laws. By the time French colonialism was established in Senegal, the system of customary or indigenous law which was put in practice was a thorough confusion of Islamic and preexisting legal systems. How much so-called customary law emphasized Islamic law depended on which commune one inhabited.

Following the independence of Senegal in 1960, the first and succeeding constitutional documents set up a system of secular law modeled on that of France and the West. This was a continuation of the colonial system by which two sets of laws (the Western code and the "indigenous codes" which included Islamic law) had coexisted. The Senegalese government never adopted a system by which all parts of the law system were subject to interpretation by Muslim scholars as such. Instead, lawyers and judges were trained in the manner of French legal education, thus continuing a secular law system despite the fact that most of the legal officers were Muslim.

Under the Senegalese system there are, however, two different codes of law: the *droit civique* or civic law gives *all* citizens, male or female, the right to vote. Both males and females have an equal right to education and to health benefits guaranteed by the state, and to impartial treatment by the courts. All of them, male or female, have an equal right to the minimum wage. Neither men nor women are proscribed from occupying any position. Laws pertaining to political rights, to criminal behavior, and to administrative regulation, are written without distinction between the rights of men and women. Codes of family law are different, however. In colonial times, families in the communes of Dakar and St.-Louis had the right to follow either French law, or to seek redress in indigenous courts which followed predominantly Islamic law. In 1972, a new Family Code was passed which equalized the position of men and women. This law caused considerable resentment by Muslim leaders throughout Senegal. As a result, in a tradition made familiar from the colonial era, the government left the law on the books, but provided considerable latitude for people to elect to follow Islamic law, under which, as indicated above, women inherit half of what their brothers received, do not have custody over any but very small children, and can be divorced at will by their husbands who have no obligation to pay maintenance for them (except when they are caring for infants). The right to select the Islamic versus the secular family code is determined by the head of household who controls the family and who is, by and large, a man.

Ruth Sivard, in her book on women's rights throughout the world, cites Senegal as a country which ratified the United Nations' conventions to guarantee women equal political rights, equal rights to education, equal pay for equal value, and equality in employment. She notes that Senegal signed the United Nations' convention on the elimination of all forms of discrimination against women (passed by the UN General Assembly in 1979), including their inequality before the law and inequality with respect to contracts and property. This, however, seems to be a signature based on the intent of the government rather than one founded on the actual legal rights of women as they are observed in Senegalese society. It is perhaps not surprising that in the end Senegal did not ratify the latter convention.[20]

Aside from examining the written law in Senegal, observation of custom and habit in daily interactions among men and women is the best indicator of the position of women. Women are not veiled nor do they live in seclusion in Senegal. Women sell produce—their own products from individual plots, from family fields, from vegetable gardens—in the markets. Women work in factories and drive cars. Sheldon Gellar writes that women have improved their position markedly since the 1960s. Whereas less than one percent of women could speak or write in French in 1965, in 1988 almost fifty percent of school age girls were in school (using French). Not only were girls attending French secular schools, but female attendance at Qu'ranic schools increased sharply in the 1970s and 1980s. Where women had held no major political office in colonial times and immediately thereafter, by 1978 all three parties had women candidates among their electoral choices. Two women (Caroline Diop and Maimona Kane) were named to ministerial positions following these elections. There are now a few women professors at the University of Dakar, and there is an Association of African Women for Research and Development in Dakar (headed by Marie Angelique Savane). Women are beginning to participate in the adult literacy programs in the countryside, to receive assistance from the government (such as mechanical grain mills) to reduce their domestic drudgery, and to be encouraged to participate in rural economic and political institutions. In the urban areas, primarily near Dakar, women have entered the labor force as typists, clerks, secretaries, and unskilled factory workers. One-third of the students in the university are female.[21]

It is men, however, who head the government, men still are mainly the shopkeepers, the business people, and the professors, and it is men who act for the family in negotiations with the government or banks and who generally get title to the land when it is regularized out of the former land holding system (where land was not owned by individuals). In a recent study by John Waterbury and Mark Gersovitz, the lack of power for women in predominantly rural Senegal (more than 60 percent of the Senegalese population lives in rural areas) is strikingly illustrated. It is men who act as the *chef du ménage* (family head) and men, in these capacities, who control the allocation of land, money from loans, and tools either purchased or loaned. Women, like young unmarried males, will work on the fields of the *carre* or *ménage* (for money or in kind payments) and will have their own plots only in the farthest reaches of less desirable family land or *toll keur*. Although married women are permitted to keep the proceeds of their own production on their plots, their ability to benefit from this right is vitiated by the requirement that they also grind the millet, prepare the food, get water and firewood, care for the children and household, and work in the family fields. They are the last to get the use of equipment, and will receive minimal amounts of fertilizer.[22]

What then is the impact of Islam and the state, variously and together, on women in Senegal? The answer is complicated by the fact that, however poor the existing sources, it seems clear that women in pre-Islamic society were treated as second class citizens, under the control of the males in their families. Although they had certain rights guaranteed by custom and tradition, these rights did not make them equal politically or socially to men. Islam, as it was introduced, did not change this fact markedly. It may have regularized customs pertaining to marriage and divorce, but even this is not absolute. For example, among the major Muslim leaders who headed the brotherhoods, marriage and inheritance rights were not followed in a strictly Islamic pattern. The Cheikh Al Hajj Falilou MBacke (d. 1968) had two hundred wives (approximately), rather than four, and was succeeded as *Khalif* of the brotherhood by his brother, Al Hajj Abdou Lahat, rather than by his son.

Islam was a revitalizing force in the politics of Senegal in the nineteenth century. Adherence to Islam was a way for a society to find a new identity in a period when its political system, as well as its customs and traditions, were crumbling under the impact of the French. This new identity was a composite, however. The Wolof and Tukulor people did not shed all their habits, myths, and assumptions. These were absorbed and then transformed into a Senegalese version of the Islam which was brought from North Africa.

Over the intervening years, more and more of the Sengalese population has become Muslim, more mosques have been established and more children exposed to Qu'ranic schools (including girls). There is much greater awareness of what is happening in North Africa and the Middle East. Senegal, however, has remained under the influence of the French. Continued close ties with France have shaped the political system in a Western mode, although this was superimposed on, and reshaped by, the traditional Senegalese system of politics. The education of most Senegalese politicians, business, and professional persons was in French. The official national language of the country is French. Thus, in the 1980s, when Senegal faces major and long run economic problems, Islam is again gathering force as a revitalizing movement against the secular values and habits of the West. There is a clear parallel to what occurred in Egypt in the 1970s. In Egypt, veiling became more and more widely accepted by women in social groups which two decades before had been quite successfully pushing for emancipation along Western lines.[23] In a society undergoing rapid social change and suffering severe economic problems, veiling (and its symbolic and consequent loss of political and social rights) could represent security, self identity, and status to many women.[24]

Senegal has been more closely linked with Western and secular thought than was Egypt, and less connected to the Middle East. Thus, it would be much more dramatic here were Senegalese women to be forced into seclusion. In this context, however, it would not be surprising if Islam began to be used in its fundamentalist form to reduce or nullify some or all of the slowly accumulating rights of women as part of a move to disentangle Senegalese society and politics from the West. As part of a criticism of the loss of moral values and the decay of modern society, women may be pushed backwards. It is not predicted here that Senegalese women will be veiled, but it will be increasingly difficult for them to advance in their move for equal rights in the present political climate.

Until recently, the Senegalese government has been a defender of women's rights. Although almost all government leaders were

Muslim, they have acted in the French colonial tradition to put into law secular rights guaranteed in French society to men and women alike. They have done this with considerable ambivalence, both because they were Muslim and were influenced by the teachings of Islam as propagated in Middle Eastern and North African countries, and also because they were dependent on Muslim leaders in the countryside who were conservative and opposed to secularization for anyone, not only women.[25] The French colonial rulers cannot be said to have made women equal to men in their own society, much less in Senegal. Many observers have said, to the contrary, that Western values, including those of the French, helped to strip women of rights they previously had in subsistence African agricultural systems.[26]

In Senegal, indeed, the influence of the French may have helped to marginalize the economic role of women and thus cost them a degree of independence which they had had. Nonetheless, French law in the colonial period, especially after World War II, did give women many more equal rights relative to men than did Middle Eastern countries which adopted the *Sharia*. It is this aspect of the Western tradition which must be said to have strengthened (rather than undercut) the position of women in relation to men. Thus, the state in Senegal worked for the advantage of women and against Islamic law as understood in North Africa, although in a very limited fashion.

ISLAM, WOMEN, AND THE STATE IN NIGERIA

Assessing the interplay between secular law and the role of *Sharia* law in Muslim areas of Nigeria in defining and establishing the position and rights of women is not easy. Although a majority of Nigerians are not Muslim, Muslims form the largest single religious group. Perhaps because they are not an absolute majority, Muslims in Nigeria are more consciously Islamic. In Kano, a large state of over ten million people in the far north, Islam is older and more deeply entrenched than in Senegal. Kano City has been a commercial center since the twelfth century and Kano State is the most Islamic state in Nigeria, its population being 98 percent Muslim.

Early written records (in Arabic) and king lists suggest that the ancient Hausa city-state of Kano was walled around A.D. 1050 and that the first Muslim missionaries arrived from Mali about 1150.[27] Two centuries later, it is recorded that the Hausa king, Yusa, received forty Muslim missionaries (c. 1380), built a mosque, and ordered the people to pray five times a day.[28] Kano was one of the first Hausa states to be affected by Islam and today rivals Sokoto as the center of Islam in Nigeria.

Under Mohammad Rumfa (1463-99), the city reached its "golden age." Rumfa established wide trade connections and brought Muslim missionaries directly from the holy city of Medina in Saudi Arabia to Kano. The missionaries found the soil of Kano to be "the same" as that of Medina, thus establishing a special and mystical connection between it and Kano. Rumfa introduced seclusion for women (or *kulle* in the Hausa language), and decreed that his thousand concubines be secluded in the enlarged palace that still occupies the center of the city.[29] Thus, by the end of the reign of Rumfa, Islam was firmly established in Kano, and women of high social standing (both wives and concubines) were secluded. For several centuries, most women not in seclusion were slaves and worked in the fields. Hence, once slavery was abolished in the area by the British at the turn of the century, one symbol of nonslave status was wife-seclusion. Today, unlike in Senegal, virtually all women in Kano live in some form of seclusion.

By the mid-fifteenth century, Fulani traders from the region of present-day Mali had become a significant presence in Kano, and had begun to settle permanently, intermarrying with the Hausa. The Fulani were also Muslims and greatly expanded the Islamic presence. Fulani teachers, or *mallams*, began to voice their disapproval of those portions of the surrounding Hausa culture that were not yet fully Islamic. In particular, they protested the passing of inheritance through the female line, the "nakedness of women," and the mingling of the sexes in public—all of which, according to them, defied Islamic law.[30]

As devout Muslims became increasingly dissatisfied with the contrast between daily Hausa life and the Islamic ideal, the stage was set for the Fulani reformer, Shehu Usman dan Fodio. The Fulani *jihad* (or holy war) from 1804-1807, led by dan Fodio, completed the Islamization of Kano Emirate, a process that had been occurring peacefully in Kano, as throughout Hausaland, over the course of several centuries.

In pre-Islamic times Hausa women of royal lineages held titles and positions of authority over other women.[31] By the sixteenth century, the growing influence of Islam contributed to the erosion of the standing, influence, and authority of women title holders. Vestiges of these positions remained, however. At the time of the *jihad*, the

Fulani regarded this authority of women over women as one of the fundamental manifestations of the un-Islamic nature of Hausa society: "One of the ways of their government is that [a man] put the affairs of his women into the hands of the oldest one, and every one [of the others] is like a slave-woman under her."[32] While the leader of the jihad, Shehu Usman dan Fodio, denounced the inappropriate roles of royal women in the Hausa states, he deplored the virtually universal ignorance of common women (that is, ignorance of the *Qu'ran*) and advocated that they be taught basic Arabic literacy and Islamic religious doctrine. This admonition was used in the late 1970s to encourage fathers to send their daughters to school.

The Shehu's second son, Muhammad Bello, founded the town of Sokoto, which became the Fulani capital, and Kano came at least nominally under the control of Sokoto as did the other six Hausa states or emirates. The Fulani rulers established the *Sharia* as a uniform code throughout the empire and ruled "in the name of Allah." Over the years, through intermarriage and cultural assimilation, the once conquering Fulanis have adopted the language and customs of their postjihad subjects. Fulanis are part of Hausa society; hence the common ethnic amalgamatory term "Hausa/Fulani." At the same time, virtually all the Hausa have embraced Islam, creating that higher level of unity that transcends supposed ethnic differentiation. Within this unity, however, the politics of inter-Islamic brotherhood forces are at play. And, underlying Islamic ties to North Africa through the Fulani are the deeper ties in Hausa Kano to the more fundamentalist Islamic brotherhoods of Saudia Arabia.

Clearly, whatever the political experience of pre-Islamic ruling class Hausa women, it had declined gradually but dramatically over the centuries of Islamization, with a final and fatal break at the time of the jihad and shortly thereafter. That all women in postjihad Kano were already political minors when the British colonial state was imposed is apparent from the dearth of reference to them in official documents, except for the inevitable mention of marriage and divorce patterns. Presumably the subordination of women accorded with British predilections for a male-controlled society. In the years following the arrival of the British and until independence in 1960, the notion that women bore any interests that would warrant their having a political place in Kano had no relevance to either the British or the traditional rulers. Here "modern" colonialism reinforced an already entrenched social norm—women belonged in the home, not in public places.

The early twentieth century brought another sharp change in

historical direction in the area of the Hausa states. Most of the Fulani empire, centered in Sokoto, came under the domination of the British. Kano fell to British-led troops in 1903. In that year, British rule was also effectively extended over all of Nigerian Hausaland when British military forces defeated the sultan of Sokoto at the battle of Burmi. Unlike the French, for whom colonialism in Africa entailed the policies of Direct Rule and assimilation, (the extension of French cultural norms and administrative structures to colonial subjects), British colonial rule, as formulated by Sir Fredrick Lugard, the first Governor of Northern Nigeria, had a more laissez-faire quality about it. For Indirect Rule, as it was to be called, entailed the retention of the precolonial forms of government (i.e. the Fulani emirate system) in an attempt to gradually encourage the evolution of the Hausa political culture and system toward the British mold. Thus Indirect Rule would occur within the more familiar (and theoretically less disruptive) framework of traditional indigenous rule.

The British felt an innate empathy for the Hausa-Fulani system of government, which parallelled, they believed, Britain's own history of constitutional monarchy, political and social stratification, and empire building. The British found among the Hausa-Fulani a structure with which they could identify—one characterized by strong leadership, centralized government, and established religion. Official British policy was thus to accept, entrench, and relegitimize the prevailing "religio-political orthodoxy."[33] Islam was accorded the status of "native law and custom" and, with a view toward protecting the Islamic integrity of the North, laws were passed severely restricting Christian missionary activity, thus ensuring that Islam there was protected from liberalizing forces at work in Southern Nigeria. Islam became ever more deeply entrenched, and the Shehu's legacy of ideas remains part of the ethos of the area to the present day. The colonial state provided the stable conditions necessary for Islamic culture to grow and develop. Under Fulani rule and British protection, the Islamic (or *Sharia*) courts were very much a part of this system. An elite, conservative, and orthodox class of Muslim teachers (*mallams*) flourished with considerable influence under the protections provided by Indirect Rule.[34] To this day, when there is a conflict between Islamic orthodoxy and modern ideas, the *mallams*, who have considerable influence over their adherents, give evidence of a deep-seated hostility to change. Hence, any effort in this environment to enhance the rights of women without Islamic sanction is probably doomed to failure.

The period of British colonial rule in Nigeria was very short.

By the 1940s, a southern based nationalist movement was already well underway, and demands for immediate and full independence could be heard. In 1960 Nigeria became an independent state. The next five years brought tension and trouble for the civilian regime, culminating in a controversial and violence-plagued second election at the end of 1964. The intense struggle between regional, ethnic, and religious elites and a central federal government that appeared too weak to check their excesses led to the demise of the First Republic by means of a violent military coup in January 1966. After waging a civil war along ethnic and religious lines (between Hausa and Igbo and between Christian and Muslim) the northern military elite continued to rule Nigeria until 1979, when a Muslim dominated civilian government was returned to power.

In 1967 Kano became a state within a reconstituted Nigeria without any alterations of its traditional boundaries. Citing the teachings of the Shehu, the first military governor (Alhaji Audu Bako) established primary, secondary, and teacher training colleges for girls and women. In 1976 the federal government introduced a scheme of Universal Primary Education (UPE) and all parents were urged to send all their children, male and female, to school. In 1978, the military government granted Muslim women the right to vote for the first time in the new elections called for 1979, which returned Nigeria to civilian rule for four more years. As a result of these innovations, the numbers of educated women and of girls in school in Kano increased manyfold, while the presence of women as teachers and as low-level administrators in various government agencies also grew steadily. By 1982 the Kano state government had founded 130 new elementary schools, five secondary schools and, two teacher training colleges for girls and was actively urging parents to enroll them.

In the national elections of 1979, the People's Redemption Party (PRP) came to power in Kano State. The PRP was a popularly based political party that presented itself as a radical Muslim party with a public commitment to the "emancipation" of women. In fact, women voting for the first time are credited with having elected this party to power. Before he died in April 1983, Mallam Aminu Kano, the national leader of the PRP and a popular Kano religious leader and presidential candidate in the 1979 elections, announced that his vice-presidential running mate in the 1983 elections was to be a woman. From 1979-1984 (when the civilians were again overthrown by the Nigerian military), the Kano state government aggressively sought to encourage women's education and participation in the political domain. The real impact of these efforts is yet to be felt, but observations on the scene suggest that real reform will be limited.

In spite of the right to an education and the right to vote, Islam as practiced in Kano presents a major constraint upon any state effort towards dramatic change in the public role of women, limiting freedom of choice and movement by gender and according privileges to men while defining restrictions for women. In spite of their right to an education, Muslim women in Kano must present their husband's written consent to work. In spite of their right to vote, Muslim women are not afforded the protections of the Nigerian Constitution of 1979, which relegates to the states matters covered by "Islamic personal law." Hence, matters of vital concern to women (marriage, divorce, child custody, property) are regulated by the state according to *Sharia* (Islamic) law.[35] Wife seclusion (*kulle*) is nearly universally practiced in Kano, and while this is an Islamic tradition, in Kano its practice takes the extreme form of actual physical seclusion rather than the more modified form of veiling as practiced in many other Muslim societies. Over the decades more and more women have entered *kulle*; at present, it is the general pattern of life for women in both urban and rural areas in Kano State.

For centuries Kano had reflected the religion and culture of North Africa and the Arabian peninsula. From the beginning of the twentieth century, Kano was also being pulled towards the southern coast with its Christian and European influences. Since 1952, when regionally based political parties were formed, Kano has been associated with radical and populist Islamic movements. It has retained its position as the acknowledged seat of Hausa and Fulani traditions and culture and of Islamic learning. The juxtaposition of opposing currents represented by Islamic culture and traditions, on the one hand, and Western education and radical politics on the other, has produced great tension in the society evidenced by the outbreak of Islamic fundamentalist violence in 1981 in which 10,000 people were killed.

In Kano, the call for a fundamental reconsideration of the position of women within an Islamic framework has occasioned public controversy. The issues seem inseparable from a more general anxiety over the nature and direction of change. A sharpening perception of the claims and consequences of programs of social modernization goes hand-in-hand with a sensation of threat to a society that prides itself on its adherence to Islamic teachings.

The subordination of women to men and their exclusion from

the world of men is central to the conception of Islam as practiced in Kano. In Kano today the emphasis of traditional Hausa culture remains on inherited family status, stratification of classes, ascription of roles, continuity of institutions, and conformity of behavior to prevailing interpretations of Islamic doctrine. In this culture, as in Senegal, women are positioned in effect as the minor wards of their fathers and husbands; they are induced to marry early, to confine their activities to the domestic sphere of social relationships and functions, and to observe postures of deference and service toward men. They cannot own property or apply for loans. Girls marry young, generally at the onset of puberty. Upon marriage, most women enter *kulle* or seclusion: they do not go out to shop, trade, or to attend the market. Because they cannot go out, their opportunity for paid work is severely limited. Most engage in some sort of small-scale trade, especially the preparation of cooked food for sale by their children, but the profits are small. Life expectancy is forty-five years for men. For women it is thirty-six, which is in part the consequence of high mortality during childbirth; this in turn is in part related to the fact that most girls in Kano will be married by age twelve.

The belief that the home must be more closely ministered to by females than by males in order to nurture the young in the Islamic way of life and that women must be educated, particularly in obtaining a knowledge of the *Qu'ran* in order to so nurture the young, is a constant theme in this culture. Thus, although encouraged to go to school, women face a multitude of restrictions: their sexual activities are circumscribed, their roles are more closely defined, and their access to social and economic institutions is more limited than men's in order that their families may be the focus of their lives. Within the limited social context of female adult life, Hausa society reinforces women's conservatism and traditionalism, and encourages them to accept or at least rationalize their subordination in accordance with Islamic teachings.

Religious education has been a concern of political and religious leaders alike in Kano for the past several decades. The Northern Muslim Congress was established in Kano in 1950 for the purpose of upgrading and expanding Islamic schools and was strongly encouraged by the *mallams* who advocated instruction in Arabic (rather than English, the language of Christianity) in all schools in Kano. Mallam Aminu Kano, the Emir of Kano, and large merchant families all established schools that tried to graft Western education onto an existing Islamic one. Although English in fact did become the language of official instruction in Kano schools, both political and religious leaders strongly encourage the study of Arabic. The federally supported university in Kano (Bayero) requires a knowledge of the language in certain curricula, such as law. Arabic is described as "the language of the Prophet" and hence, of true Islam. Thus, while education for women is advocated and indeed a majority of girls now attend up to three years of primary school, the purpose of education is clearly seen to be to teach girls to be proper wives and mothers in the Islamic way.

Likewise, the genesis of religious political themes, constantly reiterated in the language of politics, gives Kano politics a very distinct cast. The effort to relate political positions to Islamic themes on the part of all major political parties is relevant to the efforts after 1979 to develop public policies affecting women and to involve them in the political process. Clearly all such efforts must be justifiable by Islamic principles.[36]

Islam recognizes basic human rights, including life, justice, minimum standard of living, and the equality of human beings regardless of race, color, or nationality (but not sex).[37] Although they have never been invoked by women, human rights in Islam also include the right to protest government tyranny, the right to equality before the law, and the right to participate in the affairs of state (*Qu'ran* 24:55).

In a society in which deeply ingrained patterns of female subordination generally are believed to find sanction primarily in religious rather than secular prescriptions, any attempt at redefinition must also proceed on religious grounds. Mallam Aminu Kano repeatedly challenged the near total exclusion of women from the public world by emphasizing that no Qu'ranic text denied full political participation for women.[38]

However, fundamental notions of social place are challenged in addressing this area of deeply ingrained social mores. As Aminu Kano and other reformers succeeded in introducing female equality as an accepted ideal in religious life, the daily lives of women moved, if anything, farther from such a reality. Radical politics and progressive religious ideas continued to do battle with conservative and retrogressive notions of "right" concerning women's proper place. While exhortations for education and political emancipation of women were increasingly voiced, more and more women were moving deeper into total seclusion, which is now virtually universal in both the rural and urban areas of Kano State. This fact of life for Hausa Muslim women in Kano is reflected in developments at the national level in Nigeria. While women in the southern states of

Nigeria voted in the elections of the 1960s, women in the northern states did not vote until the 1979 elections, after having been enfranchised by a military decree.[39]

Perhaps it is in the field of law that Islam has the greatest impact on women. In Kano, Islamic law has increasingly become a fundamental symbol of Muslim identity. During the colonial period, Islamic law was protected in the northern part of the country, including in Kano. At independence in 1960, four categories of law (criminal, land, subversion, and taxation) were assigned to the civil code that was, theoretically, legislated and secular. The Islamic legal code (*Sharia*) continued to apply to a fifth category of law; family law continued to be religiously based on a part of the Islamic system left under the authority of the emirs and *Sharia* courts. This provision became very contentious during the debates in 1979 concerning the adoption of a new Nigerian Constitution.[40]

The issue of concern in these debates was the provision for the creation in Nigeria of a Federal *Sharia* Court of Appeal that would review cases of Islamic law heard at the state level. In the end a compromise was reached wherein the Federal Court of Appeal would include judges versed in Islamic law, who would, when the occasion arose, form a subunit of the Court in order to hear such cases. During the course of the debates, several important issues were raised, including the proper relationship between sacred and secular law in general, the position of Islamic law in a secular state in particular, and the separation of Islamic "personal law" out of the general body of Islamic law.[41]

While it was stressed in the debates that Islam is a "total way of life" and the *Sharia* sacred in its totality and not subject to change in order to suit changing social conditions, the Muslim members compromised in this instance, as they had with the British, in order to make a separate Islamic court system more palatable to non-Muslims. They argued that the *Sharia* courts would deal only with Islamic personal law, except where the parties concerned voluntarily submitted other issues to these courts, as provided under the provisions regarding "customary" law in the new constitution.

The final version of the constitution as promulgated into law established a *Sharia* Court of Appeal in each of Nigeria's ten Islamic states (Nigerian Constitution, Sec. 240[1]). The grand *kadi* (chief justice) of such courts and the number of *kadis* in each state are prescribed by the state houses of assembly (Constitution, Sec. 240[2]) and must have considerable experience or be distinguished as scholars of Islamic law (Sec. 241[3]).

The constitution makes it clear that marriage laws are under the jurisdiction of the states. Thus, for Islamic women, matters that most deeply affect them—marriage, divorce, child custody, and property—are not under the protection of the Nigerian Constitution but rather, under the sole jurisdiction of the states; in states with Muslim majorities, they are relegated to the *Sharia* courts. The appeal from these courts is not to higher secular courts, but to a subcommittee of the federal appeal court composed of Muslim men "learned in Islamic law."

In Hausaland, customary forms of behavior are accepted as Islamic injunctions, even where varying interpretations of Islamic law are possible. According to the grand *kadi* of Kano State, all legislation must be held within the limits prescribed by the law of the *Sharia*. "No legislation can alter or modify an injunction of God and his Prophet. The responsibility for determing the real intent of the Sharia must rest with people with specialized knowledge of the Sharia, with men learned in Islamic law."[42]

At present large families as well as early and arranged marriages limit choices and options for women. With education, some women will perceive their situation as disadvantaged and mobilize politically for individual rights—for the right to work, to have custody of children, to pursue education, to make choices in marriage. But, in daily life, the difficulties of social radicalism—of the appearance of disaffection from one's culture—are too great to attract many women or men. The promotion of women's education has become socially acceptable. But notions of female autonomy, the possibility that a young woman might live outside of marriage or that birth control or family planning might be practiced, for example, are still generally unacceptable. Thus, it appears that while in Senegal the state may have improved the position of women in relation to men, in Islamic Nigeria it has not. In Nigeria, a nation-state with a large Muslim plurality but not a majority, Muslim fundamentalists play a more pivotal political role, and hence the state is more cautious in advancing women's rights if such rights appear to conflict with Islamic law.

CONCLUSION

Islam was introduced to Kano by Arab missionaries in the twelfth century and came to Senegal through missionaries from North African societies in the eighteenth and nineteenth centuries.

This critical time difference turns out to be a crucial variable in the use of Islam in the two societies. In the Senegalese case these Muslim missionaries were similar in culture and expectations to the peoples of the ethnic groups among whom they spread the religion. Thus, Islam spread more rapidly and widely in the area than did Christianity which had been brought by missionaries from Europe whose culture and habits were alien. In Europe, in the eighteenth and nineteenth centuries, the Industrial Revolution began, and with it came the Christian Reformation. Economy, society, and religion were transformed together. Protestantism and more latterly, Catholicism, adapted their doctrines and their teachings to the advancing wave of reform and liberalism. North Africa and the Middle East did not experience this set of changes, except through their contact with Europe. Liberalism and democracy, which grew out of the industrial revolution, were exported by the West as part of colonialism and imperialism. Christian missionaries reflected these values. Northern Nigeria was more protected from these forces than was Senegal due to differing philosophies concerning the nature of the colonial state on the part of the British and the French. Christian missionaries were not permitted to work in Muslim areas of Northern Nigeria, and thus Islam here was more isolated from liberalizing influences than was the case in Senegal.

Muslim scholars have argued that what prevented a kind of Islamic reformation similar to the Protestant Reformation in Europe and what preserved Islamic teachings in their original form was an unfavorable balance of power which kept the Islamic world under foreign domination until very recently.[43] This may be true. In any case, the attitudes of Islam toward women can be best explained by understanding that Islam as taught in West Africa was a religion exported by a preindustrial, rural and underdeveloped society in which paternalism and inequality were parallel social conventions. Liberalism, equality, and secularization were introduced as products of European imperialism and in many cases are rejected for that reason. Societies, however, in the Middle East and North Africa have not yet modernized economically, nor are they industrialized. Inasmuch as the Industrial Revolution was a precondition for the Enlightenment in Europe, we cannot expect such changes to occur in societies which are still economically dependent and underdeveloped. The prospect for a reformation in Islam which would affect the roles for women prescribed by it is made more difficult by the fact that Islam is an organic religion. It does not distinguish between the sacred and the secular, and it does prescribe in detail the rules which should govern family and social life. It was written down by men in a pre-industrial society and preserved in this archaic form to the present day. This makes the problem of reform of Islam greater; but it does not make such reform impossible.[44]

Many scholars have pointed to the great variation in the application of the *Sharia* in Muslim countries as evidence that Islamic law can be reinterpreted should those who control the brotherhoods in a given society choose to do so. Christianity too in preindustrial society was used to justify the submission of slaves and the dependence and inferiority of women. The Christian Bible does not prescribe a complete set of family laws as does the *Qu'ran*, but it does admonish women to hide their "beauties" and extols women to be in subservient, dependent roles. Various Pentecostal groups have used literal quotes from the Bible to justify existing and unequal social rules. Islam has been similarly used by conservative and reactionary religious leaders.

In West Africa, in particular, the version of Islam adopted by a country depends on the characteristics of those in power. The more fundamentalist and conservative the men in office (or in power in the countryside), the more they will turn to a fundamentalist form of Islam. At the present, more liberal minded Muslim politicians confront the influence of nationalism and reaction against the West in the Khoumeni Muslim form. This reaction is easily understandable; when countries face economic crises and political impotence they look for a strong ideology to provide a national identity. In both Nigeria and Senegal this combination of circumstances may lead to a conservative backlash in society which will damage the position of women with Islam provided as the justification. What is at issue, however, is not primarily the nature of a religion but the way it is being used and the characteristics of men (seldom women) in power in the country as a whole and the political circumstances at any particular time.

Contemporary Islamic male writers have a strong and negative reaction to any identification that the patriarchal relationship between men and women might be challengeable. As do men elsewhere, Islamic men appear comfortable with women as subservient and obedient wives whom they marry in order to legitimate conception and procreation. Any challenge to this relationship will most likely be resisted vigorously and the authority of the state will be used to support this resistance. Secular reform cannot trespass on the domain of sacred law. Reform cannot be imposed by the state, but must come through changing interpretations of the law initiated by Islamic scholars themselves.

GENDER AND THE STATE: PERSPECTIVES FROM LATIN AMERICA

*Susan C. Bourque**

Academic attention to both "the state" and gender has flourished in the study of Latin America. These lines of inquiry have revised our understanding of the region, its politics and political culture. Significant theoretical questions have been raised by these parallel lines of research, and while discussions of the state and gender are currently distinct (as suggested in the editors' introduction) there are important points of intersection. The study of gender has enriched our understanding of the differential impact of state policy on men and women and revealed the symbolic components of power. Similarly, renewed attention to the state has revised our understanding of the relationships between state elites and civil society and underscored the significance of women's efforts to organize politically.[1] Most significantly, research on the state has rekindled interest in political culture, a concept which in turn is enriched by the current research on gender.

GENDER AND THE STATE

Feminist theory is grounded in analyses of power but no scholarly consensus has been reached on the ideal role of the state. Feminist analyses of the state's impact on gender relations have run the gamut from unquestioned faith in the ability of a socialist state to promote an egalitarian ideology, to complete rejection of the state as hopelessly masculine, militaristic, and authoritarian. While one still finds feminists distributed along this spectrum, scholars now emphasize the need for greater sensitivity to the particular context of states and to their internal cultures. Feminist theorists share the growing awareness among political scientists that the values, attitudes, and world views of the incumbents of state offices and bureaucracies are varied. Thus, state elites are both potential sources of access as well as critical actors in the creation and maintenance of hierarchies. Just as the research on the state by political scientists has revealed a more complex and varied institution, so too, research on gender has identified the wide-ranging significance of gender-based ideologies as key components in state policy and action.

Feminist scholars have raised a series of questions about gender and political life. First, how did Western political culture develop so as to exclude women from formal political activity? What have been the available styles of political action for women? How have women leaders functioned in relation to their constituencies? What has been the relationship between leadership and sexuality? At the level of the state, they have asked a series of very practical questions: How have state policies in the past affected women? How can the state be used to improve women's status? What impact would shrinking or expanding the state have on women's access to political life?[2]

These questions are asked in the context of a new understanding of gender. Rather than an immutable category given in biology, feminist scholars now argue that our concepts of gender are socially constructed; they change historically and vary cross-culturally. They are open to conscious manipulation. "The production of culturally appropriate forms of male and female behavior is a central function of social authority, mediated by the complex interactions of a wide range of economic, social, political, and religious institutions."[3] We have come to understand gender relations as processes in flux. Thus subordination or domination are not fixed states; rather they are the current outcomes of dynamic and interactive processes, and as such, open to challenge and change. Further, gender relations are systemic, they permeate and intersect most levels of social life; change in gender relations will have reverberations throughout the social system. This understanding of gender leads feminist inquiry to ask of the future, what alternative conceptions of authority and legitimacy would provide an altered conception of female leadership and political behavior?

The symbolic content of gender and power is a central element in thinking about gender and the state. "Meaning," we have come to recognize, is central. As Michelle Rosaldo wrote in 1980, "sexual asymmetry is a political and social fact, much less concerned with individual resources and skills than with relationships and claims that guide the way people act and shape their understandings." Thus she concludes, "we must begin to analyze the social processes that give appearances their sense."[4] Similarly, Joan Scott writes, "concepts of gender structure perception and the concrete and symbolic nature of all social life."[5]

Given this point of departure, what does a systemic approach to the study of gender and the state imply in scholarly terms? The most successful efforts in this direction combine attention to four levels of analysis, or four dimensions of state elites' responses to gender. First, scholars must identify the mechanisms of access to control over society's resources. This includes attention to the legal and property systems and the restrictions or opportunities structured by gender, the entitlement systems (including education and health provisions, as well as employment), and the creation and use of new knowledge and tools. Second, we must understand the prevailing attitudes toward sexuality and its control through policies toward birth control, abortion, and the family, as well as the treatment of issues of sexual preference and the control of sexual violence and rape. Third, feminist research has been especially insightful in illuminating how competing and intersecting hierarchies are used, either in conjunction or opposition, to achieve social control. Thus we must understand how gender is used in conjunction with or in opposition to class, racial, and ethnic divisions to serve state purposes. Finally, we must understand the symbolic: the use and manipulation of gendered symbols of state authority. How is the association of male and female used to convey ideas about political relations? Appreciating how authority and legitimacy are conveyed through gender imagery may reveal important, yet unarticulated assumptions within the political culture. Unravelling the symbolic uses of gender may reveal unspoken but nonetheless key components of a society's political culture.

While I have separated these analytic dimensions of gender-state relations, they operate in conjunction with one another; we would expect change in one dimension to trigger change throughout the system. Two examples of recent scholarship from Latin America demonstrate these dimensions of gender-state interaction.

GENDER AND STATE FORMATION

Scholars of gender relations have been concerned with the origins of sexual subordination. The starting point of such research is state formation, the moment when institutions are either created or imposed. To what extent do regimes fashion policy in gendered terms? What functions do these policies serve? Irene Silverblatt's study of the Inca and Spanish conquests uses political history to illuminate both state action and gender relationships. Silverblatt argues that both conquering powers constructed and consolidated their new states on the basis of rewritten gender relations.[6] In the case of the Incas, it was the assertion of access to the women of the conquered groups which symbolized the group's submission to the lords of Cuzco. While the Incas did not alter women's traditional control over resources, the conquest of the communities of the Andes and the establishment of the bureaucratic apparatus to run the empire created inequities where they had not previously existed. The Inca conquest infused the sexual division of labor (which predated the conquest) with sexual hierarchy by exalting the male role of warrior and creating a new exclusively male role of state administrator. The Inca empire changed the rewards available to men and women and set new limits on what each could become. Women were not exalted as warriors nor did they have access to the new administrative posts necessitated by the creation of the empire. These new opportunities changed material conditions for men and women and replaced the Andean understanding of complementarity with hierarchy.

The Spanish conquest kept the class differences of Inca rule in place, and further alienated women from their control over resources by restricting their rights to land and property as well as their religious responsibilities, privileges, and autonomy. While theoretically releasing women from the responsibilities for tribute to the crown, colonial practices exacerbated the financial dependence of women on men. Silverblatt argues that Spanish policies which separated Andean women from their traditional property rights often favored their male kin. This manipulation of male Indian peasants, she argues, enhanced male compliance with the Spanish state.[7]

In her account Silverblatt combines all four dimensions of gender-state relations: the control of resources, the control of sexuality, the manipulation of competing hierarchies, and the symbolic representation of gender and power. Furthermore, she demonstrates how each aspect of state action affects the others. With regard to women's access to resources, the Inca state and the Spanish empire created new opportunities available only to men and in some cases separated women from previous sources of independence; with respect to sexuality, the concept of virginity was linked to service to the Inca state and the dedication of young women to the needs of the empire became a key mechanism for enhancing the position of one's family within the empire. Under the Spanish, the control of women's sexuality became a thinly veiled mechanism for dislodging women from their previous realms of authority, particularly with respect to Andean religious observances. At the symbolic level, during the Inca conquest marriage was the metaphor for state authority, and women's subordination in marriage emblematic of the new status of conquered groups. Under the Spanish, the Andean concept of complementarity was replaced with the claim of female inferiority and vulnerability and consequently, women's need for male protection. This claim legitimated the state's efforts to eliminate women's religious prerogatives and property rights. Silverblatt illustrates the intersection of gender hierarchies with class and ethnicity by demonstrating that during the Spanish colonial era, peasant Indian men's pursuit of self-interest brought them into collusion with the Spanish. In their rush to appropriate the goods women lost under the Spanish, peasant men became unwitting collaborators with the Spanish in the destruction of Andean society.[8]

GENDER AND AGRICULTURE POLICY

In studies of the contemporary period, scholars have been concerned to understand the constraints on women's access to resources, and to the mechanisms which perpetuate economic subordination. In Latin America, this has meant reassessments of women's participation in the agricultural sector where governments have been pressed to develop reforms. Two issues have become central: First, how can women gain access as beneficiaries of land distribution policies, either through the assignment of a land parcel or membership in the governing organization of collective or cooperative schemes? Second, what kinds of policies and programs would facilitate a wider range of options for rural women and what are the ideological constraints on such access? Related to both issues are the overarching questions: What role should the state play in the promotion of gender equity and what would induce it to play that role? What role can rural women's organizations play in prompting, guiding, or substituting for state action?

While these issues appear to address only one of our four dimensions (that is, access to and control over resources), a closer look at recent studies of state policy toward women and agriculture suggests that at least three of the four dimensions come into play. First at the symbolic level, policy reform depends on the state recognizing women's labor. State elites must be able to see woman's contribution to development in the agricultural sector. This means not only her labor, but distinguishing her contributions and her rewards from those assigned to the household.[9] Freeing policy makers from the assumption that the concerns of women would be met if the needs of peasant households were adequately addressed requires a major analytic shift, a major change in perceptions of how the peasant family operates, and an altered conception of women and their needs. As Staudt has written:

> Women's invisibility in policy is perpetuated by treating them as analytically indistinct from the family or from men. . . . The household lens blinds analysts to the existence of female-headed households, to the distribution of income, status, and opportunities within households . . .[10]

A major thrust of the scholarship on gender and agriculture in the past fifteen years has been to end the invisibility of women's labor force participation. This is a symbolic issue rooted in both gender expectations and class relations. Class hierarchies intersect with gender to obscure women's contributions to agriculture. Both men and women deny women's contributions to agriculture when such contributions would suggest lower status for the household. As Carmen Diana Deere and Magdalena Leon point out: "Although class and gender can be separated analytically, in practice they are difficult to distinguish. . . ."[11] Even explicit efforts on the part of states committed to gender equity have found this profound perceptual change difficult to achieve.

In a comparative study of how women have fared in agrarian reforms throughout Latin America, Deere notes that although we now have extensive data documenting rural women's participation in agriculture, in most Latin American agarian reforms only male household heads were incorporated into the new structures. Women's participation in agrarian reform structures "has taken place only in countries where the incorporation of women is an explicit objective of state policy."[12] But even then the law may not be enough. Citing data from Honduras, where the law explicitly included women, Deere writes, "The predominant norms of the gender division of labor served as a barrier to women's incorporation within the agrarian reform, even though the law explicitly provided for at least female heads of households to be potential beneficiaries."[13] Research in rural Peru suggests similar forms of local resistance to state initiatives designed to promote sexual equality.[14]

Scholarship on gender has clarified the complexity and constraints in the rural sector by demonstrating the intersection of class and gender, the tenacity of sexual stereotyping and the symbolic significance of gender in limiting access to resources. We need to combine this research from the local level with a closer look at the mechanisms operating at the state level. In this respect, the Mexican case study by Lourdes Arizpe and Carlota Botey[15] is an instructive first effort. Arizpe and Botey tell us that despite the central role women play in rural life, agrarian planners had failed to take that participation into account until 1971 when women gained equal rights in the Agrarian Reform. At least four provisions of that 1971 Federal Law of Agrarian Reform were designed to protect women's rights. A related provision of the law created agro-industrial units for women (*Unidad Industrial de la Mujer*). Arizpe and Botey record that much of the change inherent in the 1971 law was undermined by women's lack of access to credit and technology. It was not until 1983 that the government undertook large-scale initiatives toward rural women through the creation of PROMUDER (*Women's Program for Rural Development or Programa de la Mujer para la Consecusion del Desarrollo Rural*). PROMUDER explicitly responded to women's needs to earn cash, to gain greater access to technology, and for more information about their legal rights in employment. Despite the difficulties that arose in the rural center for women, Arizpe and Botey conclude "the very fact that such projects were proposed at the upper policymaking echelons and that they were initiated throughout the country with a ripple effect meant that rural women found new avenues for participation open to them."[16]

Arizpe and Botey's study suggests the importance of state policy in the rural sector. Yet despite that recognition, we still do not fully understand what stimulates change at the state level. Those who have looked at socialist regimes find some hope in the ideology of equality promoted by the state, but it is a qualified hope. "Even socialist states, or those in transition, cannot will away the association of the female gender with reproduction or male privilege within the domestic unit or society."[17] It is at this juncture, when the importance of a more comprehensive understanding of the motivations of state elites is obvious, that we turn to the new research on the state, and the intersection of the two currents of scholarship.

THE STATE IN LATIN AMERICAN POLITICS

"The state" has returned to prominence in scholarship on Latin American politics. Several concerns rekindled the interest of political scientists. First, there was growing puzzlement within the scholarly community about the conditions for achieving simultaneous economic growth and political stability. The initial formulations of modernization theories, which assumed that economic modernization would bring about political democracy and stability, proved inaccurate. Similarly, approaches which stressed regime type as an explanation for political or economic performance were of limited utility. Dependency theory offered an important perspective on the interdependent and unequal terms of development, but its sweeping tenets were overly deterministic and ultimately static.[18] Dependency theory failed to illuminate important variations and sources of change within the "dependent" nation. The need to look more closely at the internal processes of the state and the choices of political leaders became apparent. This led many to look at public policy, and from public policy to turn new attention to the internal culture of states. How were state elites thinking about development? How did their ideologies affect their choices and calculations about change?

These questions about the impact of the values and attitudes of state elites on policy choices have led to a reconstituted notion of political culture. This is emphatically not the notion of political culture which relied upon sentimental, stereotyped or self-serving pronouncements about "national character," (such as "the emotional, hot-blooded Latin ill suited for deliberative democracy"). Rather the new focus on political culture looks directly at the beliefs and assessments of those state leaders involved in the formation and implementation of state policy. The concept admits the likelihood of more than one version of the culture, and the potential for conflict among competing visions of development and change.[19]

A second component to the new research on the state is a reassessment of the relationship between state elites and civil society. The formulations of both liberals and neo-Marxists[20] have been rejected in favor of an emphasis on the independent identity and interests of state elites and their impact on civil society. Thus state elites can actively shape interaction with civil society, influencing the very nature of political life, giving rise to "various conceptions of the meaning and methods of politics itself, conceptions that influence the behavior of all groups and classes in national society."[21]

Two recent studies merit close attention as examples of the superb work being done on the state. Merilee Grindle in *State and Countryside: Development Policy and Agrarian Politics in Latin America* examines the changes in agricultural policy in Mexico, Colombia, and Brazil, and Alfred Stepan in *Rethinking the Military* analyzes the role of the military in the process of redemocratization in Brazil, Argentina, and Uruguay. Each study, while not focused on gender relations, has important implications for research on gender.

Grindle takes issue with both Marxist and pluralist positions toward state elites. She points out that proponents of both perspectives view state elites as unimportant to the initiation and content of policy. Grindle argues on the basis of evidence from Mexico, Brazil, and Colombia that one finds regular instances in which state elites have subordinated specific interests in order to implement what they defined as national economic interests.

With respect to Mexico, Grindle traces the growth of the state's role in agriculture from 1940 to 1980, and concludes that while state policies initially fostered the export-oriented production of the small capitalist entrepreneurs, this policy was reversed in the 1970s when state elites determined that their policies had exacerbated rural poverty and instability. State elites responded with programs which derived from their new understanding of the agrarian situation, not from the dictates of the small capitalist class they had initially favored. In short, changed world views led to new policies.[22]

Among the changes, although not directly addressed by Grindle, was a 1971 Law of Agrarian Reform which granted equal *ejido* (communal ownership) rights to women and established the programs to address the needs of rural women, described by Arizpe and Botey. When state elites change policy in response to an altered understanding of the impact of previous policies, or in response to an altered vision of how they hope to alleviate poverty or achieve economic growth and development, then it is of enormous importance to understand what stimulated change in the direction of gender equity in the rural sector. When these policies explicitly address the concerns of women, we must ask if altered perceptions led to a new vision of social relations? It is equally possible that new policies toward women may not include revised gender relations, nor a new view of men's and women's roles. Thus, understanding the values and attitudes of elites is of critical importance.

Feminist scholars have signalled the important cultural and political uses of gender imagery. Grindle's work reminds us that the internal culture of state elites also includes perceptions of men and women. Jointly these two lines of inquiry lead us to ask some further questions about agricultural policy: What led state elites to perceive the changes necessary and to begin to address the needs of rural women in 1971? Where did the policy initiate? Grindle tells us that the Luis Echeverría administration was deeply concerned about the inequities suffered by rural peasants that had been generated by export led production. The intersection of the research on gender and the state would lead us to ask, who in the Echeverría administration targeted the needs of women? What analysis of the problems of rural life motivated the change? And what understanding of rural women and their needs did they bring to their policy recommendations?

In the case of the PROMUDER program we understand some of the state process which led to its development and its implementation. The project was developed in the office of Beatriz Paredes, who was then undersecretary for Agrarian Organization. Paredes, who became governor of Tlaxcala in 1987, led an office staffed by distinguished feminist scholars who had seen the need to turn to action and involvement in political life.[23]

While Grindle's analysis helps us appreciate the utility of an emphasis on the changing attitudes and values of state elites, research on the state has been equally concerned with the interaction between state elites and civil society: "The forms of collective action through which groups make political demands or through which political leaders seek to mobilize support are also partially shaped in relation to the structures and activities of states."[24] Stepan's work on the military and the process of redemocratization emphasizes this dimension.

Throughout Latin America, the military establishments or the national police force play a significant if not determining role in the state. Fluctuations between civilian and military governments occur in Central America, the Southern Cone, and the Andes, and for these regions military regimes must be analyzed as key state actors. Stepan examines the values and attitudes of military leaders as they returned their nations to civilian control. He explores the motivations for such decisions and the key elements in moving toward new relationships between the military and civil society. His study reveals the tensions and cross-currents within military governments, as well as the sources of change which encouraged redemocratization.

In the case of Brazil, Stepan concludes that it was the "growing autonomy of the security community both within the state and especially within the military" which led the regime to look for allies in civil society and to a process of "regime concession and societal conquest."[25] In brief, Stepan argues that President Ernesto Geisel and the key figure in the military's scheme of liberalization, General Golbery, realized that in creating the national security system they had created a monster. Moreover, the extreme repressive tactics of torture and "disappearances," long after any real threat had been eliminated, did not serve the long-term interests of the military nor their vision of the development of Brazil. Moving against extremists within the military and limiting the security community required finesse and carefully constructed alliances with civil society and even with the opposition to the military regime. Stepan recounts President Geisel's efforts to support civil society's protests over torture and his contacts with both the Church and human rights organizations in efforts to identify himself with civil society and allow him to move against military extremists. Stepan's work raises new questions for us about how to interpret the responses of authoritarian military regimes to women's protests over torture, disappearances, and human rights, as well as the larger questions about women's interaction with the state under various types of regimes.

What do these closer readings of internal dynamics of Latin American states tell us about the role of gender in the political system? Neither Grindle nor Stepan is explicitly concerned with gender, yet their studies highlight where the link between research on the state and gender would be mutually beneficial. Our understanding of the development ideologies of state elites will be more complete and our understanding of their policy initiatives more comprehensive to the extent that our questions probe the concepts of gender relations which inform their policies. Similarly, Stepan's insights into the relations between the military's internal culture and its links to civil society lead us to broaden feminist analyses of women's political behavior. This becomes especially apparent when we consider the interaction between authoritarian regimes in Latin America and current trends in women's political participation.

GENDER AND STATE BUILDING: MILITARY REGIMES AND WOMEN'S POLITICAL PARTICIPATION

A main focus of Latin American politics has been state building and competing views of the kind of state desired. As in the case of the European state, we would expect concepts of gender to be a crucial component in this process. In Latin America the military's role is central to both state building and the concepts of gender involved. The overwhelmingly male nature of military organizations suggests a gendered territory of enormous symbolic importance. If we are concerned with the question of why women have been excluded from formal politics in Latin America, this association of the public sphere with the military is a key issue. Women's attempts to influence military governments are an unalloyed case of gendered interaction. Similarly, the response of the military to women's overtures and protests tell us a great deal about how gender images and expectations operate with respect to the authoritarian state. In the case of military governments, context is essential. There are enormous differences among regimes, and as demonstrated in Stepan's work, significant cross-currents within regimes. With those caveats in mind, how has research on gender illuminated our understanding of military governments?

Two dimensions of military regimes demand our attention: their response to protest and the conditions they create for political participation. Each has an important gendered element. Women's protests and appeals to the military, whether these are in the nature of a demand for military intervention (as in Brazil in 1964 or Chile in 1973) or in opposition to the abuses of military regimes (in the *Madres de la Plaza de Mayo* in Argentina or the human rights movements of Brazil, Guatemala, or Chile) have stressed the gendered nature of the demand. In the case of demonstrations calling for military intervention against leftist regimes, women emphasized their identities as housewives and mothers and protested shortages in foodstuffs or the perceived threat to the family posed by communism. When women protested against a military regime's abuse of human rights in Argentina, Brazil, or Guatemala, it was as mothers of children or the wives of loved ones who had "disappeared." Both interactions included an appeal to the military's masculinity. In the case of the demonstrations in favor of military intervention, Maria de los Angeles Crummett reports that the women mocked the military for their failure to move against Salvador Allende, throwing chicken feed at them to suggest they lacked the necessary virility.[26] In the case of the protests against the disappearances, there was at least some sense that this type of protest, if it came from women, would be less likely to invoke the military's wrath. Women would be an unworthy target for virile men.

Why was the strategy chosen? Was there a sense on the part of women that their appeal would be more effective if phrased in gendered terms? To which elements in the ideological assumptions of state leaders would a gendered protest appeal? The historical potency of the ideology *marianismo* in Latin America may trigger this manipulation of the concept of motherhood. There is an ample record to suggest that women have sought their ends in the political system through the extension of the image of an exalted self-sacrificing mother from the privacy of the home to the public arena.[27] This appeal to sexual and gender difference as the basis for political participation suggests that other strategies are either unavailable or deemed to be less effective. The invocation of motherhood also suggests a potential basis for cross-class alliances among women. Motherhood and common family responsibilities might provide the basis for short-term agreement among diverse groups of women. To the extent this strategy works, it is of potential use to both the right and the left.

We must recall that protests against the abuses of the military were not without cost, and women were far from immune to the punishment brought upon regime opponents. The complementarity and male protection of the female, assumed in the *marianismo-machismo* contrast, has always been an illusion. Thus, the cultural image of women as self-sacrificing mothers and wives did not prevent the Argentine military from abusing the *Madres de la Plaza de Mayo,* or the Chilean, Guatemalan, and Brazilian military from torturing women as well as men. Ximena Bunster-Burotto argues that the forms of torture applied against women were aimed at sexual humiliation and the destruction of gender identity. Torturers, according to Bunster-Burotto's account, emphasized to their victims that they had deviated from proper female subordination and silence in the face of male authority. Thus, even in the case of torture, gender remains a central element in assertions of power and dominance.[28]

In her study of Chile, Patricia Chuchryk has correctly emphasized the courageous acts of the women in the human rights movements. She argues that this type of women's political participation represents a redefinition of both motherhood and politics. The women's protests represent a redrawing of the "gendered lines" of public space to include the claims of mothers against the state.[29]

Stepan's work leads us to ask a slightly different question: What state purpose was served by allowing women to protest against authoritarian regimes? He describes a scenario in which the leaders of the military government consciously allowed opposition to the human rights abuses of their regimes in the belief that they could use civil protest to curb internal excesses. He suggests the military allowed civil protest to signal new limits they wished to impose within the military and security apparatus. Were women a relatively nonthreatening group to carry forward the protest and the military's project of reform? That military elites may be willing to allow such protests from women may also suggest that they intend to restrict sharply the limits of acceptable protest. Certainly, as Chuchryk notes, General Pinochet was very anxious to disband *El Poder Femenino* after Allende had been toppled.

CONCLUSIONS: POLITICAL PARTICIPATION, AUTHORITARIANISM, AND POLITICAL CULTURE

Throughout the Southern Cone and the Andes, women's political participation expanded in the 1970s despite the presence of military governments. In the case of the Peruvian military, the regime's ideology from 1968 to 1975 actively promoted such participation. In contrast, the regimes in Argentina and Brazil were committed to "values of machismo, female subordination, heroism and patriotism."[30] Despite such contrasting ideologies, feminist groups flourished in both Peru and Brazil. Furthermore, the return to democracy in both nations has seen further evidence of women's political organization and participation. Such parallel expansion of participation, despite differences in regime type, underscores the need to look closely at state processes, the beliefs, values, and attitudes of state elites for a better understanding of what promotes change.

In the case of Peru, women's organizations have developed across the political spectrum and independently of it. The economic crisis brought new forms of collective action, including communal kitchens and children's milk programs, which also served as important vehicles for organizing women in the populous sections of the city. New research on urbanization has revealed the significant role that women and their organizations are playing in the profound process of urbanization and migration in Peru.[31] Nor have women ignored the state. Feminist lawyers have rewritten the civil code to rid it of its discriminatory elements and the 1979 Constitution contains an equal rights clause. Feminist activity in Peru has been extensive and has built significant cross-class alliances. All of this portends a new understanding of gender by both state elites and women's popular organizations. To illustrate, since elections have been held in 1980, women have constituted a higher proportion of the Peruvian legislature than the United States Congress, and under the García administration women served as the secretaries of Health and Education.[32]

In the case of Brazil, a fascinating and complex relationship has developed between feminists and the state. Alvarez reports the success of the recently established National Council for Women's Rights and attributes it to the recognition by feminists that they can accomplish positive change through key points of entry to state elites. The Brazilian case is especially noteworthy for women's active roles in redefining equity in the justice system and eliciting a response to violence against women. As Alvarez recounts this history, Brazilian feminists made strategic decisions to rephrase their agenda in gender neutral terms. Thus they allowed daycare to become a "workers" and "children's" and "health" issue rather than a women's issue, and they achieved greater state responsiveness. In the area of population policy, feminists were wary of an extensive and unchecked role for the state. They feared a male-dominated state would impose policies insensitive to women's needs. In response to these fears feminists forged contacts with sympathetic state officials to ensure a policy which addressed women's concerns.[33]

There can be no doubt that authoritarian regimes have attempted to limit women's political roles. Nor can there be much doubt that a solid and independent local grassroots movement is essential to keeping women's concerns on the agenda and preventing cooptation. Both patterns exist in Latin America. These diverse patterns suggest that there is no simple correlation between a regime's ideology, its hopes and claims, and the results for its citizens. In the case of the authoritarian regimes in Brazil and Argentina, Scott Mainwaring and Eduardo Viola suggest that the rupture in political life forced by the closing of established channels of political expression and dissent forced Brazilians to think about new ways of "doing" politics and stimulated speculation about better ways of organizing social life.[34] Similar questions occurred in Peru under a military regime that actively encouraged the reassessment. Regime type may be less important than the concerns of state elites, but to make such a claim we must have a clear understanding of the internal culture of state elites and their use of concepts of gender in pursuit of state goals.

Politically, the expansion of the state in the development of national intelligence and security systems has had a chilling impact on political participation. Despite the return to democratic politics in many nations of the Southern Cone and the Andes, the size and influence of the military has not been dramatically reduced and tensions over the appropriate balance between the state's authority and the rights of citizens to participate are heightened by the possibility of a return to military rule.

Yet the Latin American experience also indicates that there is the potential to use the state's view of its needs to expand women's political realm, to redefine their political space, and to broaden women's claims. Before we can fully assess this potential, however, a host of questions remain. We have noted the significance of grassroots organizations and cross-class alliances as women have sought to influence state policy. Equally significant has been the gender imagery which has accompanied this behavior. Feminist scholars have taught us to examine the cultural and political purposes served by gender imagery and that insight leads us to recognize the ambiguity of concepts such as *marianismo* in structuring expanded political participation. Will a revised and empowered notion of *marianismo* emerge in Latin American politics? Or, will this conceptualization of gender relations be challenged by an alternative view stressing "sameness" and basing its claim for participation on equality? Similarly, as the limits of cross-class alliances are reached, will differing political solutions be expressed in contrasting views of gender relations? Certainly research to date would lead us to expect this to be a mode for expressing changing notions of leadership and authority.

As political scientists recognize the interpretive potential inherent in a more sophisticated concept of political culture, we can expect them to encounter the significance of gender. On the basis of these early attempts, we can look forward to a more profound understanding of political change as the research on gender and the state begins to intersect.

SUBVERSIVE MOTHERS: THE WOMEN'S OPPOSITION TO THE MILITARY REGIME IN CHILE

*Patricia M. Chuchryk**

The 1973 military overthrow of the democratically elected government of Salvador Allende ushered in a period of intense political expression and economic crisis. Traditional institutional channels of political expression were systematically dismantled, including Chile's bicameral parliamentary system, trade unions, political parties, and to some extent, the universities. Fortified by the Doctrine of National Security and the notion of "internal threat," as well as by the experience and expertise of their Brazilian colleagues[1] the Chilean military declared war on the Chilean people.

The first "transitional" phase,[2] from September 1973 to June 1974, was a violent, chaotic, and bloody reign of terror, with no one appearing to be accountable to anyone for anything.[3] As the world watched in horror, thousands were exiled, executed, imprisoned, and tortured. Many disappeared. Although it is difficult to estimate accurately the actual number of victims, even the most conservative estimates are devastating. A U.S. Embassy unofficial report suggested that 5,000 people were executed during the first months after the coup.[4] A report from the Inter Church Committee on Human Rights estimated that as many as 30,000 were killed.[5] A 1974 Amnesty International report cites Church sources which estimated that by the end of September 1973 there were 45,000-50,000 political prisoners—7,000 in the National Stadium alone.[6]

With the creation in June 1974 of the DINA (*Dirección de Inteligencia Nacional*, Pinochet's private secret police force), disappearances began to be carried out in a much more systematic manner. It is estimated that up until its dissolution in August 1977 (and subsequent replacement by the *Central Nacional de Inteligencia*— CNI), the DINA was responsible for well over 2,000 disappearances—unofficial estimates are much higher—and to this day the military junta does not acknowledge them.[7]

Given the circumstances of this reign of terror and its consequences, it is not surprising that women—as the mothers, wives, sisters, daughters, and grandmothers of the victims of repression—were the first to mobilize in opposition to the dictatorship. Men were the victims of repression more often than women, in part because women had tended to play what were considered marginal or secondary roles in the targeted organizations, principally political parties and trade unions. In this sense, it was precisely women's traditional public invisibility which allowed them to become political actors during a time when it was extremely dangerous for anyone to do so.

Two of the organizations which emerged as a direct response to the repression, the Association of Democratic Women (*Mujeres Democráticas*) and the Association of the Relatives of the Detained and Disappeared (*Agupación de los Familiares de Detenidos-Desaparecidos*)[8] are especially worthy of note. In these two groups we see an outstanding example of how traditional roles provided women with the impetus and initial motivation to organize against the military state. Indeed, women of the *Agrupación* were the first to demonstrate publicly against the junta.[9]

Following a description of these two groups—what they do, how they are organized and the women who comprise them—I would like to begin my analysis with a discussion of two related but distinct historical trends. The first addresses the question, "Why mothers?" and examines the importance and contradictory role of the traditional ideology of motherhood and women's place in contemporary Chile. The second situates these groups and the experience of their participants within the larger context of the emergence of the women's opposition to the military dictatorship in Chile.

Mujeres Democráticas

Less than three weeks after the coup, on October 1, 1973, the Association of Democratic Women was formed to do solidarity work with political prisoners and their families. The group began work with five members; later, their numbers swelled to 120 but as of November 1983, there were roughly sixty women involved.[10] Their activities include helping to provide basic foodstuffs for prisoners and their families, strike support work and taking food to soup kitchens in poor neighborhoods. Especially during the early years, much of their work had to be done clandestinely. For precisely this reason, their organization is comprised of women. Participants suggest that it was easier for women than for men to work in the underground, in part because the military itself tended to ignore women.[11]

In the beginning, while their numbers were still small, they met as one group, knowing each other on a first name basis only, and using traditional female activities as the mechanisms to facilitate meetings. That is, the women organized tea parties and group knitting sessions to camouflage their meetings. In many cases, their families had no knowledge of their activities and indeed believed that they were only going to tea or knitting parties. As the organization grew, its structure was transformed for reasons of security and necessity. Women now meet in small groups of ten or twenty. Each group elects a representative (*cabeza del grupo*). The *cabezas del grupo* meet from time to time to coordinate the activities of the group.[12]

Over the course of its existence, this group has expanded not only its sphere of activities but also its self-definition—although its principle task (*tarea*) has always been, and continues to be, defined as solidarity work with the victims of political repression. They situate their organization, now as in the beginning, within the political framework of the struggle for the return of democracy. They see themselves as a flexible organization which changes in accordance with the circumstances and demands of the moment. What is interesting is that now they also see themselves as having a political role *after* the return to democracy in Chile. This role consists of encouraging and participating in the political education of women (*for-*

mación política) so that women can begin to participate in traditional political organizations on an equal footing with men. During a group interview I conducted in 1983, several women pointed out that women have held few leadership positions in other organizations, in part due to women's familial responsibilities, and in part due to *machismo*. They also emphasized that while theirs is a women's organization and not a feminist group, they have no argument with the feminists and indeed, find some of the issues raised by the feminists "extraordinarily interesting." The Association of Democratic Women is also a member of MEMCH 83, an umbrella group which was formed in 1983 to coordinate women's opposition to the military junta.[13]

Most of the women involved in this group are older, middle class housewives and professionals.[14] Many had never before engaged in political activity. During the interview several of the older women pointed out that one of the reasons they initially became involved in the group was that there was no "space" for older women, they didn't seem to fit in anywhere else ("and younger women could organize in the university"). It was emphasized that this group is political but nonpartisan.[15] While some individual members may be active in a political party, the group itself has no institutional links to any political party.

While in some sense, perhaps, much of the work of this group could be seen as a kind of "Ladies Auxiliary"—providing baskets of food and clothing to poor, needy families, visiting political prisoners and their families, working with children[16]—nevertheless, it is the context itself which makes this work politically necessary as well as politically dangerous. During the first months after the coup, many of these women acted as liaisons between political leaders who had gone underground. They played an important role in taking the first tentative steps toward rebuilding political networks. Many women, especially wives and sisters of political leaders who were dead, imprisoned, or disappeared, were forced by circumstances to take on leadership roles for the first time. Some of these women were also involved in the formation of the *Agrupación*.

AGRUPACIÓN DE FAMILIARES DE DETENIDOS-DESAPARECIDOS

Groups seeking the whereabouts of detained and disappeared family members have emerged in a variety of Latin American countries although perhaps the most internationally well known of these is the *Madres de la Plaza de Mayo* formed in 1977 in Argentina.[17] The first such group appeared in Guatemala in 1967, following the escalation of repression and massive disappearances in that country in 1966. In 1980 the Latin American Federation of Associations of Relatives of the Detained-Disappeared (FEDEFAM) was organized. At its first congress, held in 1981 in Costa Rica, it was estimated that during the previous twenty years, there had been over 90,000 disappearances in Latin America.[18]

The Chilean *Agrupación* was formed in 1974. It emerged in response to the same conditions and circumstances which produced similar organizations—the implementation of military strategies consistent with the Doctrine of National Security and designed to eliminate the internal enemy—and as such is part of a continent-wide phenomenon. Nevertheless, the *Agrupación* is at the same time uniquely Chilean, born as it was within the Chilean historical context.

As was the case in other countries, in Chile, the same women kept running into each other outside of prisons, in hospitals, and in government offices, all seeking information about the whereabouts of a loved one. After a time, these women tentatively began to trust each other and, with the help of the Committee for Peace (*Comité Pro Paz*), an Inter Church organization formed shortly after the coup to help the victims of repression and their families, they formed a group, thinking they could do more and get more answers if they worked together. The Committee for Peace was eventually forced to discontinue its activities by the government. It was replaced by the Vicariate of Solidarity, a Roman Catholic organization directly under the authority and protection of the archbishop of Santiago. It was about this same time that the list of 119 detained-disappeared appeared. These 119 are the only detained-disappeared who have been recognized by the military regime, only because they were found and declared dead in Argentina. The appearance of this list had the effect of consolidating the efforts of the *Agrupación* which, since that time, has worked closely with and has been supported by the Vicariate of Solidarity.

There are now roughly 150 members of the *Agrupación*, of whom between forty-five and fifty could be considered active members. Only two of the present membership are men. The rest are primarily middle and working class housewives and mothers, some of whom are also professionals. They range in age from fifteen to seventy years old.[19] All are missing a loved one, often a husband or son, sometimes a brother, sister, or daughter. As a result of their participation in the *Agrupación*, many have been arrested, some as many as ten times.

From the beginning, the objectives of these women were and are clearly defined. They want to know where their family members are. They want the truth about these disappearances to be known. They demand justice and that those responsible be prosecuted. At first, their efforts focused on the traditional mechanisms of the criminal justice system, for example, *habeus corpus*, and court depositions. When these strategies proved useless, they began to use more unconventional methods such as hunger strikes and chaining themselves to the gates of the government palace and the Supreme Court. As indicated earlier, these women were the first to take to the streets to protest against the military regime.

What is interesting is how their objectives and activities have evolved within a political framework. Many, if not most of the women initially involved, had never been politically active, and sought the emotional support of the group, seeing themselves as individual and accidental victims of history. The problem of the detained and disappeared was not, at first, conceived as a political issue. After the central committee of the Chilean Communist Party fell in 1976, however, many Communist Party members became integrated into the *Agrupación*, engendering a tension which culminated in an internal crisis during 1982-83. Those already politicized sought to educate those who were not. The consequences of this tension and its subsequent resolution are several.

While maintaining its "absolute autonomy" from any particular political party, members of the *Agrupación* are no longer as reluctant to identify themselves (to each other) as political party members. The issue of the detained and disappeared has been redefined as a political one. The objectives of the Agrupación now include the need to politicize the issue both nationally and internationally. It is a member of the Latin American Federation of Associations of Relatives of the Detained-Disappeared (FEDEFAM). The *Agrupación* also participates in the general struggle for the return to democracy, and includes such demands as rights for workers and the return of exiles.[20] It is also a member of MEMCH 83.

Their political activities are both internally and externally directed. In 1978, fourteen members formed a folkloric group designed not only to articulate protest in a different and new way, but also to provide a therapeutic function for its members. There are workshops in political education, public relations, and leadership training for the membership. A youth group has been formed, which is comprised of the children, grandchildren, nieces, and nephews of the members. Externally oriented political action is directed at raising public awareness, politicizing the issue within Chile itself, mobilizing international support,[21] and using the criminal justice system to exert pressure on the Pinochet regime.

Participation in either or both of these groups, the Association of Democratic Women and the *Agrupación*, has had important personal consequences for the participants. The following discussion situates the emergence of these two organizations and the consequences of participation in them, within both an ideological and a contemporary historical context.

MOTHERHOOD: THE SUBVERSION OF AN IDEOLOGY

The traditional ideology of women's roles is the usual explanation for women's assumed, and often all too real, political conservatism. General readers on Latin America, for example, explain women's lack of political participation by focusing on women's confinement to the private sphere of the family.[22] Feminist scholars also use an analysis of the public-private dichotomy to examine and explain the relationship between women and politics. It is often argued that women tend to resist social change because of their relative social powerlessness.[23] Furthermore, given that women have been defined almost exclusively in terms of their reproductive function, that is, motherhood and housewifery, it is not surprising that their isolation in the home and concomitant lack of personal identity outside of those roles have inhibited political participation.[24] In this way, as Jane Jaquette pointed out in 1975, the family acts as an agent of social control, not only by making it difficult for women to participate actively outside of the home but also in terms of reproducing those traditionally conservative values on which the patriarchal family is based.[25] Women are often considered incapable of organizing themselves politically[26] in part because women's roles lie outside the realm of that which traditionally has been considered political.

There are three important assumptions made by these arguments, all of which will figure importantly in the analysis which follows. The first is related to women's presumed interest in maintaining the family, and that this vested interest somehow precludes their active participation in politics. The second has to so with the assumption that women lack the knowledge and skills to become politically active, and the third involves a very conventional notion of what constitutes politics.[27] All of these assumptions derive from an analysis based on separate spheres, but as Charlton, Staudt, and Everett argue, ". . . this private-public distinction is actually a distortion of reality."[28] The public-private distinction falsely implies that women's reproductive activities and the family lie outside of the political realm when in fact they form an essential part of it. That is to say, that not only do women perform important reproductive activities for the state but also that the state has historically played an active role in defining and delimiting those activities. As Sonia Alvarez has argued:

> The Latin American State has confined women to their ostensibly natural functions within the family or the "private sphere" by politically and institutionally reinforcing the boundaries which have delimited women's lives socially and historically.[29]

Nowhere is this as clear as in the case of Chile where women were organized against the government of Salvador Allende on the basis of their vested interest in preserving the family and where now, the government of General Pinochet actively encourages for women only those roles related to the glorification of motherhood.

Without a doubt, the ideology of motherhood was the single most important factor which mobilized primarily middle and upper class women to form *El Poder Femenino* (EPF) in 1971 in opposition to Allende's *Unidad Popular* government. The leaders of this profoundly conservative (and anti-feminist) organization invoked images of the family under attack by the spectre of communism. In the words of one EPF leader:

> Women felt their fundamental values of family and motherhood threatened at the onset of Marxism; it touched the insides of women's being . . .[30]

By preying upon values associated with women's domestic roles, EPF attempted to unite women in political action against the Allende government. And although the organization was initially formed by upper class women, it did appeal to middle and working class women as well.

Despite conflicting class interests, it was possible for the EPF to use the traditional woman's role in domestic work and her responsibilities for household consumption to recruit a large number of middle-class and poor women.[31]

The use of the "preservation of the family" was a politically motivated strategy which attempted, at the same time, to maintain the status of the family as "above" or "outside" politics. EPF manipulated values which traditionally justify women's place in the home, in order to encourage women to take public political action to defend their roles as homemakers. Ironically, Pinochet had no doubt as to the political nature of EPF when, much to the dismay of many of the participants, he ordered it to disband after the coup.[32]

Since its takeover in 1973, the military has made conscious and deliberate use of the traditional ideology of motherhood and the family. Pinochet has assigned to women, as mothers, the sacred duty of defending the integrity of the Chilean family and saving the Fatherland. Through their self-sacrifice and abnegation, through their suffering, through their dedication to the family, and through their unwavering loyalty to the *Patria*, women—in Pinochet's plan—will ensure that Chile's sons and daughters grow up to be patriotic (that is, nonpolitical) citizens.

The two key institutions used by the military to promote this image are the Mothers' Centers (*Centros de Madre*) and the National Secretariat for Women (SNM). The latter was created in October 1973 with Pinochet's wife, Lucía Hiriart de Pinochet, as its director.[33] The Mothers' Centers (CEMAs), orginally created by the Christian Democratic government of Eduardo Frei, were substantially reorganized and converted into an ideological tool to promulgate the images of the self-sacrificing patriotic housewife. CEMA-Chile is also directed by Mrs. Pinochet.

It is extremely important not to underestimate the role played by Pinochet's control of these two organizations.[34] In 1983 it was estimated that throughout Chile there were approximately 10,000 CEMAs, with 230,000 members and 6,000 volunteers.[35] CEMAs are directed primarily at lower class women whose activities are controlled and directed by middle and upper class women volunteers, many of whom are military wives. The SNM is an organization primarily for middle and upper class women in their capacity as volunteers. Its principle objective is an ideological one: the dissemination of family and patriotic values.

Through the vehicles of their respective publications (*Revista Amiga* and *Revista CEMA-Chile*) both of these organizations promote the same image of women—an image defined exclusively in terms of women's reproductive function. Women are conceived of as pillars of the society who defend and transmit spiritual values. Sacrifice, abnegation, service, honesty, diligence, and responsibility are women's chief characteristics, according to the official discourse.[36]

Furthermore, Pinochet has reinforced this ideological project through the implementation of new policy. All of the progressive provisions of Chile's Labor Code have been eliminated. Employers are no longer required to provide or subsidize childcare for female employees. New law also makes it possible for employers to fire pregnant employees.[37] In addition, by adopting a pronatalist population policy and by actively supporting the Catholic Church's position against divorce, Pinochet has made it quite clear that the only appropriate roles for women are those of mother, wife, and homemaker.

It is important to underline that the Pinochet government did not *create* the image of the suffering, self-sacrificing, patriotic mother who is the Chilean woman. Allende, for example, also invoked this same very traditional and very conservative ideological image of women. It is a testament to its historical longevity that this image has long defined the nature of the relationship between women and the state, not only in Chile but in the rest of Latin America as well. As Lois Wasserspring comments,

> The fact that Allende and Pinochet, despite the cavernous political gulf between them, could share similar views about woman's proper role and sphere amply dramatizes the vitality of the tradition which relegates men and women to very different economic and political "space" in Latin America.[38]

By focusing on motherhood and the family, Pinochet is, in effect, using the state to manipulate women's reproductive roles for its, and his, own purposes and, at the same time, attempting to depoliticize women and situate them outside the realm of that which is traditionally considered political.

The mothers' groups in Latin America represent a radical departure from the way in which the ideology of motherhood has traditionally been manipulated and exploited by conservative forces. Yet, it is motherhood (or women's traditional roles in a more general sense) which justifies the entry of women into the public political sphere. Clearly, motherhood and the family also motivated women to participate in EPF. This was true also of the Women's Patriotic

Front, an organization of workers, housewives, professionals, students, and union activists formed in 1972 to support Allende, and indeed, of nineteenth and early twentieth century feminists in both North and South America who based their arguments on the moral imperatives of motherhood.[39] Perhaps the feature which most distinguishes the mothers' groups from other forms of women's political activity based on traditional conceptions of motherhood is the process of individual empowerment, one of the more dramatic consequences of participation in these groups. Motherhood, in this case, has also motivated a politics based on resistance to, rather than acceptance of, traditional, conservative political values.

What indeed is the process by which women have become self-conscious political subjects? What is it that has transformed women-as-mothers into, as Marysa Navarro has so eloquently described it, symbols of resistance against oppressive authoritarian regimes?[40]

> [as women we participate in the *Agrupación* because] we are the women and mothers of this land, of the workers, of the professionals, of the students, and of future generations.[41]

Of the women of the *Agrupación* who were interviewed, many pointed out that they had always been outside of politics—their husbands, fathers, and sons were the ones who occupied political roles. When they (the men) were imprisoned, detained, and disappeared, what enabled women to overcome their terror was their sense of obligation as wives, mothers, sisters, and daughters. It was the state's direct assault on family life, in the form of disappearances, executions, torture, and imprisonment that drove women to engage in the political process.[42] It was devastatingly clear that the home was no longer a safe place for anybody. In fact, one of the early demands of the *Agrupación* was the right to "reconstruct their families" which were destroyed by disappearances.

When asked why these organizations are comprised primarily of women, the women considered the question to be irrelevant. Men were those more affected by the repression, and women have organized simply out of necessity—to search for a missing son or husband. Upon reflection, some suggested that above all, men are the heads of families and therefore could not and cannot get involved for fear of losing their jobs. It was also suggested that the men who had participated during the beginning probably felt isolated, whereas the women felt companionship with other women. Furthermore, they felt that they, as women, had more time than men to devote to such activity. In any case, all of the suggestions were based on some notion of women's traditional roles.

In a sense, this discussion underlines the potential flexibility of the traditional ideology of women's roles. Although not conceptualized by the participants in these terms, their activity has involved both a confirmation and contradiction of their traditional roles as women. On the one hand, it was precisely women's political invisibility and the exclusion of mothers and motherhood from the political sphere which not only enabled them to act but at the same time, legitimated their demands because they *were* wives and mothers. As Navarro points out with reference to the *Madres de la Plaza de Mayo*, participation in mothers' groups expressess, ". . . a coherent acceptance of their socialization, of their acceptance of the dominant sexual division of labor and of their own subordination within it."[43] But it seems, at least in the Chilean case, that once active in these organizations, they began to view traditional womanhood critically, as a barrier to full political participation. Like the women interviewed for Elsa Chaney's study, *Supermadre*, the women who participate in these groups often see their activity as an extension of their domestic roles—roles which have involved, nevertheless, considerable personal sacrifice. In some cases this has meant marriage breakdown and dissolution.[44] Women whose husbands do not want them to be involved are often forced to choose between their activity in the group and their marriages. One woman interviewed, who previously had never been involved politically, became politicized as a result of her husband's imprisonment. When he was eventually released from prison, he demanded that she become "uninvolved." She refused, and subsequently left her husband. Some women also experienced considerable guilt because they felt that, to some extent, they were not giving their children the attention that they required, and hence they were not being good mothers. This feeling of guilt, however, was not enough to prevent their participation.

Most important has been the impact of this participation on the women themselves. All of the women I spoke with indicated, to a greater or lesser extent, that their experience in these groups has had tremendous personal consequences. Although it is not necessarily a self-conscious process, many of the women had acquired a new sense of themselves as political beings. They see themselves as occupying a public political space that they had not occupied previously. For them, their participation has also involved the process of becoming politically educated. These experiences together constitute a process of individual and personal empowerment.

Many women suggested that for them, the group had become a second family, a means of personal integration. More importantly, many also indicated that their participation also signified a form of personal liberation.[45]

> Many times I have cursed these four walls of my house, that in spite of having contained so much joy, have also isolated me from the world, from other people, from the problems we all share, and from those whom I love and whom I no longer have at my side.[46]

> As a person, I have changed a great deal. Before I was shy, I never spoke up . . . I've grown as a woman, now, I am much more aware . . . (Interview)

> At the beginning, my husband and I participated together but later he decided that we shouldn't continue . . . but I insisted and that was my liberation . . . (Interview)

Without exception, these women talked about their personal growth as a result of being involved in political activity with other women. There is no consciousness of this process itself as a collective political process, however. Rather, it is conceived as an individualized consequence of their individual participation. Nor has it been perceived, in any way, as a contradiction of their traditionally defined roles as women. Nevertheless, some of the more important aspects of the growth of mothers' groups are common to, and consistent with, the formation and emergence of a wide variety of Chilean women's oppositional organizations. For this reason it would be useful to situate this process within the context of the growing women's opposition to the military regime.

THE GROWTH OF THE WOMEN'S OPPOSITION IN CHILE

Since the mid-1970s, there has been a remarkable growth of nongovernmental women's organizations in Chile. As one feminist activist described it, "Like mushrooms after a rain, organized pockets of women are springing up in unions, in shanty towns, and in neighborhoods all over the country."[47] These groups range from human rights organizations, (for example, the Women's Committee of the Chilean Human Rights Commission, or CDM), to all-women soup kitchens, to union organizations like the Women's Department (DF) of the National Trade Union Coordinator (CNS), to autonomous shanty town women's groups, like Women's Action (*Acción Femenina* or AF), MOMUPO (Movement of Shanty town Women), MUDECHI (Women of Chile), and CODEM (Committee for the Defense of Women's Rights), and finally to feminist organizations like the Feminist Movement (MF), the Movement of Women for Socialism (MMS), and the Center for Women's Studies (CEM).[48]

As indicated earlier in this chapter, the first groups which began to mobilize against the regime were largely comprised of women. The first large demonstration to be held after the imposition of military rule was organized by women trade unionists (of the then recently formed DF) to commemorate International Women's Day, March 8, 1978. However it was in 1976 that formally structured women's political groups began to appear. One of the first was the Women's Department (DF) of the CNS, a proscribed organization at the time. This group united women union leaders and the women's departments of the various unions affiliated with the CNS. Its two objectives were: (a) to organize women workers and to encourage women (both workers and wives of workers) to participate actively in the Chilean trade union movement, and (b) to struggle for the rights of women workers both in the workplace and in the union. The focus of this organization is to integrate women into the trade union movement given women's historically low level of participation in unions as well as other kinds of political organizations. In 1978 the DF organized the First National Women's Conference, attended by over 300 women. This group also took up the struggle against the 1979 Decree Law No. 2200—a law which effectively wiped out the few protections women workers had. In June 1987 the DF organized a conference on women's rights in the workplace, taking up such issues as sexual harassment, and the insistence of some employers that prospective women workers submit to a gynecological examination (to assure employers that the prospective worker is not pregnant).

In 1979 the Women's Committee of the Chilean Human Rights Commission (CDM) was formed and in 1982 began to publish a newsletter called *Hojita*. The work of these women, among them professionals, housewives, union leaders, and representatives of other organizations, includes solidarity work (especially with women who have been imprisoned and/or tortured), popular education, and public consciousness-raising around women's rights issues. They have done a considerable amount of work documenting the legal situation of women in Chile, although in recent years they do not appear to be as active as during the 1983-84 period.

CODEM (*Comité de Defensa de los Derechos de la Mujer*) was formed in 1980 and MUDECHI (*Mujeres de Chile*) in 1981. Both of these are more self-consciously political given their early connections to political parties. The basic objective of CODEM, which has groups in a variety of Chilean cities and towns, is to encourage and educate women to become active participants in the political process. In the early years, CODEM focused its work on the dramatic consequences of the economic crisis—issues such as the lack of drinking water in poor neighborhoods, and the lack of adequate health care and education. Added to the group's central demand for an end to military rule are demands for free childcare, equal rights and opportunities for women, and free, safe and reliable birth control. This group is especially interesting given its origins in conventional Chilean partisan politics and its identity as a grass-roots organization. In the beginning, there were very few women involved in CODEM who would identify themselves as feminists, and the group self-consciously defined itself as nonfeminist (if not anti-feminist). After an internal process and struggle, in 1987 CODEM defined and identified itself politically as a feminist organization. This is particularly significant given this group's earlier position, borrowing from left-wing rhetoric, that feminism is middle class and divisive of the working class.

Like CODEM, MUDECHI is a grass-roots organization comprised primarily of poor women (*pobladoras*) who live in the shanty towns (in Chile called *poblaciones*). This group, too, has member organizations in many Chilean cities and communities and by 1987, had over thirty-six groups in Santiago alone. MUDECHI defines its basic political priority in terms of the struggle for the return to democracy. The members of MUDECHI engage in a variety of activities: from participating in public demonstrations and organizing the unorganized, to gathering small donations to buy cigarettes for political prisoners, providing children with clothes and Christmas gifts, protesting price increases, and denouncing instances of repression. While MUDECHI does not define itself as a feminist organization (viewing feminism as anti-men), it does nevertheless see the importance of women taking on public roles and occupying public "space", and participating in politics on equal footing with men.

Since early 1987, MUDECHI has been operating a house in central Santiago.

These two organizations have gradually begun to combine a growing concern for the specific situation of women with general opposition to the military dictatorship and its repressive tactics. They have defined their constituency as women, precisely because women have been marginalized in and by the political process and hence are assumed to lack the education and skills to become active political participants.

Other kinds of groups have emerged, although the one unquestionable and undeniable element has always been opposition to the military regime. These groups have emerged with different focus, however. Their politics take shape and substance from the perspective of women's particular daily life situation and oppression.[49] For example, MOMUPO (*Movimiento de Mujeres Populares de la Zona Norte*), formed in 1982, links approximately twenty smaller groups of *pobladoras* living in the northern sections of the city of Santiago. These smaller groups were formed with the goal of self-education: skills training workshops, political self-education, and workshops on childcare, sexuality, women's legal rights, and women's history. In 1984 this group founded a women's center, *Casa El Domos*, in an attempt to meet some of women's most urgent needs, for example, in the area of health and legal information. In 1985 MOMUPO began to define itself as a feminist organization and has begun to combine these "inner-directed" activities with public activism.[50]

In 1981 a collective of socialist feminist women began to publish a magazine called *Furia* (meaning rage in Spanish). Their objective was to put women's issues on the socialist agenda and their journal focused on an analysis of patriarchy. In part due to lack of funding and in part due to the untimely death of one of the members of the collective, the last issue was published in 1985. But in its place, other socialist women's groups have emerged. For example, in the fall of 1983, a group of women organized a discussion group called *Mujeres Socialistas* (Socialist Women). Women who considered themselves small "s" socialists[51] united across class and sectarian lines in order to discuss the issues important to them as women and to define the role that feminism might play in the political process. Now called the *Movimiento Mujeres por el Socialismo* (Movement of Women for Socialism or MMS), this group combines an analysis of capitalism and the need for major socioeconomic transformation with an analysis of patriarchy and the need for women's autonomy and self-determination in the political process. MMS often takes up particular issues within the opposition and organizes public forums. For example, in June 1987 they organized an extremely well-attended forum on the issue of free elections.[52]

By far one of the most significant groups to emerge was the *Círculo de Estudios de la Mujer* (Women's Studies Circle). Although the *Círculo* later (at the end of 1983) split into two groups, the *Centro de Estudios de la Mujer* (Center for Women's Studies or CEM) and the *Centro de Análisis y Difusión de la Condición de la Mujer—La Morada* (Center of Analysis and Diffusion of the Situation of Women—La Morada), it has left the Chilean women's movement with an important legacy. The *Círculos's* roots go back to 1977 when a small group of primarily professional, middle class women began to meet to discuss their situation as women. A year later, this group grew to include several small collectives under the name ASUMA (*Asociación Para la Unidad de Mujeres* or Association for the Unity of Women). In 1979, the group, under the name of the *Círculo*, was incorporated into the Academy of Christian Humanism, an umbrella organization of the Church designed to protect the various research centers which had formed after the coup. The underlying motivation for the formation of the *Círculo*, was the lack of knowledge about women in Chile. Its activities focused on both generating that knowledge, and generating consciousness. In addition to a core group of feminist researchers associated with the *Círculo*, there were grass-roots activists, ongoing consciousness-raising groups on women's oppression, a feminist theater collective, courses on the situation of women, publications, a documentation center, and public forums. For a long time, the *Círculo* was feminism's only public face in Chile. It was the organization which played a central role in placing women's issues on the political agenda.

In December 1983 the Academy of Christian Humanism withdrew its support of the *Círculo*. After an extended period of crisis, two groups emerged. CEM became a research oriented organization, fashioned after other alternative research organizations which have sprung up since 1973. *La Morada* took on the political, activists, and consciousness-raising activities. Today, *La Morada* has roughly 120 women participating in a variety of ongoing workshops and provides a meeting place for a variety of feminist groups, including the Feminist Movement and the *Frente de Liberación Femenino* (Women's Liberation Front). It has an open house every Monday evening to which all women are invited.[53]

In 1983, three other important organizations emerged: the *Movimiento Feminista* (Feminist Movement), MEMCH 83, and *Mujeres*

Por La Vida (Women for Life). The *Movimiento Feminista* emerged as a consequence of the political mobilization of the opposition around the Days of Protest. For the first day of protest, May 11, 1983, two women (then members of the *Círculo*) and their children made and distributed flyers (*volantes*) which read "Democracy in the Country and in the Home!"—a slogan which has since become the catch phrase of the feminist opposition movement (and indeed has been appropriated by the nonfeminist women's opposition). It was a spontaneous action, a way in which the women felt that they, as feminists, could make their own modest contribution to the protest. By the third day of protest (in July) between eighty and one hundred women were involved in a network to initiate and organize feminist political opposition activity. On August 11, 1983, in conjunction with the fourth day of protest, approximately sixty women staged a five minute sit-in on the steps of Santiago's National Library under a banner which read "Democracy Now! The Feminist Movement of Chile." This was the first public demonstration by a feminist group and, in a real sense, put feminism on Chile's political map. The MF continues to grow both in membership and public visibility. To celebrate International Women's Day, March 8, 1987, feminists organized a women's lunch which was attended by roughly one thousand women.

MEMCH 83 is an important example of how a concern for women's rights has gradually become incorporated into a program for political change. The original intention was to create a united women's front against the military government, and to facilitate the flow of information among the various groups. The specificity of women's situation was not, at first, considered a fundamental part of this opposition. Later on, however, demands for women's rights, such as equal pay and the right to work, were incorporated. On November 28, 1983, for example, MEMCH 83 organized a successful women's demonstration not only to oppose the government but also in the name of peace and women's rights. Since March 1987, MEMCH 83 has been operating out of a house in central Santiago, hoping to give greater visibility to its activities and provide opportunity for dialogue and coordination. Since its beginnings many member groups have come and gone. For example, new groups such as the *Accion Femenina* (Women's Action) have incorporated and other groups, such as MOMUPO and the Feminist Movement, have withdrawn, probably because of a different conception of political agendas.

The third important group to emerge in 1983 was the *Mujeres Por La Vida*, initially an informal group of friends, many of whom

were (and are) well-known political figures representing a wide political spectrum. They were unhappy with the lack of unity among the
various forces of the opposition—a lack of unity owing in part to
political party sectarianism. Determined to demonstrate to the opposition that it was and is possible to form a united opposition, their
first action was to call for a demonstration in the name of peace and
unity in December 1983. Approximately 10,000 women showed up
at the Caupolicán Theater to participate. Men were not permitted to
attend, not even male journalists, for the simple reason that these
women wanted to demonstrate to the men of the opposition how
unity could be achieved. Since that time, despite a sometimes troubled existence, *Mujeres Por La Vida* continues to play an important
role in the women's opposition, joining with other groups to call for
demonstrations and raise the issue of women's rights within the context of the struggle for democracy.

This brief overview has been limited to only a few of the groups
which have emerged in Santiago. Recent reports suggest, however,
that a variety of different women's organizations have been form-
ing throughout the country. Furthermore, apart from those groups
which are more or less formally structured and which have a degree
of public visibility, there has been a remarkable transformation in
the Chilean social, economic, and political landscape. Due to the
devastating hardships incurred by the neo-liberal economic model
imposed by the military government, women, in unprecedented
numbers, are engaging in economic activity.[54] Much of this activity
is organized in what are called *organizaciones económicas populares* and the overwhelming majority of those involved are women.[55]
Women run soup kitchens and knitting groups, gather old clothing
and make the tapestries called *arpilleras*. In addition, in the *poblaciones* women organize workshops on parent-child relationships,
political issues, and sexuality.[56] All of this activity, even that which
has purely economic survival objectives, has a clearly defined political content. Three important consequences, however, stand out.

The first has to do with the shift in the locus of political activity from the "public" to the "private".

The shantytown has eclipsed the factory and neighborhood organizations have displaced trade unions as the locus of political
action. . . . As social and political activity becomes increasingly
rooted in the place of residence (thereby bridging the distance
between "family" and "political" life), an new *dramatis per-
sonae* shantytown women and youth—have taken center stage
in the social struggles now taking place in Chile.[57]

This is due in part to the reduction of political "space" by the military making trade unions and political parties illegal but also to the increased activity of women. Women have created new ways of "doing politics" (*hacer política*) based on the resources they have had at their disposal, so that distinctions between the public and private, between the political and the domestic and between the productive and the reproductive have begun to blur and "(t)he home and family suddenly (become) important dynamic centers of discussion, criticism, and clandestine resistance."[58]

This shift is also reflected in how traditional politics have been reconceptualized in recent years, not only in the sense of the change of locus but also in the politicization of daily life. As Chilean popular educator Horacio Walker has argued, "the reconceptualization of the political is made possible through a questioning of the public/ private sphere (*sic*)."[59] In his case study of an all-women soup kitchen in a Santiago shantytown, Walker suggests that even though in many respects the women are simply extending domestic roles into the public realm, at the same time their work represents a collectivization of those roles. Furthermore,

> By engaging in the operation of an all-woman soup kitchen, they are criticizing traditional gender relations from the bottom to the top; they are raising doubts; they are promoting questions; they are seeing themselves differently.[60]

The women in Walker's study often saw their work as somehow "outside" of that which is traditionally considered political. However, Walker makes the distinction between consciousness in discourse and consciousness in action, that is, that the language used by these women is not the language of conventional political discourse but rather the language of their reality—daily life. He further points out that the political practice of these women challenges authoritarianism in a way that conventional political discourse cannot. Also, the consequences of "seeing themselves differently" involves the recognition that they are capable of moving beyond the limits a patriarchal society has imposed on them.

> What is always pointed out by these women is their discovery that they were persons able to do other things besides rearing their children and cleaning and cooking at home.[61]

This recognition is one of the common features among most of the women's groups which have emerged since the imposition of military rule. I have found in my work with many of these groups that the right to be a person (*ser persona*) is becoming increasingly articulated not only as a consequence of political activity but also as a political demand. In the process of developing political platforms and strategies and building autonomous (that is, nonpartisan) women's organizations, all of these groups, to a greater or lesser extent, have begun to incorporate demands related to the nature of women's position in society. In the *Agrupación*, many women have come to experience themselves, for the first time, as public political actors with the right to "occupy" political "space" as well as having the capacity to occupy leadership roles. In their meetings, the Democratic Women now talk about *machismo* as one of the barriers to women taking on political roles. In all of these organizations, women are beginning to define and demand their right to be persons.[62]

Some of the groups I have discussed in this chapter are organized around traditionally defined political goals. Among these we can situate both the *Agrupación* and the Association of Democratic Women. They focus primarily on educating women politically and encouraging them to participate in the general struggle for the return to democracy. On the other hand, other groups focus on integrating women's specific concerns into that struggle, and in the process, they attempt to reconceptualize that which is traditionally defined as political.

For a variety of reasons, most of these groups reject the label "feminist." Nevertheless, whether these groups define themselves as feminist or not, whether the groups consist of *pobladoras* or of middle class women, cannot alter the important consequences women's renewed political activity has had on Chilean politics generally. Women are beginning to view themselves as equal partners in the political process. By empowering themselves as individuals they are challenging not only the state's right to define, determine, and delimit the nature of their political identities, but also the assumed political conservatism of motherhood. Furthermore, a concern with women's rights is becoming increasingly more legitimate as a political issue. Public awareness is also beginning to motivate the opposition to Pinochet to reexamine its own values—values often consistent with Pinochet's own political project for women.

The Chilean situation offers a moving example of how intense repression can foster resistance and strength. The political mobilization of women in Chile has confronted an ideology which seeks to deprive women of their right to be persons. Regardless of the nature of their political focus and strategy, women in Chile are struggling for this right. In doing so they are carving out a new chapter in their collective history.

INCORPORATION VERSUS CONFLICT: LOWER CLASS WOMEN, COLLECTIVE ACTION, AND THE STATE IN INDIA

*Jana Everett**

Lower class women have not been active participants in conventional modes of political participation. However, if one adopts a broad view of politics, they can, as Louise Tilly notes, "be seen as political actors trying to influence government authorities and those in positions of economic power in order to protect or promote their interests."[1] Under certain circumstances the survival strategies of lower class women include instances of collective action whereby groups make claims on the state.[2] Do such activities increase the power and material welfare of lower class women? How? Under what conditions?

Adequate answers to these questions require a theoretical exploration of the extent to which the state should be viewed as a potential resource for lower class women or as a lethal entity from which they need protection, as well as comparative empirical investigations of the experiences of lower class women involved in varying types of collective action under varying types of state systems. Such theoretical and empirical work has only just begun. This chapter is intended as a modest contribution to such a project. It reviews briefly U.S. feminist perspectives on the implications of the welfare state for lower class women in light of the recent literature on the state. From this review, arguments supporting and opposing lower class women using collective action to gain access to the state are advanced. The discussion then examines the involvement of lower class women in two different types of collective action in India: (urban women in self-help associations) and (rural women in grassroots movements.) It attempts to assess the costs and benefits of these two different collective action strategies toward the Indian state—strategies that can be labeled incorporation (urban associations) and conflict (rural movements). Finally, the chapter assesses the implications of the Indian experience for the arguments about the nature of the state.

Theda Skocpol and others have called attention to the independent effect of the state on politics: that state policies and structures directly shape and "indirectly influence the meanings and methods of politics for all groups in society."[3] This literature adopts a Weberian perspective on the state. For example, Dietrich Rueschemeyer and Peter Evans define the state as "a set of organizations invested with the authority to make binding decisions for people and organizations juridically located in a particular territory and to implement these decisions using, if necessary, force."[4] What implications does this conceptualization of the state have for collective action strategies of groups subordinated by class and gender? Rueschemeyer and Evans advance the notion that the state embodies four contradictory tendencies: (1) "a pact of domination" between the state apparatus and the most powerful classes, (2) "a corporate actor" with its own interests, (3) "an arena of social conflict" and (4) "the guardian of the universal interests of the society."[5] These four tendencies are expressed in activities intended to achieve state goals of economic growth, internal order, and external security. Any analysis of subordinate group strategies of empowerment should take into account the nature of state goals, the four contradictory state tendencies, and the pattern in which the tendencies are combined in particular states during specific historical periods.

Participants in the emerging feminist debate on the U.S. welfare state usually emphasize one of the four contradictory state tendencies.[6] Feminist scholars are unlikely to characterize the state as the "guardian of universal interests," but this has been the ideal behind the efforts of feminists to gain state recognition of women's rights in property, employment, marriage, education, and suffrage. In the nineteenth century feminists pointed out that the liberal state's exclusion of women was antagonistic to both the practical and strategic gender interests of women.[7] The campaign for women's rights represented a struggle by middle class women to gain entry into the state. The effects of these eventually successful efforts on lower class women were mixed. Subordinated by class and sex, and in some cases race, they were least able to exercise political rights. In the twentieth century welfare state, the political agenda broadened considerably, as policy makers sought to promote security along with liberty and equality.[8] The development of an array of welfare state programs increased the relevance of public policy to lower class women. The policies, however, reflected class and gender biases that served to perpetuate the subordinate status of lower class women.

Can lower class women utilize collective action to gain resources and power from the welfare state? Some feminists (such as Frances Fox Piven) say yes and recommend a reformist strategy. Others say no and advocate a strategy of autonomy and self-help.[9] In the U.S. context, feminists tend not to advocate a revolutionary strategy designed to transform the state. According to the reformist strategy, the state bureaucracy is potentially open to claims for increased resources and power by lower class women. To maximize chances for success, lower class women should form formal organizations focused on narrow goals but be capable of defiance in times of crisis. Furthermore, lower class women should use their organizations to forge alliances with groups already represented in the state. According to the autonomy strategy, efforts to utilize the state bureaucracy by lower class women will only result in increased social control. They will be incorporated into the system but only as a subordinate, dependent, and marginalized group. Participants may gain short-term benefits for themselves but no redistribution of power or policy changes. Increased power will come only from the formation of autonomous groups that are decentralized and participatory. This strategy rejects hierarchical organization and financial dependence on outside bureaucracies because of the internal hierarchy it creates. In these groups it is thought that women will develop a feminist discourse which will include a conception of politics centered on the needs of women and children. The implication of this strategy is that women should construct structures of collective action that are not state and market determined. Exactly how this type of action will transform the state is not spelled out.

CASE STUDIES OF LOWER CLASS WOMEN, THE STATE, AND COLLECTIVE ACTION IN INDIA

The expansion of the state in the twentieth century is not restricted to the welfare state in advanced capitalist nations. This phenomenon can also be seen in the state role in economic development in the postcolonial states of the Third World. Are feminist debates about the welfare state relevant to the efforts of lower class women seeking empowerment and material welfare in the Third World? To what extent does the Third World state represent an opportunity and /or a danger for lower class women? This paper now turns to these questions through an investigation of two different strategies of collective action in which women have participated in India: urban women's associations of informal sector workers and rural grass-roots movements.[10]

In India the effects of capitalism and the colonial and postcolonial state upon women overlay a precolonial social structure that was extremely hierarchical. The landlord-peasant political economy of classical Indian civilization was characterized by three interrelated hierarchies—class, caste, and gender. Women of the landed upper castes were extremely restricted while women of the lower castes and classes enjoyed more mobility because of their important economic role. However, they were economically and sexually exploited by the upper castes and classes. During the colonial period these hierarchies were not overturned by either the British colonial or Indian nationalist elites. The colonial state was structured to meet imperial security and economic interests. The preoccupation with security led colonial elites to rely alternatively on repression and co-optation to maintain order. In response to the development of the Indian National Congress, constitutional reforms were implemented and in turn shaped Congress strategy and organization. Social movements among the peasants and lower castes and a women's movement among urban, educated, upper caste, professional families were absorbed by Congress. Mahatma Gandhi renamed the untouchables *Harijans* (children of God), campaigned against their ill treatment, and championed the cause of women. In the postcolonial era the Indian state sought to promote economic development and social order. The political elite under the leadership of Prime Minister Jawaharlal Nehru embarked upon a national capitalist development strategy and constructed an expanded military-civilian bureaucratic apparatus and democratic political system, centering around the dominant Congress party.

THE POSTCOLONIAL INDIAN STATE

Debate on the nature of the postcolonial Indian state has not yet reached the intensity of earlier debates on the mode of production in India. Nevertheless, three different interpretations can be identified with contrasting implications for the strategies and goals necessary to achieve subordinate class empowerment. Each interpretation emphasizes different combinations of the four contradictory state tendencies put forward by Rueschemeyer and Evans.[11] The interpretations vary in the degree of primacy accorded to state or social forces in development and in the implications for progressive reforms.

A social democratic perspective emphasizing the potential of the Indian state as an arena of social conflict can be seen in the writing of Francine Frankel.[12] She views the state as currently constituting a pact of domination between dominant castes and agents of state power, but she believes the state would be responsive to pressures for reform from organized subordinate classes. The pact of domination, in Frankel's view, stems from the separation of political party organization and strategies of social transformation in the structure and policies of the Indian state. This has resulted in the ineffectiveness of the latter and increased dependence of the poor upon the landed castes. Frankel argues, "[U]nless countervailing efforts are made to organize the peasantry in new forms of class-based associations that can build their own direct relationships with outside power centers in the political parties and the administration, the superior numbers of the poor cannot be converted into a potent political resource."[13] She believes that such associations would be capable of challenging the power of the dominant castes and achieving benefits for the poor "without exacting fearful costs . . . of a violent upheaval."[14]

In a 1977 article, Bharat Patankar and Gail Omvedt offer a Marxist perspective on the Indian state.[15] For them it is a bourgeois state which facilitates the reproduction of the capitalist mode of production.)They see (no opportunity for subordinate class empowerment through state sponsored institutions: "The existence of . . . [electoral] parties, of the parliamentary system with its bourgeois elections, of the trade union struggle of the working class all have the effects of rationalising class struggle in ways conducive to the maintenance and growth of the bourgeois mode of production and the stabilisation of the bourgeois State."[16] Instead they advocate replacing one pact of domination with another: "[A]n armed mass revolutionary movement capable of smashing the bourgeois State and replacing it by a proletarian State."[17]

Recently, a statist perspective has been put forward by several scholars. Lloyd and Susanne Rudolph emphasize the state as a corporate actor. They conceptualize the Indian state as a "third actor" (vis-á-vis capital and labor) moving from autonomous to constrained along a continuum of state-social domination.[18] They view the state in India as simultaneously strong and weak. The strengths include state domination of investment and employment in the organized economy, administrative structure, centrist party politics, and state dominated interest group pluralism.) The weaknesses include the deinstitutionalization of party and state in the last two decades, the increasing political mobilization of demand groups overloading the state, and rising caste, class, and religious conflict.) The Rudolphs perceive state autonomy as having both (progressive and regressive potential: while autonomy defends the state from social forces appropriating it for their own ends, autonomy also exposes the state to the danger of state elites' appropriating it for their own ends.

More radical scholars agree with certain aspects of the Rudolph's characterization but emphasize the capture of the Indian state by dominant classes. According to Rajni Kothari, the present state is characterized by a decline in autonomy and in its overall role in society. Two factors have led to this decline: the state's institutional incapacity to meet the aspirations of the poor, and its capture by the global world order, the "universal union of elites and affluent classes."[19] Kothari believes that the state pursues technological modernization to render the poor superfluous, expands the machinery of coercion to protect the affluent from the poor, and eradicates diverse indigenous cultures to further elite control.[20] Pranab Bardhan argues that the state has been captured by a heterogeneous and unstable coalition of classes (industrial capitalists, rich farmers, and bureaucrats and professionals) leading to a proliferation of subsidies reducing the surplus available for development.[21] Atul Kohli attributes the failure of reform to an alliance between state leaders and property owners.[22]

There is disagreement among the radical scholars on what to do to achieve reform and redistribution. Bardhan does not spell out his recommendations. Kohli argues that disciplined ruling parties of the left can be agents of redistributive capitalist development and bases his argument on the experience of the Communist Party of India (Marxist) in West Bengal. Kothari appears to have a bottom-up perspective in contrast to Kohli's top-down perspective for reform. Kothari appears hopeful that political movements of the disadvantaged can transform the state and society. He observes:

> There are many indications that out of the present struggle between a centralised and increasingly repressive State and various movements of protest and defiance based on local organisations of the poor and ethnic minorities, peasants' movements and movements for regional autonomy and decentralisation of power may emerge an alternative formation that will prove more sensitive to India's indigenous cultures.[23]

Kothari sees such movements "as new forms of organisation and struggle meant to rejuvenate the State and make it once again an instrument of liberation from exploitative structures."[24] Unlike Frankel he does not believe the poor can be incorporated into the state as it now exists. Unlike Patankar and Omvedt, he doesn't see the solution as smashing the state. Unlike Kohli, he doesn't support the idea of a Leninist party as the best hope for eradicating poverty within a democratic capitalist context. Kothari believes that the current social context renders irrelevant the theories of both reformers and revolutionaries:

> Today's oppressed will need to wage their struggle from *outside* the existing structure, not just dethroning the ruling class and "smashing" the state and taking it over but to redefine the whole concept and structure of politics with a view to empowering the masses for a transformation at and from the very bottom of society.[25]

His goal (which is somewhat vague) appears to be a state which could be both autonomous and the guardian of universal interests.

The nature of the Indian state has not been addressed explicitly in the women's studies literature in India. Implicitly, this literature views the Indian state either as an arena of social conflict or as a mechanism of social control. The first view appears in the policy oriented studies growing out of the 1975 ground breaking government-sponsored report, *Towards Equality*, which documented the abysmal situation of lower class women and the failure of state laws and programs to reach them.[26] This literature adopts a critical perspective on the operation of state policies but generally assumes that through organized pressure by women, these policies can be improved. The second view can be seen in the work of some Marxist scholars who view state programs (such as credit and training) targeted at lower class women, and the associated efforts of women's organizations, as intended to subject women to capitalist domination.[27] These writings provide a critique of the first stance but do not offer any ideas on how to respond. The second view can also be seen in feminist writing, such as the journal *Manushi*, which argues that the state is in alliance with the rural elite and cautions against relying on the state for support.[28] Instead, editor Madhu Kishwar recommends,

> [T]he more they [poor women] can confront their oppressors directly with their own organizing power, and the more we can prevent the police and government from intervening on behalf of the rural elite, the better their chance of wresting some rights for themselves.[29]

Kishwar implies that male domination is a component of the pact of domination between state and ruling class. This stance emphasizes the connections among caste, class, and gender oppression and advocates struggling against all forms of oppression.

Which characterization of the state seems most useful in understanding relations between the state and subordinate classes, and state, class, and gender relations in India? In what patterns are the contradictory state tendencies combined? Two recent case studies of policy implementation offer some insight into the operation of government programs targeted at the poor in one urban and one rural context. It would be unwise to draw any generalizations covering all of India based on only two cases. The cases, however, do suggest some alternative hypotheses for further study.

Mira Savara and I studied the operation of the nationalized banks' business loan programs for the poor in Bombay.[30] We viewed the programs as a strategy of political assimilation directed at informal sector workers. Contrary to the initial impression given by the public sector banks, the relationship between bank and borrower was usually indirect, arranged by an intermediary—a political broker, slum leader, or raw materials supplier—whom the banks referred to as "social workers." The strings attached to social worker assistance included payments, obligations to buy raw materials, votes, and participation in party demonstrations. Involvement with the (male) social worker was one factor depressing repayment rates. We concluded that the process of obtaining benefits from government programs should be seen as a form of political participation, and the (mostly female) lower class borrowers as participants in a system of patron-client ties.[31]

In South Gujarat, Jan Breman studied the operation of the Rural Labour Ministry charged with supervising compliance with the minimum wage for agricultural laborers.[32] He found that,

> [T]his office, set up to provide a counterweight to the economic and extra-economic pressures exerted by the dominant farmers, in fact very often confirms the great and increasing inequality between landowners and landless, through its mode of operation.[33]

Very few laborers risked bringing charges of subminimum payment, even fewer cases were found in their favor, and landlord retaliation was sure to follow. Breman attributed this pact of domination between state and large landowner class to the strategy of capitalist development. According to him, government programs were designed merely to "soften the misery" of the rural poor, but "even this purely remedial policy arouses opposition because it lessens the beneficiaries' dependence on their opponents."[34]

These cases suggest two alternative ways of characterizing state and subordinate class relations. On the one hand, it could be that differences in the nature of the pact of domination between urban and rural India result in the conversion of urban programs into political resources for elites and the complete obstruction of rural programs. On the other hand, it could be that within the same overall pact of domination differences in the perceived impact of distributive versus regulative state policies lead elites to adopt different strategies toward the groups targeted by these two types of state policies: a manipulative strategy toward the former and a repressive strategy toward the latter.

URBAN WOMEN AND COLLECTIVE ACTION:
ASSOCIATIONS OF FEMALE INFORMAL SECTOR WORKERS

During the 1970s three women organizers with long histories of involvement in union and party politics started associations of women informal sector workers.[35] Through their political work these middle class women became aware of the problems of lower class women working as vendors, home-based producers, and service providers. (For example, there were *khannawallis*, women who cooked meals for the male workers who came to Bombay alone.) These problems included indebtedness to moneylenders, harassment by the police, and exploitation by middlemen. At the time bank business loan programs for the poor were just starting and apparently not accessible to women. In all three cases the organizations that were formed initially focused on providing their members access to low-cost credit by serving as intermediaries between the banks and borrowers.

These organizations—the Self Employed Women's Association (SEWA) of Ahmedabad, Working Women's Forum (WWF) of Madras and the *Annapurna Mahila Mandal* (a *khannawalli* women's association named for the goddess of food) of Bombay—developed innovative strategies to tailor banking to the needs of lower class women. The core of the organization was the loan group—a group of women borrowers in a neighborhood who would act as guarantors of the loans and as a support group for each other. Group leaders investigated prospective members, attended organizational meetings, and assisted in loan collection.

These organizations were quite successful and grew rapidly. SEWA disbursed 8,000 loans from 1973-76, WWF 7,000 loans from 1978-82, and Annapurna 6,000 from 1975-82. In general, repayment rates were very high. For example, repayment rates of 3,500 Annapurna borrowers from 1976-78 ranged from 94 percent to 98 percent. SEWA, WWF, and later Annapurna, became dissatisfied with their intermediary role and started their own women's cooperative banks. All three organizations expanded their roles to meet other needs of their members. SEWA was explicitly started as a union for self-employed women and represents its members in conflicts with merchants, factory owners (who operate "putting-out" systems employing home producers), and the government. SEWA provides social insurance schemes for members and operates an economic wing which runs training programs and production cooperatives. WWF provides welfare programs, day care centers, and training programs, and Annapurna has opened a center that includes a catering unit, a women's shelter, and other services. The leaders of all three organizations have been involved in lobbying efforts for policy changes in the interest of self-employed women.

Although the organizers have backgrounds in party politics, the women's associations have generally tried to be "nonparty" groups. This is sometimes an asset and sometimes a liability in their efforts to operate as both a union and a development agency for their members. While these emphases are complementary—pressure group tactics help get needed services—they also can be conflictual. As a SEWA organizer puts it, "You can't do union work and development work at the same place and time. . . . When working within the system, you can't think of struggle." All three organizations seem to share the perspective on the Indian state held by the policy oriented women's studies scholars: they believe state policies have disadvantaged women, but they believe that organization and pressure can ameliorate the situation.

RURAL WOMEN AND COLLECTIVE ACTION: GRASS-ROOTS MOVEMENTS[36]

In the last fifteen years grass-roots movements have emerged among various sections of the rural poor: tribals, *dalits* (a term meaning "oppressed," used to refer to Harijans), agricultural laborers, and poor peasants. Young educated activists from the cities initiate struggles among the poor over deeply felt grievances and/or channel on-going protest activity. Grass-roots movements have tried to confront divisions, internal oppression based on class, caste, and gender, and harmful practices among the poor, and have tried to build coalitions across these divisions to confront the external enemy—landlords, commercial interests, and in some cases, the government. Issues central to the daily life of the poor—subsistence rights, health, ecology, violence against women—"get defined as political and provide areas of struggle."[37] The methods utilized include strikes and demonstrations and an array of innovative tactics drawn from the local traditions of the participants.

On the basis of available information, six movements were selected for analysis: (1) The Shahada movement arose among the Bhil tribals in the Shahada subdivision of Dhulia district, Maharashtra, in the early 1970s and, as of 1981, covered over two hundred villages;[38] (2) Two related movements, one called Anti-Alcohol and one called Chipko, emerged in the Uttarkhand, a mountainous region in Uttar Pradesh, in the 1970s;[39] (3) The Rural Community Development Association started to work among *dalits* in Chingleput District of Tamil Nadu in 1974, and by 1983 had enlarged its focus to include all agricultural laborers and included over 3,000 members and fifteen full-time organizers;[40] (4) The Ryotu Coolie Sangham (a peasant worker association) started in the Bhongir subdivision of Nalgonda District in Andhra Pradesh in 1976-77 and by 1981 there were *sanghams* in at least eighty four villages;[41] (5) The Chhatra Yuva Sangharsh Vahini (Student Youth Struggle Movement) was formed in Bihar in 1975, and began to organize agriculture laborers in the Bodhgaya Movement;[42] and, (6) In 1978 the Kashtakari Sangathana (Toilers Organization) was formed in the Dhanu subdivision of Thane District, Maharashtra, among landless and poor peasants who were primarily tribals, and by 1981 covered more than twenty five villages.[43]

The militance and extent of women's participation has been noteworthy in these movements. The earliest movements, Shahada and Chipko, were especially important in this respect. At Shahada's first women's *shibir* (training camp) in 1973, women discussed sexual harassment by landlords and the police, the burden of housework, alcoholism among their men, and the associated wife beating. Then the women spontaneously marched to a village, smashed the illegal liquor still, and *gheraoed* (encircled) the police inspector to protest his acquiescence in illegal liquor productions. In 1974 in Uttarkhand, twenty-seven women blocked sixty forest department employees from selling thousands of marked trees by hugging the trees. These examples awakened the grass-roots organizers to women's potential for militance, and in the four other movements the organizers paid increased attention to mobilizing women and they set up separate women's associations (within the movements) and/or initiated discussions of women's issues.

FORMATION OF ORGANIZATIONS

Researchers have identified two sets of factors as crucial in the formation of social movement organizations.[44] These factors—structural changes increasing the relevance of collective action and the efforts of organizers—appear to apply in the Indian case studies examined. The structural changes involve the growth of the state and of capitalism. The growth of capitalism has increased the insecurity of subsistence for the lower class. Wage labor replaces long-term bondage to particular landlords in rural India. The (partial) freeing of feudal bonds means that the oppression of the poor is in some ways less brutal and they have greater independence, but their struggle for subsistence becomes more precarious as they suffer high rates of unemployment and underemployment. Many lower class individuals migrate to the cities and become part of the informal sector. Capitalist farmers and entrepreneurs utilize a variety of methods to take control of land and forest resources formerly used by tribals and other lower class groups. The growth of the state also increases both the need and the opportunities for collective action. On the one hand, many state policies such as the commercialization of the forest, exacerbate the insecurity of lower class groups. The expansion of state institutions—police, courts, development agencies—provides additional mechanisms for the domination of the poor by local elites. On the other hand, state policies and institutions also offer potential protection and resources for lower class individuals. Local elites adapt old forms of caste and class domination to maintain their power in the changing system. State policies prohibiting caste discrimination and forced labor, imposing land ceilings, and providing benefits for the poor offer the disadvantaged some recourse against oppression.

The instances of collective action examined illustrate that state programs and laws do provide resources for the organization of lower class groups. However, state programs are in themselves not enough, as the cases described above in Gujarat and Bombay show. The case studies of the urban women's associations and the rural grass-roots movements show that middle class organizers are able to facilitate the organization of lower class groups in order to gain access to state programs and in order to have state laws enforced. Furthermore, in the case of the urban women's associations, lending programs were the crucial organization-building resource.

In both the rural and the urban cases of collective action studied, middle class organizers were extremely important in initiating the action and/or in channelling on-going protest activity. The urban women's associations were started by experienced women organizers. Ela Bhatt of SEWA had worked for two decades with the Gandhian Textile Labor Association of Ahmedabad. Prema Purao of Annapurna had been expelled from Goa as an adolescent because of her work as a "freedom fighter," and then she and her husband were trade union organizers for the Communist Party of India (CPI). Jaya Arunachalam had worked for the Congress Party. The organizers in the rural grass-roots movements were (mostly male) students and intellectuals dedicated to social change and disillusioned with party politics. Many had been inspired by the Naxalite uprising in Bengal in 1967 or by the J. P. Movement in 1974–75. Their ideologies were diverse—Marxist, Gandhian, and Christian.

Selective and collective benefits are sought for and won: access to bank loans and famine relief programs, enactment of prohibition, and enforcement of antidiscrimination laws. The power of the organization is demonstrated through symbolic and substantive recognition by the state. Ela Bhatt received a prestigious national award from the government. After an agitation of several years by the Bodhgaya Movement, the government agreed to distribute 1,000 acres of temple land to landless laborers. The organizers structure opportunities for building solidarity. In addition to loan group and other associational meetings, the women's associations organize a number of events to build community among their women members—the dedication of the new SEWA headquarters, mass intercaste marriages celebrated by WWF, and trips around India set up by Annapurna. The grass-roots organizers mobilize the poor through *shibirs* and village meetings where issues and strategies are discussed. Cultural performances are also held to build solidarity. Villagers sing traditional and protest songs, and perform skits illustrating such topics as relations with landlords or wife beating.

The organizers vary in important ways across the groups studied; differences are most striking between the urban women leaders and the rural grass-roots organizers in age, life-style, and strategies. The three women's association leaders are middle-aged and live in comfortable though not luxurious surroundings. The grass-roots organizers tend to be younger and live among the rural poor, sharing their desperate conditions. The urban women leaders retain and utilize their political and class connections, while the grass-roots organizers eschew party politics.

GOALS AND FORMS OF PARTICIPATION

The women's association leaders appear to be following a reformist strategy to promote the interests of urban informal sector women. Their goal appears to be providing informal sector women workers access to the state. They use conventional procedures and only rarely use direct-action tactics. In contrast, the grass-roots organizers appear to be following a strategy that is both autonomous and conflictual to advance the interests of the rural poor. They form autonomous, participatory, and decentralized organizations which engage mainly in direct action tactics. Electoral politics and the state-defined political agenda are rejected. So is the idea that radical change occurs through " 'smashing' the state and taking it over."[45] Their long-term objective is the democratization of economics, politics, and culture. In this ambitious undertaking they "suffer from the absence of a relevant theory of transformation,"[46] as they have rejected both the reformist and the conventional Marxist strategies of change.

Joan Nelson notes that the political participation of lower class people is primarily oriented toward relatively modest goals concerning distribution and regulation.[47] Lower class men and women use political participation to obtain resources and protection from the state. In the Indian cases examined both patron-client networks and self-help organizations structured the participation of the lower class. Both patterns of participation provided access to the system, by, for example, bank lending and food for work programs. The difference between patron-client networks and self-help organizations appears to be the conditions under which access occurs. When urban, lower class borrowers are recruited by social workers, the patron-client relationship establishes vertical ties that the social worker can use to his advantage but no horizontal ties through which the borrowers can fight for collective goals. Under these conditions the lending program merely provides new channels through which ties of dependence and exploitation are established, maintained, or strengthened. When urban and rural lower class men and women join self-help organizations, the creation of horizontal ties through meetings and group problem solving and the development of local leaders facilitates the struggle for collective goals.

In the cases studied slum leaders facilitated access to on-going programs while the women's associations and grass-roots movements got government officials to expand the implementation of existing programs to groups (women) and districts previously not covered. SEWA has been particularly successful in gaining access to government funds and programs to provide training, social insurance, raw materials, and markets for its members.

In general, women's association and grass-roots movements used different methods to obtain access to government benefits. Grass-roots movements used direct action and women's associations used elite representation, with the women leaders meeting with bank and government officials. Women's associations usually encountered less opposition than the grass-roots movements but in some cases they also came up against an entrenched, unrelenting power structure. SEWA had to wage a multi-pronged attack before *bidi* (indigenous cigarettes) workers in Patan, a district town, were able to get access to medical services supposedly available through the *Bidi* and Cigar Workers Welfare Act.[48] The owners refused to give the women the necessary identity cards and gave in only after two years of petitions, meetings, correspondence between SEWA leader and the state welfare and labor commissioners, and a question raised in Parliament. Then ,the *bidi* factory owner retaliated against the women in a number of ways, provoking a *dharna* (demonstration) of SEWA members in front of one of the owner's shops.

Both the women's organizations and grass-roots movements have sought protection through government policies demanding the implementation of existing regulations, changes in regulations, and the formulation of new policies. SEWA has campaigned for the enforcement of minimum wage legislation applying to some self-employed workers, and for regulations to protect street vendors from police harassment. Several grass-roots movements have demonstrated against commercial forest policies, charging they take away their livelihood and contribute to deforestation. The anti-alcohol movement demanded the reimposition of prohibition in Uttarkhand. Pressure on the government for policies redistributing wealth and power has been much less common, and the only examples occurred in the grass-roots movements. The Shahada and Bodhgaya movements demanded a redistribution of land from caste Hindu landlords in Shahada and from a temple trust in Bodhgaya. The second case ultimately resulted in a partial redistribution by the government after a protracted struggle.

Further research is necessary to determine the extent to which the above differences between urban women's associations and rural grass-roots movements are due to differences between rural and urban political economies, differences between the policies under contention, and/or to differences in emphases between the two types of groups. Do rural power holders perceive lower class groups obtaining access to the state in redistributional terms as a threat to their own welfare and power, while urban power holders perceive access in less threatening distributional terms? Are women's associations more concerned with increasing the allocation of benefits from the state? Are grass-roots movements more concerned with regulating the behavior of the power holders and redistributing economic and political power?

Ultimately, both groups seek a redistribution of power between classes, castes, and genders through self-help activities to empower their members. Several of the groups provide informal education to members. More assertive strategies also exist. Members of the women's associations and the grass-roots movements have evolved ways of protesting abuses of power, stopping their occurrence, and preventing further occurrences. A common abuse of power is sexual harassment of lower class women by landlords, merchants, and police. Annapurna members have come to Prema Purao with stories of indebtedness leading to coerced sexual relations with merchants. They have discussed the situation in meetings, and the members (and the bank loans) have helped to repay the debts and end the sexual exploitation. In Shahada women resorted to a mock trial after a landlord had beaten a tribal woman severely and had torn off her blouse. Drawing on folk traditions, two to three hundred women gathered, garlanded the landlord with sandals, blackened his face, paraded him on a donkey, and beat him. The urban women's associations and women's associations in the grass-roots movements have treated male drunkenness, wife beating, and the verbal abuse of women by the men of the same community as serious issues. Annapurna women organized night patrols to overcome drunken men. In Nalgonda, a women's association decided that a man who beat his wife should leave his house and should be denied food and water by the community. Women have encountered male resistance but have continued to struggle over these issues.

DEFINITION OF INTERESTS

As participants in patron-client networks in bank lending programs, in urban women's associations and in grass-roots movements, Indian lower class women seem to define their interests primarily in terms of family survival. Participation in politics is relevant, insofar as it helps to obtain the resources necessary to provide for the basic needs of the family. In the groups that permit horizontal ties to develop, women also act on behalf of class, community, and gender interests. Their own economic advancement clearly affects family survival so women in SEWA and the Shahada movement have demonstrated for higher wages, and women in several of the grass-roots movements have sought access to land and to forests. In the Bodh-gaya movement women were able to gain movement acceptance of the demand that the land redistributed by the government would be accepted in women's names only. Male organizers had argued that this would weaken class unity. The response of women organizers was as follows:

> [E]quality can only strengthen, not weaken, an organization, but if it does weaken our unity, that will mean that our real commitment is not to equality or justice but to transfer of power, both economic and social, from the hands of one set of men to the hands of another set.[49]

Women in the grass-roots movements and in the urban women's associations link issues of family survival with issues of women's self-respect. Their struggle to feed their families involves confronting landlords, merchants, and petty government officials. These are individuals who use violence against lower class women to demonstrate their power, maintain their power, and regain their power when threatened by lower class activism. As mentioned above, women in both urban and rural organizations have evolved innovative ways to articulate gender interests against abuse by male power holders. Women link issues of self-respect and family survival when they articulate gender interests against the alcoholism of their men: men's drinking is a serious drain on family resources and when drunk, men may physically and verbally abuse women.

Women also link gender issues and issues of caste-tribal discrimination. One thousand Shahada women marched to a nearby town to protest a film that portrayed tribal women in a degrading manner. Women *dalits* in Tamil Nadu organized a march to a village pond which had been banned from *dalit* use by caste Hindus. They selected menstruating women to be the first to draw water in order to symbolize the interrelation of caste and gender prejudices. The urban women's associations have also campaigned against caste discrimination, and Ela Bhatt was one of a few public figures in Ahmedabad who took the side of the *dalits* during the caste riots in that city.

Several factors facilitate women's ability to define their interests in terms of family, class, community, and gender and to see these interests as interconnected. One important factor is the existence of separate women's associations. Another is the development of capitalistic relationships of production so that family household production has been replaced by either wage employment (men and women as agricultural laborers) or by different income earning activities by men and women (urban men in factory jobs and women in informal sector work, or in Uttarkhand, men migrating to cities in search of work and women remaining in subsistence production). The development of capitalistic relationships of production facilitates organizations of the poor along lines that transcend caste-tribal affiliations. Finally, the organizational models constructed by the urban women organizers and the rural grass-roots organizers are at least somewhat receptive to both class and gender issues.

IMPACT

What has been the impact of participation on Indian lower class women—either through patron-client networks or through collective action in women's associations or grass-roots movements? They have gained access to some benefits and protection from state programs and policies. Yet neither the benefits nor the protection has changed their position as informal sector workers, agricultural laborers, or poor peasants, nor enabled them to transform the system which disadvantages them. The dynamics of programs such as lending to the poor tend to erase the distinction between formal and informal sector workers in terms of political participation. The visibility of formal sector workers enables them to win some benefits from a government dependent on the electoral support of the masses; however, they are also vulnerable to being used as "block" support.[50] Government programs that target benefits for the poor provide visibility to informal sector workers and the rural poor which in turn offers them some material benefits and increased vulnerability to manipulation. As political participants, the lower class women studied are vulnerable to manipulation by their leaders. As the leaders have gained national recognition, they have tended to compete among themselves for political influence. However, the existence of democratic procedures and the opportunity to develop horizontal ties through collective action provide a check on the leaders not available in the patron-client networks. Furthermore, collective action provides a forum for politicizing relations of domination within the household.

Studies show that borrowers in lending programs for the poor experience small increases in income but remain below the poverty line.[51] Borrowers associated with women's associations are likely to do somewhat better than other women borrowers, because their higher repayment rates and the advocacy role of the women's associations ensure they will get additional loans. Borrowers associated with the social workers are less likely to get additional loans. Although continuing in the role of intermediary depends on achieving acceptable recovery rates, the social workers lack the skills, resources, and motivation to generate these rates. Even when borrowers associated with the social workers do repay loans, they are likely to experience long delays in getting additional bank loans because of the poor record overall of these borrowers. Even continued access to the bank loans does not lead the majority of women's association members to get out of poverty or even to get out of debt to moneylenders.

In the rural areas, members of grass-roots movements gain access to some benefits from poverty-focused programs, and they sometimes are able to get the state to intervene on their behalf against landlords, commercial liquor and forest interests, and discriminatory caste practices. These movements also encounter a high level of repression by dominant economic interests, the police, and in some cases, by left political parties. It is not possible to tell whether the level of repression is higher or lower than before the formation of these movements that have politicized the relations of domination. The emergence of rural grass-roots movements has also led to efforts by political parties to co-opt them.

For lower class women both the urban women's associations and the women's associations within the grass-roots movements have provided a base for continued mobilization on issues of class, caste, and gender inequality. Surveys of women's association members report increased awareness, confidence, and assertiveness on the part of members, and group leaders show greater attitudinal changes than other members.[52] Anecdotal evidence suggests similar changes among women in the rural movements. These changes are in keeping with other studies of the effects of associational participation by lower class people.[53] The existence of these associations has increased opportunities for women to act politically by carving out organizational spaces and developing local women leaders. These organizational spaces have enabled women to articulate their grievances, evolve their own solutions, and sustain their participation.

The differences between the two types of involvement of lower class women in collective action reflect the different contexts in which they occur and point to their respective strengths and weaknesses for women's empowerment. The greater sexual differentiation in income earning activities in urban versus rural lower class households shapes separate urban women's associations and rural women's associations that are components of rural grass-roots movements.[54]

Some degree of separate organization seems necessary to encourage women to participate and to sustain the incorporation of gender issues into the political agenda. The separate urban women's associations and their female leadership mean that gender interests are less likely to be compromised but the "integrated" grass-roots movements provide a better forum for struggle over gender issues.

The larger presence of the state in the big cities—regulations, government officials, banks, and other bureaucracies—as well as the more open exercise of domination by rural power holders shapes the reformist strategy of the urban women's associations and the conflictual strategy of the grass-roots movements. On the one hand, the urban women's associations pursue narrower goals and their leaders seek alliances with sympathetic policymakers. They provoke less resistance and can count on more allies in powerful places when they do encounter resistance. On the other hand, the grass-roots movements have a greater role in defining their political agenda and may be evolving a new theory and strategy of political change. They are beginning to gain allies among progressive professionals—academics, journalists, and lawyers—who are attempting to build a coalition of grass-roots movements and their sympathizers.

Grass-roots movements seem to have facilitated raising a broader constellation of issues feminists consider central to women's empowerment (strategic gender interests) than the urban women's associations. At the same time these organizational spaces for women are more vulnerable to being crushed by dominant interests than the less threatening urban women's associations are.

The experiences of women in both types of collective action have much in common in spite of their differences. Opportunities have been created for the development of leadership, discussion of problems, and the construction of solutions. These organizations and their women members face tremendous obstacles. Yet both the grass-roots movements and the urban women's associations have asserted—in their own ways—that development is a struggle for economic and political rights, and they have challenged the separation of political participation from social change in India. While their strategies have varied in the extent to which conflictual direct action tactics have been utilized, both urban and rural organizations have achieved similar "small victories" from the state: policy enactment and implementation providing access to state resources and protection from dominant interests. They also face a common challenge of reconciling their nonparty political stance with the reality of a party dominated political system.

Conclusion

The grass-roots movements and urban women's associations share a strategy of empowerment through self-help activities, but they differ in their stance toward the state: the urban women's associations seek incorporation in the state primarily through conventional political means and occasional direct action tactics, and the rural grass-roots movements confront the structures of state and dominant class power primarily through direct action. These differences in strategy appear to reflect variations in three factors—the political-economic contexts of urban and rural India, the policies under contention, and the groups themselves, which in turn have some effect on the first two factors.

What insights do these two collective action strategies offer to the debates on class, gender, and the state in India? The achievements of both the urban women's associations and the rural grass-roots movements provide support for the social democratic arguments of Frankel and the policy oriented women's studies scholars: through organized pressure lower class groups "can build their own direct relationships with outside power centers . . . in the administration" and obtain benefits from state programs.[55] In the urban women's associations this occurs without patron-client ties siphoning off benefits and subjecting women to dependency relations with male "social workers." The grass-roots movements provide a counterweight to the entrenched power of the rural elites: by being able to defend themselves the rural poor can gain some concessions from the state.

The achievements of the urban women's associations also support the argument of the Marxist scholars that these associations facilitate the incorporation of women into the capitalist mode of production. According to a Marxist perspective, this process strengthens capitalist domination and offers no hope for substantive improvement in the material welfare and power of lower class women. Women's association members may win some short-term benefits but without challenging the pact of domination, the redistribution of power necessary for overall improvement in the lives of lower class women will not occur. The strategy of the grass-roots movement is on a better track but remains seriously flawed because it doesn't seem to offer the potential of taking over the state.

Both the social democratic and the Marxist arguments appear one dimensional. They assume a predetermined set of consequences will follow subordinate class organization. Instead, if the state is

viewed as a combination of the four contradictory tendencies identified by Rueschemeyer and Evans, there are both opportunities and
dangers for subordinate class empowerment created by organizing to
demand benefits and protection from the state. In addition to em-
bodying a pact of domination and an arena of social conflict, the
state is a corporate actor and claims to guard universal social interests. Subordinate class efforts enable the state to become more autonomous from the dominant classes. Subordinate class organizations—with the help of sympathetic journalists and lawyers—can
invoke the ideal that the state is the guardian of universal interests.
Neither the state nor the dominant classes, however, will cease in
their own efforts to control the subordinate classes through co-optation and repression. Co-optation appears the more serious threat to
the women's associations for some of the reasons advanced by the
Marxist scholars. Repression appears the more serious threat to the
grass-roots movements.

The cases of women's collective action reviewed in this chapter
cannot settle the scholarly debates on the most feasible way to accomplish redistribution through the state—through top-down left
parties (Kohli), bottom-up movements (Kothari), or through armed
struggle (Patankar and Omvedt). However, the experience of the Naxalite movement decisively crushed by the government casts doubt
on the revolutionary alternative.[56] Although Kohli writes favorably
about the Communist party of India (Marxist) in West Bengal, a study
by Amrita Basu reveals an organization that has promoted practical
gender interests to the exclusion of strategic gender interests:
"Women's articulation of their own problems and needs, however,
has been negligible, because male-dominated political parties have
initiated organizing."[57]

The bottom-up organizations examined here have articulated
both practical and strategic gender interests. Will the efforts of these
(and other) groups lead to greater gender, class, and community
equality in India? Several obstacles and dangers can be identified.
Kohli argues that there are layers of obstacles and his points can be
expanded to include gender as well as class constraints. These constraints to successful redistributive policies include the established
definition of the role of the state, which is biased against women and
the lower classes; the structure of bureaucratic authority, which was
designed by upper class men; and the reality that redistributive policy implementation disrupts stability and efficiency.[58] According to
Kothari, international capitalism, global development institutions,
and the Indian state have identified nongovernmental organizations

(NGOs) as a model superior to private firms or state bureaucracy in penetrating society. The danger facing lower class women is that their organizations are vulnerable to being used by this "pact of domination":

> For the NGO sector, the new temptations of being development agents in the Corporate State's model may make them overlook the new threat to their voluntarism, their ability to critically evaluate government policies on behalf of the people and both their will and their power to intervene justly and creatively.[59]

Bringing the state in as an actor in its own right leads to more sophisticated analyses of the causes and consequences of collective action strategies. However, there is the danger in a state-centered approach that the state is seen as the only source of change. Kothari's contention that the fundamental transformations required to humanize politics and the state will come from outside the state provides another perspective. The importance of the internal mobilizational and self-help activities in both the women's associations and the grass-roots movements indicates that their collective action strategies should not only be seen as shaped by the state-defined political agenda but also as an autonomous challenge to oppressive structures based on class, caste, and gender. Since the state and dominant classes have used male domination and caste hierarchy to enforce their rule, any struggle for the economic and political rights of the poor must also be a struggle for gender and caste equality. It is too early to assess the long-term limitations and/or accomplishments of the urban women's associations and the rural grass-roots movements. They do, however, represent a new stage in the politicization of lower class women in India. Women's involvement in collective action around practical gender interests has created a forum for articulation and struggle around strategic gender interests as well.

What light does the exploration of lower class women's involvement in collective action in India shed on the debates about gender and the state in Western countries? The Indian case points out the insufficient attention to class and to the interconnections among gender, class, and racial inequality in the American debates, although Europeans appear more sensitive to these linkages. It also points out the need for a more sophisticated feminist analysis of the state: there is some value in each of the feminist perspectives on the state, but instead of being seen as mutually exclusive positions, each should be seen as identifying one of contradictory tendencies that are combined in particular patterns to constitute the state.

Most importantly the Indian case casts doubt on the distinction between reform and autonomy as the mutually exclusive and only available stances for lower class women vis-á-vis the state. The urban women's associations seeking incorporation into the state are pursuing a reformist strategy. State program benefits (loans for the poor) represent an organization building resource. Yet the activities of the urban women's associations promoting women's autonomy are central to these organizations. Providing a forum where issues of gender, caste, and class oppression can be raised and strategies pursued encourages the women members to approach their husbands, merchants, and government officials empowered instead of dependent and victimized

The rural grass-roots movements represent a third stance toward the state. Instead of seeking incorporation into the state or rejecting involvement with the state in favor of a completely autonomous strategy, they adopt a stance of conflict toward the state and dominant classes: demanding resources and protection from the state but in many cases seeking the reversal of state policies and the redistribution of resources. At the same time the internal activities of the grass-roots movements promote autonomy. As in the urban women's associations, providing a forum for issues of gender, class, and caste oppression is essential to women's participation. Grass-roots movements not only promote autonomy, they also offer a forum for struggle between men and women of the rural poor over gender issues.

The Indian collective action strategies suggest that a completely autonomous strategy may be unrealistic for lower class women who lack the privileges of middle class existence. The state infringes upon the lives of lower class women mainly in negative ways, and any benefits to which they are entitled are not easily accessible. Thus lower class women must adopt a stance toward the state—somewhere along a continuum extending from seeking incorporation into the state to seeking confrontation with the state. At the same time, however, lower class women must develop their own independent base through discussion and action around the issues that they encounter in their daily lives. Only through the autonomy facilitated by the organizational spaces they have created do lower class women have any chance in their struggle against the hierarchical structures of caste, class, gender, and state.

9

CONCLUSION

Jana Everett
Kathleen Staudt
Sue Ellen M. Charlton

The preceding chapters have examined the relationships between gender and the state under varying political and economic circumstances. The contributors have adopted a statist orientation—viewing the state as a significant force in its own right—and have avoided the reductionism of approaches that explain politics completely by economic and social factors. The state is conceptualized as a bureaucratic, coercive, and normative order, and the implications of the state for gender relations are examined on three levels: state officials, state institutions and policies, and state definition of politics. The interest in state officials concerns their "purposefully undertaken actions" that make binding rules to guide the behavior of their citizens.[1] The structure of state institutions and the content of public policies are viewed as important factors shaping politics. Finally, the state is seen as constituting a normative order that expresses a particular conception of politics, of power, and of the goals and values of collective life.

Development policies are among the priorities of the contemporary state. From the perspective of state elites, development entails capital accumulation, industrialization, and increased agricultural productivity and typically involves greater state penetration of society. Both development policies and the concomitant state penetration of society affect gender relations in ways that are seldom predictable. The preceding chapters' investigations of how state policies and definitions of development have affected gender relations suggest that the impact of the state's developmental role on gender relations should be given more emphasis. A great deal has been written about the implications of economic systems and economic transformations for gender relations, but the impact on gender relations of the state's role in capital accumulation and industrialization has been neglected.

The contributors recognize that the state is a set of institutions situated in a social context. State-gender relations form one dimension of state-society relations interconnected with other dimensions (including class, race, and religion). The contributors also share a feminist perspective on society, viewing existing societies as characterized by varying degrees and types of gender inequality that are interconnected with other forms of structured inequality. From this perspective, the impact of the state on gender is seen to be partly shaped by historically specific patterns of gender relations in society, and partly shaped by historically specific state leaders, policies, and definitions of politics (ideologies). This volume represents a modest start in the project of developing a comparative theoretical framework on women and the state. Such a framework must address the implications for gender relations of variations in state autonomy and capacity. It must also address variations in gender relations across class, racial, and religious lines. Finally, it must be dialectical; it must understand gender relations to be structured by the state but also to be the product of complex interactions between classes, genders, and the state.

As noted in the Introduction the authors seek to extend feminist theory and enrich political science by formulating a gender-sensitive approach to the theoretical analysis of states and development. Our goal is to promote intellectual dialogue between those scholars studying comparative political economy or international studies, and those scholars studying gender relations. On a practical level, the state, or at least aspects of the state—government leaders, policies, agencies, ideologies—are important items on the agenda of feminist movements worldwide. But there has been little reflection by activists on the implications of reliance upon the state. Fundamental questions remain to be addressed: Can women look to the state for their emancipation? Or does the state merely represent a mechanism for women's subordination? How do differences among states affect the extent to which the state contributes to women's emancipation or subordination? Under what conditions and through which strategies can women make their presence felt in the state or effectively protect themselves from the state? Although feminist theory has only begun to answer these questions, it is important to build on and extend this theory as a guide to practice.

In this chapter we set out some questions to guide our thinking about women and the state:

1. What roles have states played in the maintenance and/or transformation of gender relations?
2. How have women responded to the imposition and/or expansion of the state?
3. What have been the consequences for women's practical and strategic gender interests of women's responses to state imposition and/or expansion?

STATE ROLES IN GENDER RELATIONS

From the preceding studies we can draw some insights concerning the gender implications of the processes of state imposition and state expansion. For the most part, the state has reinforced or increased female subordination. How and why has this happened? We can offer only the beginnings of answers here, with more definitive answers requiring further research. At this stage, it is helpful to examine the state's impact on gender relations as the product of three interrelated levels of state activity: the strategies of state elites, the policies enacted and institutions constructed, and the political discourse and practice shaped by state institutions and ideologies. The survival of state elites depends on their success in international economic and military competition as well as in the maintenance of internal order through a mix of authority and force. In their attempts to ensure survival, state elites fashion ideologies selectively, manipulating existing and new cultural values perceived to be consistent with elite goals; they construct civilian and military bureaucracies and pursue policies to advance economic development, military security, and social order.

Each level of state activity contributes to gender inequality, but at each level of state activity there is some potential for action to reverse this dominant tendency. State leaders opportunistically draw upon existing patterns of gender inequality found in most societies, but in some cases the degree of female subordination interferes with state development goals and is ameliorated by state leaders. The strategies of elite survival themselves both reflect and promote male domination. However, the potential exists for excessive male domination to threaten both the internal order and the economic development requirements of states. Thus public policies may reflect both of these contradictory tendencies—a major tendency promoting gender inequality and a minor tendency promoting gender equality. Policies may also have unintended consequences affecting gender relations.

State elites have discovered that promoting male domination contributes to the maintenance of social order in a period of state formation. As Charlton points out for early modern Europe and Staudt for colonial Africa, leaders of new states share a set of problems: how to eliminate rival sources of power and authority and at the same time provide material resources for the state and allegiance to the state. A common solution involves offering a bargain to (some) men: in return for ceding control over political power and social resources to the state, they gain increased control over their families.[2] Not only does this solution promote male domination, but it also establishes or strengthens a distinction between public and private spheres, and subordinates the private sphere to the public. Women are relegated to this private sphere creating a state-constructed obstacle to their political action. Issues defined as male by the sexual division of labor are the concern of state-defined politics: war, foreign policy, international trade, long distance communication, and resource extraction. Female issues such as housing, food, health, and childcare are rendered politically invisible. For other issues that involve tension between men and women—sexuality, family relations, property rights—a male perspective is institutionalized in state-defined laws. The impact of state imposition in dissimilar social contexts differs: in Western Europe existing gender inequalities are reinforced, but in Africa gender relations may either be reinforced, as Callaway and Creevey suggest, or transformed with new content in gender roles and attributes, enhanced male control of women in the family, and greater male access to economic resources and political power, as Staudt argues.

Wolchik's discussion of the initial period of state socialism illustrates a case where the degree of female subordination interfered with the strategies of state elites to promote internal security and economic development. This led to certain state-directed changes in gender relations toward equality. Communist leaders sought to counterbalance patriarchal family structures perceived to be power bases of the revolution's opponents. Because of capital shortages, they also needed to mobilize all labor resources for economic development and thus sought to bring women into the labor force. State policies promoted women's legal rights, education, political participation, and increased power in the family. The state definition of politics embodied in Marxist ideology initially represented a progressive force for gender relations through its official commitment to gender equality.

In general, during the process of state consolidation and expansion, gender inequality continues to be instrumental in elite survival strategies. State policies promoting male domination and female subordination have served to gain the support of men in the society and to economize on resources in a variety of types of states. Although the initial revolutionary upheaval in the Soviet Union and Eastern Europe led to some transformation in gender relations, the consolidation of power by socialist states has in general reinforced traditional gender relations of male domination. Wolchik points out that women in leadership positions have all but disappeared, state policies have promoted the family as the building block of socialism, and state mobilization campaigns have reassured men that female employment wouldn't interfere with women's domestic duties. In another case of socialist revolution, Judith Stacey argues that in China state development strategies have had the effect of moderating family patriarchy but of extending it to all households.[3]

Turning to West European states, Charlton shows how the welfare state has reinforced the gender division of labor at home and at work. In Third World states, development policies have primarily focused on men's activities. In Latin America and other dependent capitalist states the sector of the economy regulated by the state (the formal sector) is a male preserve while women remain invisible in domestic service and petty commerce activities in the informal sector.[4] Here women's work remains unrecognized by the state as it is also in the private plots of socialist states. Callaway and Creevey show how in the context of economic and political crisis, state leaders in Nigeria and Senegal (to varying degrees) promote Islamic law in family matters and do little to advance women's rights. Elite survival strategies lead state leaders to try to win the support of Muslim leaders who are increasingly fundamentalist in the current climate.

Although in general these state policies subordinate women, there are some unintended consequences with potential for reducing female subordination. Linda Gordon points out that American welfare state programs offered some resources to women seeking to escape from patriarchal family relations, and this is also the case in some Third World states today, as noted in our introduction.[5] In the Soviet Union and Eastern Europe the double burden state policies have imposed upon women has led to a decline in the birth rate that alarms state officials. The commitment to development among Third World elites, as Charlton notes, provides a potential opportunity for women to argue that development policies which do not include them are illegitimate. In the 1970s poverty-focused policies were enacted in many Third World states to address inequities and unrest. Some of these policies provided mechanisms of access enabling women to gain some control over social resources. This was the case in the 1971 Mexican Federal Law on Agrarian Reform, as Bourque notes, and in the lending programs developed in the 1970s by the nationalized banks in India that Everett discusses. Such policies may not initially benefit women, but they represent openings that can be utilized by officials or by activists with feminist sympathies. Thus both the work of the Mexican PROMUDER (Women's Program for Rural Development) and the informal sector women's organizations in India were made possible by the prior existence of state policies that legitimized and facilitated the access to social resources by some groups of women.

The structures of bureaucracy and of state-defined political discourse also have contradictory implications for gender relations. In modern states they represent increased state control of the private sphere imposing values of hierarchy, specialization, and rationalization upon women, children and family life. However, there is a contradictory aspect to this control. As Sonia E. Alvarez has noted, state penetration also "engenders" the political, inserting issues of the family, reproduction, household subsistence, and sexuality into the state-defined political agenda.[6] This potentially creates a political base for women from which to speak of their needs, priorities, and visions.

Bureaucratization involves specialization, experts, and objectivity, all of which are at odds with the female worlds of family, locality, and daily life—however much these worlds may vary across class and nation. Militarization of the state is the clearest illustration of the state as male dominant. As Charlton notes, the military is an important channel of recruitment to positions of political leadership from which women are effectively excluded. Policies appropriating a growing share of the gross national product to the defense budget mean a diversion of societal resources away from areas of women's traditional concerns. World Wars I and II did represent periods of some gain for women in the economic and state structures, as their labor was necessary to replace men gone to war, but recent research reveals the continued importance of a gender division of labor, even during these periods.[7] Nationalism and militarism promote increased state intervention in the family to ensure a labor force of sufficient quality and quantity to win the military and industrial competitions between states. State militarism also contributes to a growing militarization of culture that reinforces male domination at the ideological level. However, as Bourque and Chuchryk make clear, the overwhelming male nature of the military state generates its own internal contradictions. In its use of torture and sexual humiliation against dissidents, the Latin American military regimes symbolized the state as rapist. But even some state leaders appear to have been troubled by these excesses of male domination and to have encouraged civil protest to curb them. These leaders may have seen women as a relatively nonthreatening group, but on a symbolic level, they were conceding the danger of an excessively masculine state.

As discussed above, modern states' increased capacity for penetration into the private sphere poses the threat of increased control of women but also "engenders" the political. It is this contradictory and dual impact on gender relations that we can see in varying degrees in the focus on motherhood among different types of contemporary states. Islamic states have the capacity to impose the vision of gender relations found in the *Qu'ran*, restricting women to family roles. This imposition reinforces male control over women and denies women's voice in the public sphere. In the Chilean state the military's use of the ideology of motherhood also restricted women to domestic roles. However, the state's direct assault on family life through widespread terror revealed that home was not a safe place and politicized women to resist the state. The recent adoption of pronatalist policies in the Soviet Union and East European socialist states has had a mixed impact on gender relations. These policies legitimize state investigation of problems women face in combining productive and reproductive roles, although the unequally valued division of labor in the family and society is maintained. In the United States, "welfare reform" may perpetuate female poverty through low wage employment, but it also adds health and childcare to the policy agenda.

Under what conditions is the potential for reversing the dominant state tendency toward gender inequality realized? What is needed are many more historically specific studies of state structures and state-society relations as they affect gender relations. Identifying the important aspects of state and societal variation relevant for gender relations is a first step. We make a preliminary effort at this in the following discussion.

State elites do not have a free hand in devising their survival strategies because these strategies are conditioned both by aspects of the state and by social context. In the statist literature the social conditions impinging on state action—class structure, culture, religion, and the nation's position in the international economy—are viewed as limits on state autonomy. States are conceived of along a continuum, from a high level of insulation from social forces at one end, to state capture by social forces at the other end. Concerning gender relations, it is not so much the degree of state autonomy as the content of the limiting conditions—both societal and internal to the state—that matters. Conditions of variation within the state that appear to have important implications for gender relations include the composition of state leadership, the bureaucratic capacity of the state, the extent of democratic participation, and the ideological basis of state legitimacy. While it might be true that the greater the autonomy of the state the larger its impact on gender relations, this proposition does not tell us about the nature of the impact. Both socialist states and Latin American military states score high in autonomy, but differences in ideology, dominant classes, and bureaucratic capacity lead to significant differences in the ways these states have impinged on gender relations. For example, the emphasis on distribution in Third World socialist states has aided women in meeting practical gender interests in food, health care, and housing to a much greater degree than in the Latin American military states which do not meet these needs and marginalize women through the policies and processes of dependent capitalist development.

WOMEN'S RESPONSES TO STATE IMPOSITION AND EXPANSION

The chapters in this book identify a wide variety of ways in which women have responded to the imposition and expansion of the state. We can classify women's responses as either seeking *disengagement* from the state or as seeking *engagement* with the state.[8] Engagement can be further divided into seeking *access* to the state and seeking *transformation* of the state.

Much of what falls within the disengagement category has not been thought significant in conventional accounts of political activity.[9] However, if we want to understand the full range of variation in women's responses to the state, it seems foolish to narrow our analysis to those cases where women have participated in state institutions. Recent modifications in the political participation literature have some relevance for understanding women as political actors, but the literature remains embedded in a pluralist conception of the state. For example, Sidney Verba and Lucien Pye suggest that instead of starting with state institutions such as elections and asking "how responsive different segments of the mass population have been to these institutions," we should be asking "about the needs felt by the poor and the less educated, about the extent to which they believe such needs can only be satisfied by community institutions and how they go about getting from government the benefits they seek."[10] A statist perspective enables us to add to this actor-centered perspective the possibility that women might seek to meet their practical gender needs by disengagement from the state as well as by engagement with the state.

We can identify four strategies of disengagement used by women: suffer-manage, insulation, escape, and reactive collective action. First, there is what Azarya and Chazan label "suffer-manage." To cope with deteriorating circumstances, survival strategies are devised that preclude active involvement in state-defined politics. Suffer-manage refers to those situations where state policies either impose hardships or fail to alleviate hardships experienced by people (such as irregularity and scarcity in supplies of basic needs) and those people "are unable to extricate themselves from the arena of the malfunctioning state."[11] Women typically are responsible for meeting family consumption needs and, exhausted by the struggle, become disaffected from government. Suffer-manage characterizes a major response of women in the Soviet Union and Eastern Europe, according to Wolchik. She describes women's low levels of leadership participation in work and politics as partly a coping mechanism in response to the hardships of daily life.

Second, there is the response of insulation within family and kin networks and other groups not incorporated into the state. This serves as a defense against state intrusion and an alternative way of gaining recognition, power, and resources. Staudt discusses this as the major response of African women to the colonial state. Today some feminists advocate "delinking" from the state and international economy because these institutions are seen as thoroughly male dominated.[12]

Escape is the most extreme type of withdrawal, and it has become an option less and less available as modern states increase their penetration vertically to the local level, horizontally across their entire territories, and functionally throughout all sectors of social life. Irene Silverblatt describes how in colonial Peru native women fled to the high tablelands to escape the Spanish and to return to their own religion.[13] More tragically, they committed infanticide rather than subject a new generation to colonial rule.

Under some circumstances women seeking disengagement from a political order redefined by the state have engaged in collective action, confronting the state in order to resist the growth of the state. The Tillys examine what they label "reactive" collective action by European men and women opposing state intervention in their lives through food riots, tax protests, and invasions of fields in the eighteenth century.[14] Women were active participants in these locally based, relatively spontaneous protests. Examining a different place and a different time, Staudt documents women's protests against state-imposed produce prices, water fees, and produce inspection in colonial Africa.

Women have not only sought withdrawal from the state; they have also sought to enter the state and/or to transform the state to meet their needs. During the first wave of feminism, primarily middle class women in North America and Western Europe sought citizenship rights in the liberal democratic state.[15] Smaller women's rights movements developed in authoritarian European states (such as Russia) and in the colonial (such as India) and semi-colonial (such as China) states of Asia, Africa, and Latin America as part of movements for democracy, nationalism, and reform. Since the emergence of the second wave of feminism in the 1960s, there appears to have been a worldwide increase in women seeking access to state resources in order to obtain or use state conflict resolution mechanisms, benefits, services, and protection. Women have sought legal equality, economic access to resources, reproductive rights, and the elimination of sexual exploitation and violence against women. These goals have involved demands for implementing and/or changing existing policies, enacting new policies, and broadening the policy agenda. They have also involved efforts to elect and appoint women and feminists to public office. In addition, women have participated alongside men and separately in movements seeking to redirect state priorities. There have been social movements organized around policy issues—collective consumption (health, housing, transportation, food prices), the environment, nuclear war, militarism. In some cases left parties—communists, the Greens—have sought public office in order to redirect policy priorities. Finally, women have participated alongside men in revolutionary movements seeking state transformation.

Instances of women seeking engagement with the state in order to meet their needs are in large measure the result of state expansion. As mentioned above, state expansion provides potential resources for women. For example, the involvement of advanced capitalist states in economic regulation and social services provides a basis for feminist demands for equal rights, employment legislation, and increased state spending on childcare. The involvement of Third World states in development programs, especially the recent programs targeted at disadvantaged groups, enable women's groups to demand women's inclusion in these programs, as Everett illustrates in the case of the urban women's organizations in India. Welfare programs in the U.S. and lending programs in India have also served as organization-building mechanisms in certain instances. Especially in certain Third World states (such as Peru, Brazil, or India) our contributors note that feminists have recognized what Alvarez terms certain key points of entry to state elites to increase the visibility and protection of women as well as benefits to women from state policy.[16] In other ways state expansion is extremely problematic for women. It has led to a deterioration in the distribution of goods and services, environmental degradation and commercialization, the danger of extinction and diversion of resources in the nuclear arms race, and repression caused by police and military action. Women have confronted the state—both symbolically and physically—in order to influence the state to cease policies detrimental to women, as Chuchryk documents in the case of Chile and Everett in the case of rural organizations in India.

As Sonia Alvarez has noted, variations across states lead to different "opportunity spaces" for women to attempt to realize practical or strategic gender interests through engagement with the state.[17] In the military dictatorships of South America, women's options were limited to confrontation with the state, but women could use this option with less lethal personal consequences than men precisely because women were defined as outside of the political realm.

Furthermore, women could draw on their identities as mothers, an identity usually relegating them to the private sphere. In India, a state officially committed to gender equality and democratic politics, the urban self-employed women's associations could work both within the system and outside of it for the practical gender interests of informal sector workers. And civil rights and women's groups could publicize state abuse of power in police rape of low caste women and rural, upper class/caste retaliation against grass-roots movements. In socialist states the monopoly role of the Communist party discourages women from using political participation as a mechanism for getting their needs met.

CONSEQUENCES

What consequences follow from women's attempts to withdraw from the state, to gain access to the state, to transform the state? Under what conditions do women's responses to state imposition or expansion lead to improvement, deterioration and/or no change in women's practical and strategic gender interests? A thorough examination of this topic requires both an analysis of the state, of women's responses to the state and of the societal context. In this section we set out some preliminary ideas. We sketch five alternative outcomes for women that could follow from women's attempts at disengagement from the state or engagement with the state: (1) autonomy from the state, (2) repression by the state, (3) cooptation by the state, (4) incorporation into the state, and (5) transformation of the state.

Historically, women have primarily sought to withdraw from state imposition or expansion. This response has offered some protection from state policies, leaders, and ideologies, but the implications for women have been problematic for two reasons. First, most societies have been characterized by gender inequality and the growth of the state exacerbates this. Thus seeking refuge in nonstate structures, women encounter male domination. Autonomy from the state does not mean social autonomy for women. Second, modern states are totalistic states seeking to penetrate all sectors of society. It is not likely women will be able to be left alone.

Women have been the targets of state repression in a variety of types of states. Often state repression is used against women activists seeking to change state policies or regimes. The police and military have imprisoned, tortured, and raped black women protesting Apartheid in South Africa, South American women protesting military dictatorship, and tribal women protesting loss of land in India. But not engaging in political activity does not guarantee the safety of women. In many cases, state repression against women has followed from particular policy priorities and/or state definitions of policies, as in forced abortions in China or forced veiling of women in Islamic states.

While it might be relatively easy to classify particular instances as cases of autonomy or repression, distinguishing between the next two cases is more difficult. Much of the disagreement among feminists today about the stance that should be taken toward the state hinges on the issue of whether the efforts of feminists to enter mainstream politics result in co-optation or incorporation of gender interests by the state. In the past, women leaders, gendered policy issues, and even feminist definitions of politics, have been co-opted by the state, resulting in greater control by the state over gender relations. Two versions of this process can be seen. In the advanced capitalist states the co-optation has had a class basis. For example, in the United States, the "maternal reform" ideology of the beginnings of the welfare state during the Progressive Era imposed a middle class feminist ideology on the working class and made the distinct needs of working class women invisible. In socialist states, the co-optation has resulted from Communist party hegemony. There has been an official commitment to women's practical and strategic gender interests without an independent feminist movement to hold the party accountable.

Both co-optation and incorporation involve the entry of women into state leadership positions and policy changes that explicitly address women's practical and strategic gender interests. The distinction between them depends on whether an increased state role in gender relations enhances the access of all women to economic resources, political value, and social value. Another way to distinguish between co-optation and incorporation is to ask whether the entry of women into the state facilitates or impedes the redefinition of politics in a direction that meets women's practical and strategic interests, and whether by entering the state women can eventually transform the state.

The final consequence—transformation of the state—is not part of the historical record but is an aspect of the feminist vision of gender equality. As of yet, neither the vision nor the paths to it are clear. Three alternative paths can be identified in current feminist thinking: (1) insider path: women gain access to the state in order to transform it, (2) outsider path: women confront and challenge the state in order to transform it, (3) autonomy path: women develop alternative decentralized models of political economy apart from the state system. Clearly we need both further theoretical development and also empirical investigation in order to specify the conditions under which these various paths lead to state transformation and gender equality. However, it appears to us that the three paths should not be seen as mutually exclusive but as mutually enhancing.

NOTES

CHAPTER 1

1. See the study sponsored by the Social Science Research Council, *Bringing the State Back In*, eds. Peter B. Evans, Dietrich Rueschemeyer, and Theda Skocpol (Cambridge: University Press, 1985); also Alfred Stepan, *The State and Society: Peru in Comparative Perspective* (Princeton, N.J.: Princeton University Press, 1978); Eric A. Nordlinger, *On the Autonomy of the Democratic State* (Cambridge, Mass.: Harvard University Press, 1981); Atul Kohli, ed., *The State and Development in the Third World* (Princeton, N.J.: Princeton University Press, 1986); Nora Hamilton, *The Limits of State Autonomy: Post Revolutionary Mexico* (Princeton, N.J.: Princeton University Press, 1982). Vicky Randall and Robin Theobald, *Political Change and Underdevelopment: A Critical Introduction to Third World Politics* (Durham, N.C.: Duke University Press, 1985) Chapter 5, note how the political development literature converged on analysis of the state.

2. Stephen D. Krasner, "Approaches to the State: Alternative Conceptions and Historical Dynamics," *Comparative Politics* 16, no. 2 (January 1984): 224.

3. Nordlinger, pp. 151–66, contrasts pluralism and neopluralism. For influential neopluralist analyses, see Grant McConnell, *Private Power and American Democracy* (New York: Alfred Knopf, 1967); and Theodore J. Lowi, *The End of Liberalism: Ideology, Policy, and the Crisis of Public Authority* (New York: Norton, 1969).

4. Frederick Engels, *The Origin of the Family, Private Property and the State* (New York: International Publishers, 1942, 1970), 231.

5. Nicos Poulantzas, *Political Power and Social Classes* (London:

New Left Books, 1973); Stephen D. Krasner, *Defending the National Interest: Raw Materials Investments and U.S. Foreign Policy* (Princeton, N.J.: Princeton University Press, 1978), 21–25, has a good discussion distinguishing structural Marxism on the state from other paradigms. See also Colin Crouch's reflective essay on what he calls functionalist Marxists' inability to predict capitalism's accommodation of developments that threaten its domination, "The State, Capital and Liberal Democracy," in *State and Economy in Contemporary Capitalism*, ed. Colin Crouch (London: Croom Helm, 1979).

6. Engels, *Origin of the Family*, chap. 9.

7. Krasner, "Approaches to the State," 225.

8. Max Weber, *Economy and Society: An Outline of Interpretive Sociology*, ed. Guenther Roth and Claus Wittich (New York: Bedminster Press, 1968), 1: 56.

9. Lourdes Benería, ed., *Women and Development: The Sexual Division of Labor in Rural Societies* (New York: Praeger, 1982); Joan Smith, Immanuel Wallerstein, and Hans-Dieter Evers, eds., *Households and the World Economy* (Beverly Hills, Calif.: Sage Publications, 1984). Susan C. Bourque and Kay B. Warren, in "Technology, Gender, and Development," *Daedalus* 116, no. 4 (Fall 1987): 173–97, critique the global economy approach, noting that by using the household as a unit of analysis, the approach downplays competing interests within the family.

10. Gianfranco Poggi juxtaposes the views of David Easton and Carl Schmitt, German legal theorist of the 1920s, to make his argument, in *The Development of the Modern State: A Sociological Introduction* (Stanford, Calif.: Stanford University Press, 1978), Chap. 1.

11. Skocpol, *States and Social Revolutions: A Comparative Analysis of France, Russia and China* (Cambridge: Cambridge University Press, 1979), 30.

12. Gita Sen and Caren Grown for DAWN (Development Alternatives with Women for a New Era), *Development, Crises, and Alternative Visions: Third World Women's Perspectives* (New York: Monthly Review Press, 1987); and Marilee Karl and Ximena Charnes, *Women, Struggles and Strategies: Third World Perspectives* (Rome: ISIS International, no. 6, 1986).

13. Adele Mueller, "The Bureaucratization of Feminist Knowledge: The Case of Women in Development," *Issue of the Decade: Feminists and State Processes, RFR/DRF,* 15, no. 1 (March 1986): 36–38. By the late 1980s, the boundaries of the women and development literature had stretched beyond bureaucratic priorities as a result both of criticism of those priorities and of a shift in them.

14. Jane Flax, "Postmodernism and Gender Relations in Feminist Theory," *Signs: Journal of Women in Culture and Society* 12, no.4 (Summer 1987): 629.

15. Catharine A. MacKinnon, "Feminism, Marxism, Method, and the State: Toward Feminist Jurisprudence," *Signs: Journal of Women in Culture and Society* 8, no. 4 (Summer 1983): 656.

16. Wendy Sarvasy, "Rethinking the Welfare State: An Overview with Some Policy Implications" (paper presented at the Annual Meeting of the Western Political Science Association, Las Vegas, Nevada, March 1985).

17. Maxine Molyneux, "Mobilization without Emancipation? Women's Interests, the State, and Revolution in Nicaragua," *Feminist Studies* 11, no.2 (Summer 1985): 232. Because there is no consistency of vision among feminist theorists, a concept of "strategic gender interests" designed to realize such a vision continues to be problematic. For the debate as it relates to the U.S., see Joan Hoff-Wilson's analysis of the problems associated with the goal of equal rights between men and women in "The Unfinished Revolution: Changing Legal Status of U.S. Women," *Signs: Journal of Women in Culture and Society* 13, no. 1 (Autumn 1987): 7–36.

18. Frances Fox Piven, "Women and the State: Ideology, Power and the Welfare State," *Socialist Review* 14, no. 2 (March-April 1984): 18.

19. Zillah Eisenstein, "The State, the Patriarchal Family and Working Mothers," in *Families, Politics and Public Policy: A Feminist Dialogue on Women and the State*, ed., Irene Diamond (New York: Longman, 1983), 41–58. Although usually classified as a socialist feminist, Eisenstein's argument is essentially a liberal one.

20. Eileen Boris and Peter Bardaglio, "The Transformation of Patriarchy: The Historic Role of the State," ibid., 70–93.

21. MacKinnon, "Feminism, Marxism, Method, and the State," 658.

22. Cynthia R. Daniels, *Working Mothers and the State* (Ph.D. diss., University of Massachusetts, 1983).

23. Bell Hooks, *Feminist Theory: From the Margin to the Center* (Boston: South End Press, 1984).

24. Molyneux, "Mobilization without Emancipation," 232.

25. For example, Boris and Bardaglio argue in "The Transformation of Patriarchy" that the growth of the liberal state has led to increased rights for middle class women and increased dependence for working class women. Many writers have discussed how the emergence of the liberal state expanded male rights while constricting female rights among the middle class.

See, for example, Drude Dahlerup, "Overcoming the Barriers: An Approach to How Women's Issues are Kept from the Political Agenda," in *Women's Views of the Political World of Men*, ed., Judith Hicks Stiehm (Dobbs Ferry, N.Y.: Transnational Publishers, 1984). Michele Barrett discusses a number of studies that argue that the expansion of the British state in the twentieth century has promoted the extension of patriarchal family relations to the working class in *Women's Oppression Today: Problems in Marxist Feminist Analysis* (London: Verso, 1980).

26. The arguments vary depending on whether the state is seen as an important actor in the reproduction of class and gender relations or is reduced to "the administration of a power structure whose roots lie elsewhere." Barrett, ibid., 245. Some see the state as enhancing both capitalist control and male dominance. Some see the state and male dominance as mechanisms of capitalist control: Mary McIntosh, "The State and the Oppression of Women," in *Feminism and Materialism: Women and Modes of Production*, eds. Annette Kuhn and Ann Marie Wolpe (London: Routledge and Kegan Paul, 1978), 254–89. And some see the state and capitalism as mechanisms of male domination. The first view is less reductionist than the latter two, but in focusing solely on social control, they are all inadequate to convey the complex interactions among a variety of political actors and structural forces.

27. *Barrett, Women's Oppression Today*, 246.

28. Barbara Wolfe Jancar, *Women Under Communism* (Baltimore and London: Johns Hopkins University Press, 1978), 113–14.

29. Catharine A. MacKinnon, "Feminism, Marxism, Method, and the State; An Agenda for Theory," *Signs: Journal of Women in Culture and Society* 7, no. 3 (Spring 1982): 522–23. See also Judith Stacey, *Patriarchy and Socialist Revolution in China* (Berkeley, Calif.: University of California Press, 1983); Gail Lapidus, *Women in Soviet Society* (Berkeley, Calif.: University of California Press, 1978); Elisabeth J. Croll, "Women in Rural Production and Reproduction in the Soviet Union, China, Cuba and Tanzania: Socialist Development Experiences," *Signs: Journal of Women in Culture and Society* 7, no. 2 (Winter 1981): 361–74; Hilda Scott, *Does Socialism Liberate Women?* (Boston: Beacon Press, 1974); Sharon L. Wolchik and Alfred G. Meyer, eds., *Women, State, and Party in Eastern Europe* (Durham, N.C.: Duke University Press, 1985), especially Section IV; and Jancar, *Women Under Communism*.

30. Kathleen Staudt, "Women, Development and the State: On the Theoretical Impasse," *Development and Change* 17 (1986): 328.

31. Fatima Mernissi, "The Moslem World: Women Excluded from Development," in *Women and World Development*, ed. Irene Tinker and

Michèle Bo Bramsen (Washington, D.C.: Overseas Development Council, 1976), 36.

32. Fatima Mernissi, "Morocco: The Merchant's Daughter and the Son of the Sultan," in *Sisterhood is Global*, ed. Robin Morgan (Garden City, N.Y.: Anchor Books, 1984), 448.

33. Kathleen Staudt, in *Women, Foreign Assistance and Advocacy Administration* (New York: Praeger, 1985), emphasizes the threat which gender redistribution poses to decision makers. Judith Stiehm has argued that we must focus as much on men (as women) in men's institutions to understand gender conflict. See her *Bring Me Men and Women: Mandated Change at the Air Force Academy* (Berkeley, Calif.: University of California Press, 1981).

34. In *Bureaucrats and Politicians in Western Democracies*, Joel D. Aberbach, Robert D. Putnam and Bert P. Rochman (Cambridge, Mass.: Harvard University Press, 1981) find that women constitute less than one percent of senior civil servants sampled in the six countries analyzed. "Being male," they say, "is little short of a necessary condition for obtaining power" (p. 47). Elise Boulding estimates that women represent six percent of policymakers worldwide; *Handbook of International Data on Women* (Beverly Hills, Calif.: Sage Publications, 1978), 36. See also Ruth Leger Sivard, *Women . . . A World Survey* (Washington, D.C.: World Priorities, 1985), 33–34.

35. For example, Marianne Githens and Jewel L. Prestage, eds., *A Portrait of Marginality: The Political Behavior of the American Woman* (New York: David McKay, 1977); Sandra Baxter and Marjorie Lansing, *Women and Politics: The Visible Majority*, Rev. ed. (Ann Arbor, Mich.: University of Michigan Press, 1983); Janet K. Boles, *The Politics of the Equal Rights Amendment* (New York: Longman, 1979); Kathleen Newland, *The Sisterhood of Man* (New York: W. W. Norton, 1979); Ruth B. Mandel, *In the Running: The New Woman Candidate* (New Haven, Conn.: Ticknor and Fields, 1981); Irene Diamond, *Sex Roles in the State House* (New Haven, Conn.: Yale University Press, 1977); Susan J. Carroll, *Women as Candidates in American Politics* (Bloomington, Ind.: Indiana University Press, 1985); Virginia Sapiro, *The Political Integration of Women: Roles, Socialization, and Politics* (Urbana, Ill.: University of Illinois Press, 1983); Susan J. Pharr, *Political Women in Japan* (Berkeley, Calif.: University of California Press, 1981). On achievements, see Irene Tinker, ed., *Women in Washington: Advocates for Public Policy* (Beverly Hills, Calif.: Sage Publications, 1983).

36. There are now a number of studies of women in public office primarily in the United States. However, so far this issue has not been addressed. See, for example, Janet A. Falmmang, ed., *Political Women: Current Roles in State and Local Government* (Beverly Hills, Calif.: Sage Publica-

tions, 1984); James David Barker and Barbara Kellerman, eds., *Women Leaders in American Politics* (Englewood Cliffs, N.J.: Prentice-Hall, 1986); Sylvia Baskevkin, ed., *Women and Politics in Western Europe* (London: Frank Cass, 1985).

37. Ann Shola Orloff and Theda Skocpol, "Why Not Equal Protection: Explaining the Politics of Public Social Spending in Britain, 1900–1911, and the United States, 1880s–1920," *American Sociological Review* 49, no. 6 (December 1984): 730–31. For the same distinction, differently stated, see Evans, Rueschemeyer, and Skocpol, *Bringing the State Back In*, 27–28.

38. Evans, Rueschemeyer, and Skocpol, *Bringing the State Back In*, 21.

39. Samuel Bowles and Herbert Gintis emphasize the private-public distinction as a central tenet of liberal theory, in *Democracy and Capitalism: Property, Community, and the Contradictions of Modern Social Thought* (New York: Basic Books, 1987), 17ff.

CHAPTER 2

1. See the distinction between strategic and practical gender interests made by Maxine Molyneux, "Mobilization without Emancipation? Women's Interests, The State, and Revolution in Nicaragua," *Feminist Studies* 11, no. 2 (Summer 1985): 227–54.

2. I am grateful to Rose Matthews for her discussions with me on this point. For analyses of the use of the terms *private* and *public* in the discipline of anthropology, see the influential collection edited by Michelle Zimbalist Rosaldo and Louise Lamphere, *Women, Culture, and Society* (Stanford, Calif.: Stanford University Press, 1974).

3. Jean Bethke Elshtain, *Public Man, Private Women: Women in Social and Political Thought* (Princeton, N.J.: Princeton University Press, 1981), chap. 1 on Plato and Aristotle.

4. V. G. Kiernan, "State and Nation in Western Europe," *Past and Present* 31 (July 1965): 23–24; and Charles Tilly, "War Making and State Making as Organized Crime," in Peter B. Evans, Dietrich Rueschemeyer, and Theda Skocpol, eds., *Bringing the State Back In* (Cambridge, England: Cambridge University Press, 1985), 171–75.

5. Elshtain, *Public Man, Private Woman*, 101.

6. For a discussion of the actual process of state-building as it relied on military force, cf. Samuel E. Finer, "State- and Nation-Building in Europe: The Role of the Military," in Charles Tilly, ed., *The Formation of National*

States in Western Europe (Princeton, N.J.: Princeton University Press, 1973), 84–163. Herbert S. Lewis has a more generalized theoretical statement in "Warfare and the Origin of the State: Another Formulation," in Henri J.M. Claessen and Peter Skalnik, *The Study of the State* (The Hague: Mouton, 1981), 201–21. Lewis comments: "Armed military action is the mechanism or the instrument of state formation itself" (215).

7. Alexander Passerin d'Entrèves, *The Notion of the State: An Introduction to Political Theory* (Oxford: Oxford University Press, 1967), 37. Hanna Fenichel Pitkin analyzes Machiavelli's political thought in terms of his seemingly contradictory attitudes toward women as weak and contemptible, and yet powerful. *Fortune is a Woman: Gender and Politics in the Thought of Niccolò Machiavelli* (Berkeley, Calif.: University of California Press, 1984), particularly chap. 5 and 6.

8. For example, Carl Schmitt. Gianfranco Poggi, *The Development of the Modern State: A Sociological Introduction* (Stanford, Calif.: Stanford University Press, 1978), chap. 1; and Joseph W. Bendersky, *Carl Schmitt: Theorist for the Reich* (Princeton, N. J.: Princeton University Press, 1983), chap. 11.

9. In this regard, Thomas Hobbes followed Bodin's lead in seeing the state as a legal system. d'Entrève, *The Notion of the State*, Chap. 6 and 8.

10. Jean Bethke Elshtain, "Moral Woman and Immoral Man: A Consideration of the Public-Private Split and its Political Ramifications," *Politics and Society* 4, no. 4 (1974): 460–61.

11. Poggi, *The Development of the Modern State*, 75–76. The process was part of what Charles Tilly has labeled "stateness." "Reflections on the History of European State-Making," in Tilly, ed., *The Formation of National States in Western Europe*, 34–35. The terms specialization (of state structures) and bureaucratization also address the phenomenon.

12. Bertrand Badie and Pierre Birnbaum, *The Sociology of the State*, trans. Arthur Goldhammer (Chicago: University of Chicago Press, 1983), 90–91, 105–11, 121–25.

13. Poggi, *The Development of the Modern State*, 95.

14. Zillah Eisenstein, *The Radical Future of Liberal Feminism* (London: Longman, 1981), 223.

15. Max Weber, *Economy and Society: An Outline of Interpretive Sociology*, ed. Guenther Roth and Claus Wittich (New York: Bedminster Press, 1968), vol. 3, Chap. 12.

16. Max Weber, *General Economic History*, trans. Frank H. Knight (New York: Greenberg, 1927), Chap. 29.

17. Elshtain, *Public Man, Private Woman*, 122. Elshtain adds, "of course they cannot, and this is the crux of one of Marx's critiques of liberalism."

18. Kiernan observes: "Much of the mass feeling that slowly gathered round the nation-state consisted of class resentment artificially diverted into xenophobia." "State and Nation in Western Europe," 35.

19. d'Entrèves, *The Notion of the State*, 173.

20. Mostafa Rejai and Cynthis H. Enloe, "Nation-States and State-Nations," *International Studies Quarterly*, 13, no. 2 (June 1969): 142; John Breuilly, *Nationalism and the State* (New York: St. Martin's Press, 1982), part II.

21. This appreciation of ideology was one of Antonio Gramsci's most important contributions to twentieth century state theory: the bourgeoisie is ideologically an all-encompassing class and the state reflects and reinforces the hegemony of the dominant class. The state is "hegemony fortified by coercion." Martin Carnoy, *The State and Political Theory*, (Princeton, N.J.: Princeton University Press, 1984), 65–77; and Anne Showstack Sassoon, *Gramsci's Politics* (New York: St. Martin's Press, 1980), 109–19.

22. Carlson J.H. Hayes, *The Historical Evolution of Modern Nationalism* (New York: Richard R. Smith, Inc., 1931).

23. Staudt, "Women's Politics and Capitalist Transformation in Subsaharan Africa," *Working Papers—Women in International Development*, no. 54 (East Lansing, Mich.: Michigan State University, April 1984), 16.

24. Ibid., 15.

25. For an empirical analysis of the Catholic-state policy relationship in matters of birth control, see Marilyn Jane Field, *The Comparative Politics of Birth Control: Determinants of Policy Variation and Change in the Developed Nations* (New York: Praeger, 1983), chap. 5.

26. Strictly speaking, from an Islamic point of view, political theory is religious and the distinction between religion and a secular state is abnormal. Helmer Ringgren, "On the Islamic Theory of the State," in Haralds Biezais, ed., *The Myth of the State* (Stockholm: Almqvist & Wiksell, 1972), 103–108.

27. Michelle Maskiell, "The Impact of Islamization Policies on Pakistani Women's Lives," *Working Papers—Women in International Development* no. 69 (East Lansing, Mich.: Michigan State University, November 1984); Anita M. Weiss, "Women's Position in Pakistan: Sociocultural Effects of Islamization," *Asian Survey*, 25, no. 8 (August 1985): 863–80; Azar Tabari, "The Enigma of the Veiled Iranian Woman," *Merip Reports*, 12 (February

1982): 22–27; Homa Nategh, "Women: the Damned of the Iranian Revolution," in Rosemary Ridd and Helen Callaway, eds., *Women and Political Conflict: Portraits of Struggle in Times of Crisis* (New York: New York University Press, 1987), 45–60.

28. For a summary of the place of bureaucracies in state building, see Joseph LaPalombara, ed., *Bureaucracy and Political Development* (Princeton, N.J.: Princeton University Press, 1967).

29. For example, Richard Kraus and Reeve D. Vanneman, "Bureaucrats versus the State in Capitalist and Socialist Regimes," *Comparative Studies in Society and History* 27, no. 1 (January 1985): 111–22.

30. Metin Heper, "The State and Public Bureaucracies: A Comparative and Historical Perspective," *Comparative Studies in Society and History* 27, no. 1 (January 1985): 93–97.

31. I accept that the state reflects the interests of dominant classes or groups in society and that the ideology that legitimizes the state in turn incorporates this relationship of dominance. But the dominant group(s) may as well be composed of religious patriarchs as capitalist industrialists or financiers.

32. Irving Louis Horowitz argues that the bureaucratic state apparatus may, in fact, be considered autonomous when its members do not come from the dominant landed, commercial, or industrial classes, nor are they controlled by a legislative or party apparatus that itself represents dominant interests. The bureaucracy can afford to respond to particularized interests as long as these interests do not threaten its legitimacy or authority. *Beyond Empire and Revolution: Militarization and Consolidation in the Third World* (Oxford and New York: Oxford University Press, 1982), 134–35.

33. Ibid., 221.

34. Theda Skocpol comments: "State executives and their followers will be found maneuvering to extract resources and build administrative and coercive organizations precisely at this intersection." *States and Social Revolutions: A Comparative Analysis of France, Russia, and China* (Cambridge: Cambridge University Press, 1979), 32.

35. Michel Crozier, The *Bureaucratic Phenomenon* (Chicago: University of Chicago Press, 1964).

36. Gabriel A. Almond and G. Bingham Powell, Jr., *Comparative Politics: System, Process, and Policy*, 2nd ed. (Boston: Little, Brown, 1978), 139.

37. Max Weber, *Economy and Society: An Outline of Interpretive Sociology*, ed. Guenther Roth and Claus Wittick, vol. 3 (New York: Bedminster Press, 1968), 975.

38. Kathy E. Ferguson, *The Feminist Case Against Bureaucracy* (Philadelphia, Penn.: Temple University Press, 1984), pp. 30ff.

39. Ibid., 37. In discussing "disciplinary technique," Ferguson draws on Michel Foucault to merge the two meanings of discipline: self-control and training that develops self-control, and a branch of knowledge. Pages 32–33.

40. Ibid., 46–59.

41. I am using here the distinction between militarism and militarization noted by Betty Reardon. Militarism is "the *belief system* that upholds the legitimacy of military control of the state;" it is "based on the assumption that military values and policies are conducive to a secure and orderly society." Militarization is the "*process* of emphasizing military values, policies and preparedness." Reardon, *Sexism and the War System* (New York: Teachers College Press, Columbia University, 1985), 14. (Emphasis added.)

42. Nancy C. M. Hartsock, "Masculinity, Citizenship, and the Making of War," *PS* 17, no. 2 (Spring 1984): 199–200.

43. One comparative analysis of civilian and military regimes, for instance, determined that in approximately sixty percent of Third World states, the chief executive position in 1980 was filled by a member of the armed forces or the armed forces presented a potential for intervention against a weak civilian regime. Gary K. Bertsch, Robert P. Clark and David M. Wood, *Comparing Political Systems: Power and Policy in Three Worlds*, 2nd ed. (New York: John Wiley and Sons, 1982), 452–60.

44. Virginia Woolf, *Three Guineas* (New York: Harcourt Brace Jovanovich, 1938). Also Marcia Yudkin, "Reflections on Woolf's *Three Guineas*," in Judith Stiehm, ed., *Women and Men's Wars* (Oxford and New York: Pergamon Press, 1983), 263–69; and Cynthia H. Enloe's analysis in *Does Khaki Become You? The Militarisation of Women's Lives* (Boston: South End Press, 1983).

45. Reardon, *Sexism and the War System*, 15. (Emphasis in original.)

46. Michael Rustad, *Women in Khaki: The American Enlisted Woman* (New York: Praeger, 1982), 13.

47. Naomi Nhiwatiwa, "Women in the National Liberation Struggle in Zimbabwe," in *Women and Men's Wars*, ed. Stiehm, 248. See also the portrayals in Stephanie Urdang, *Fighting Two Colonialisms: Women in Guinea-Bissau* (New York: Monthly Review Press, 1979), and in Buchi Emecheta's novel, *Destination Biafra* (Isle of Man, U.K.: Fontana Books, 1982).

48. The term "welfare state" is used here in its general sense of fairly

explicit commitment in both ideology and policy to goals of economic development, social security, and minimum standards in health, education, housing, and food for all social groups and regions in the nation-state.

49. I am drawing on the distinctions made by a number of feminist writers, for example, Alison M. Jaggar, *Feminist Politics and Human Nature* (Tototwa, N.J.: Rowman and Allanheld, 1983). Socialist feminists use some Marxist analytical categories, notably that of class, for their understanding of the welfare state, but reject the comprehensive utility of Marxism for explaining gender inequality and sexual exploitation. A refined typology would distinguish between Marxist and socialist feminists as Jaggar, for example, has done.

50. Ferguson, *The Feminist Case Against Bureaucracy*, 28.

51. Catharine A. MacKinnon, "Feminism, Marxism, Method, and the State: Toward Feminist Jurisprudence," *Signs: Journal of Women in Culture and Society* 8, no. 4 (Summer 1983); and Jalna Hanmer, "Violence and the Social Control of Women," in Gary Littlejohn, Barry Smart, John Wakefield, and Nira Yuval-Davis, eds., *Power and the State* (New York: St. Martin's Press, 1978), 217–38.

52. Hanmer, "Violence and the Social Control of Women," 225, 227.

53. Diana Leonard Barker,"The Regulation of Marriage: Repressive Benevolence," in Littlejohn et al., *Power and the State,* 239. Barker analyzes the evolution of law and state policy in Britain regarding marriage from the seventeenth to the twentieth centuries, a period parallelling the consolidation of the modern state.

54. Jane Flax, "The Family in Contemporary Feminist Thought: A Critical Review," in Jean Bethke Elshtain, ed., *The Family in Political Thought* (Amherst, Mass.: University of Massachusetts Press, 1982), 232–39. Flax analyzes Marxist feminism without discussing the important modifications and qualifications in the Marxist tradition contributed by socialist feminism in the past twenty years. For the classic analysis, see Frederick Engels, *The Origin of the Family, Private Property and the State*, first published in German in 1884.

55. Jennifer G. Schirmer, *The Limits of Reform: Women, Capital, and Welfare* (Cambridge, Mass.: Schenkman Publishing Company, Inc., 1982), chap. 1 and 2. Schirmer takes corporatism to mean that the state becomes the center of economic planning and coordination, and the extraction and distribution of resources, largely in response to the competitiveness of the international economic system (26–33). In his comparative study of eighteen developed capitalist nation-states, David Cameron found the "openness" of the domestic economy to international forces (particularly trade) to be the best predictor of the extent of the expansion of the public economy—thus

recalling the importance of conceptualizing the state at the juncture of domestic and international pressures. "The Expansion of the Public Economy: A Comparative Analysis," *American Political Science Review* 72, no. 4 (December 1978): 1243–61.

56. Schrimer, *The Limits of Reform*, 33–35. (Emphasis in original.) Also p. 40, note 23.

57. Ibid., 168. (Emphasis in original.)

58. Elizabeth Wilson, *Women and the Welfare State* (London: Tavistock Publications, 1977), 9. See also Hilary Land and Roy Parker, "Family Policy in the United Kingdom—The Hidden Dimensions," *Nouvelles Questions Féministes*, no 6–7 (Spring 1984): 107–54.

59. Eisenstein, *The Radical Future of Liberal Feminism*, and "The Patriarchal Relations of the Reagan State," *Signs: Journal of Women in Culture and Society* 10, no. 2 (Winter 1984): 329–37.

60. Delphy, "Les femmes et l'Etat," *Nouvelles Questions Féministes* no. 6–7 (Spring 1984): 16.

61. See Neil Gilbert, *Capitalism and the Welfare State: Dilemmas of Social Benevolence* (New Haven, Conn.: Yale University Press, 1983), chap. 5.

62. Elshtain, *Public Man, Private Woman*, 127.

63. Ibid., 142–43. Elshtain admits the controversial nature of her assertion when she says: "Men fear the sexual and reproductive power of women. This is reflected in the lengths to which they have gone to protect themselves by projecting that fear outward into social forms, by imbedding the need to defend themselves against women in institutions and activities, including those called 'political,' historically inseparable from war-making." Ibid. In this same vein, see Elshtain's analysis of Rousseau (ibid., particularly p. 159) and also that of Eisenstein, *The Radical Future of Liberal Feminism*, chap. 4, notably pp. 60–64. Carol McMillan critiques feminist theory and its assumptions of rationality by stressing the central reality of biological (sex) differences and nature. *Women, Reason and Nature: Some Philosophical Problems with Feminism* (Princeton, N.J.: Princeton University Press, 1982). For McMillan's use of Rousseau, cf. chap. 5.

64. Elshtain, *Public Man, Private Woman*, 243. Elshtain identifies herself as being most symphathetic to psychoanalytic feminism (p. 285). Her feminist answer to the private-public dichotomy lies in reconstructing the private realm by recognizing its distinctive moral quality (pp. 335–36), and in reconstructing the public world through enhanced citizen participation (pp. 347–53).

65. Jennifer Dale and Peggy Foster, for example, contrast liberal,

socialist, and radical critiques of the welfare state, and conclude that feminists can and should make incremental improvements in state policy; *Feminists and State Welfare* (London: Routledge & Kegan Paul, 1986).

CHAPTER 3

1. See Sharon L. Wolchik, "Ideology and Equality: The Status of Women in Eastern and Western Europe," *Comparative Political Studies* 13, no. 4 (January 1981): 445–76, for a brief areawide review of women's status on several indicators of equality; Barbara W. Jancar, *Women under Communism* (Baltimore, Md.: Johns Hopkins University Press, 1978), also includes the East European countries.

2. See Sharon L. Wolchik, "The Precommunist Legacy, Economic Development, Social Transformation, and Women's Roles in Eastern Europe," in Sharon L. Wolchik and Alfred G. Meyer, eds., *Women, State, and Party in Eastern Europe* (Durham, N.C.: Duke University Press, 1985) chap. 2, for a more detailed discussion of these factors, and footnote 1 for references to additional sources on precommunist conditions in the region.

3. Richard Stites, *The Women's Liberation Movement in Russia: Feminism, Nihilism, and Bolshevism, 1860–1930* (Princeton, N.J.: Princeton University Press, 1977); Barbara Alpern Engel, *Mothers and Daughters: Women of the Intelligentsia in Nineteenth-Century Russia* (Cambridge and New York: Cambridge University Press, 1983), Richard Stites, "Women and the Russian Intellegentsia: Three Perspectives," in Dorothy Atkinson, Alexander Dallin, and Gail W. Lapidus, eds., *Women in Russia* (Stanford, Calif.: Stanford University Press, 1977), 39–62; and Dorothy Atkinson, "Society and the Sexes in the Russian Past," ibid., 3–38.

4. See Wolchik, "The Precommunist Legacy," 32–35; Karen Johnson Freeze, "Medical Education for Women in Austria: A Study in the Politics of the Czech Women's Movement in the 1890s," chap. 3; Martha Bohachevsky-Chomiak, "Ukrainian Feminism in Interwar Poland," chap. 5; Bruce M. Garver, "Women in the First Czechoslovak Republic," chap. 4, all in Wolchik and Meyer, *Women, State, and Party.*

5. Mary E. Reed, "Peasant Women of Croatia in the Interwar Years," in Wolchik and Meyer, *Women, State, and Party,* chap. 6; Mary E. Reed, "The Anti-Fascist Front of Women and the Communist Party in Croatia," in Tova Yedlin, ed., *Women in Eastern Europe and the Soviet Union* (New York: Praeger, 1980), 128–40; and Susan L. Woodward, "The Rights of Women: Ideology, Policy, and Social Change in Yugoslavia," in Wolchik and Meyer, *Women, State, and Party,* chap. 14.

6. John Kolsti, "From Courtyard to Cabinet: The Political Emer-

gence of Albanian Women," in Wolchik and Meyer, *Women, State, and Party,* chap. 8.

7. Leila J. Rupp, "I Don't Call that *Volksgemeinschaft*: Women, Class, and War in Nazi Germany," in Carol R. Berkin and Clara M. Lovett, eds., *Women, War and Revolution* (New York: Holmes and Meier, 1980), 37–54 and Gisela Bock "Racism and Sexism in Nazi Germany: Motherhood, Compulsory Sterilization, and the State," in *Signs: Journal of Women in Culture and Society* 8, no. 3 (Spring 1983): 400–21.

8. See, for example, Alfred G. Meyer, "Marxism and the Women's Movement," in Atkinson, Dallin and Lapidus, *Women in Russia,* 85–112 and "Feminism, Socialism, and Nationalism in Eastern Europe," in Wolchik and Meyer, *Women, State, and Party,* chap. 1.

9. Meyer, "Marxism and the Women's Movement," and "Feminism Socialism and Nationalism," especially 26–31; Batya Weinbaum, *The Curious Courtship of Women's Liberation and Socialism* (Boston: South End Press, 1978).

10. See Wolchik, "Ideology and Equality" for an overview.

11. Gail Lapidus, "Sexual Equality in Soviet Policy: A Developmental Perspective," in Atkinson, Dallin, and Lapidus, *Women in Russia,* 115–38.

12. See H. Gordon Skilling, *The Governments of Communist East Europe* (New York: Thomas Y. Crowell, 1966), especially 48–68; and Zbigniew Brzezinski, *The Soviet Bloc, Unity and Conflict* (Cambridge, Mass: Harvard University Press, 1967), especially 67–154, for more information concerning the East European adaptation of the Soviet model. Both authors note that diversity once again increased in the region after the death of Stalin, but the political systems remain organized according to common principles.

13. Frederick B. Singleton, *Twentieth-century Yugoslavia* (New York: Columbia University Press, 1976); Dennison Rusinow, *The Yugoslav Experiment 1948–1974* (Berkeley, Calif: University of California Press, 1977, published for the Royal Institute of International Affairs, London) and Steven L. Burg, *Conflict and Cohesion in Socialist Yugoslavia* (Princeton, N. J.: Princeton University Press, 1983).

14. See Andrew Janos, "The One-Party State and Social Mobilization: East Europe between the Wars," in Samuel P. Huntington and Clement H. Moore, eds., *Authoritarian Politics in Modern Society: The Dynamics of Established One-Party Systems* (New York: Basic Books, 1970), 212–34; Carlile A. Macartney and Alan W. Palmer, *Independent Eastern Europe* (New York: St. Martin's Press, 1962); Joseph Rothchild, *East Central Europe Be-*

tween the Two World Wars (Seattle, Wash.: University of Washington Press, 1974); and Hugh Seton-Watson, *Eastern Europe between the Wars, 1918–1941* (New York: Harper and Row, 1967) for discussions of the states during the interwar period.

15. See the sources in notes 4 and 5 for further information.

16. See Victor S. Mamatey and Radomír Luža, eds., *A History of the Czechoslovak Republic, 1918–1948* (Princeton, N.J.: Princeton University Press, 1973); David W. Paul, *The Cultural Limits of Revolutionary Politics: Change and Continuity in Socialist Czechoslovakia* (Boulder, Colo.: East European Quarterly, 1979) chap. 2, and Hans Brisch and Ivan Volgyes, eds., *Czechoslovakia: The Heritage of Ages Past: Essays in Memory of Josef Korbel* (Boulder, Colo.: East European Quarterly, 1979), for further information.

17. Stites, *The Women's Liberation Movement*, 322–45; Lapidus, "Sexual Equality in Soviet Policy," 117–24; Gail Lapidus, *Women in Soviet Society* (Berkeley, Calif.: University of California Press, 1978) chap. 3.

18. See Stites, *The Women's Liberation Movement*, Chaps. 10 and 11; Robert McNeal, *Bride of the Revolution: Krupskaya and Lenin* (Ann Arbor, Mich.: University of Michigan Press, 1972); Barbara Clements, "Bolshevik Women: the First Generation," in Yedlin, *Women in Eastern Europe and the Soviet Union*, 65–74 and Barbara Alpern Engel, "Women Revolutionaries: The Personal and the Political," in ibid., 31–43 for analyses of the roles of early Bolshevik women. See Reed, "The Anti-Fascist Front," and Barbara W. Jancar, "Women in the Yugoslav National Liberation Movement: An Overview," *Studies in Comparative Communism* 14, nos. 2 & 3 (Summer-Fall 1981): 143–46; for analyses of women's role in the Partisan struggle.

19. See Gail Warshofsky Lapidus, "Political Mobilization, Participation, and Leadership: Women in Soviet Politics," *Comparative Politics* 8, no. 1 (October 1975): 90–118; Lapidus, *Women in Soviet Society*, chap. 6; Jancar, *Women Under Communism*, chap. 5; Wolchik, "Ideology and Equality;" Sharon L. Wolchik, "Eastern Europe," in Joni Lovenduski and Jill Hills, eds., *The Politics of the Second Electorate: Women and Public Participation* (London: Routledge and Kegan Paul, 1981), 252–77; Jerry F. Hough, "Women and Women's Issues in Soviet Policy Debates," in Atkinson, Dallin and Lapidus, *Women in Russia*, 333–54; Mary Ellen Fischer, "Women in Romanian Politics: Elena Ceauşescu, Pronatalism, and the Promotion of Women," chap. 7; Daniel N. Nelson, "Women in Local Communist Politics in Romania and Poland," chap. 9; and Barbara W. Jancar, "Women in the Opposition in Poland and Czechoslovakia in the 1970's," chap. 10, all in Wolchik and Meyer, *Women, State, and Party*; Joel C. Moses, "Indoctrination as a Female Political Role in the Soviet Union," *Comparative Politics* 8, no. 4 (July 1976): 525–47; and Ellen Mickiewicz, "Regional Variation in Female

Recruitment and Advancement in the Communist Party of the Soviet Union," *Slavic Review* 36, no. 3 (September 1977): 441–54 for analyses of women's political roles.

20. See Meyer, "Marxism and the Women's Movement" and "Feminism, Socialism, and Nationalism;" Jean H. Quataert, *Reluctant Feminists in German Soviet Democracy 1885–1917* (Princeton, N.J.: Princeton University Press, 1979); and Alfred G. Meyer, *The Feminism and Socialism of Lily Braun* (Bloomington, Ind.: Indiana University Press, 1985) for analyses of the treatment of feminists in the early Marxist movement.

21. See Hilda Scott, *Does Socialism Liberate Women? Experiences from Eastern Europe* (Boston: Beacon Press, 1973); Alena Heitlinger, *Women and State Socialism: Sex Inequality in the Soviet Union and Czechoslovakia* (Montreal, Que.: McGill-Queens University Press, 1979); and Sharon L. Wolchik, "The Status of Women in a Socialist Order: Czechoslovakia, 1948–1978," *Slavic Review* 38, no. 4 (December 1979): 583–602, for discussion of the impact of this factor on women in socialist states.

22. See Jancar, *Women Under Communism;* Heitlinger, *Women and State Socialism*, chap. 7; Scott, *Does Socialism Liberate Women?* 116–17; Sharon L. Wolchik, "Elite Strategy Toward Women in Czechoslovakia: Liberation or Mobilization?" *Studies in Comparative Communism* 14, nos. 2 & 3 (Summer-Fall 1981): 123–42; and Sharon L. Wolchik, "Demography, Political Reform and Women's Issues in Czechoslovakia," in Margherita Rendel, ed., *Women, Power and Political Systems* (New York: St. Martin's Press, 1981), chap. 7 for accounts of the activities of women's organizations in Eastern Europe. See Genia Browning, "Soviet Politics—Where are the Women?" in Barbara Holland, ed., *Soviet Sisterhood* (Bloomington, Ind.: Indiana University Press, 1985), chap. 7 for an account of the recent activities of the Soviet women's councils.

23. See Dorothy Rosenberg, "The Emancipation of Women in Fact and Fiction: Changing Roles in GDR Society and Literature," in Wolchik and Meyer, *Women, State, and Party*, chap. 20 for an analysis of these tendencies.

24. Barbara W. Jancar, "The New Feminism in Yugoslavia," in Pedro Ramet, ed., *Yugoslavia in the 1980's* (Boulder, Colo.: Westview Press, 1985), 201–23.

25. See Alix Holt, "The First Soviet Feminists," in Holland, chap. 8 for a discussion of the Soviet feminists. See Tatyana Mamanova, ed., *Women and Russia: Feminist Writings from the Soviet Union*, trans. Rebecca Park and Catherine A. Fitzpatrick (Boston: Beacon Press, 1984) for an example of Soviet feminist writings.

26. See Brzezinski, *The Soviet Bloc*, 97–104, and Alex Nove, *The*

Soviet Economy (New York: Frederick A. Praeger, 1966) for brief discussions of the main elements of the strategy for economic development adopted at this time.

27. See Lapidus, *Women in Soviet Society;* Scott, *Does Socialism Liberate Women?* 72–99; Wolchik, "Elite Strategy toward Women;" Jancar, *Women under Communism;* Renata Siemieńska, "Women, Work, and Gender Equality in Poland: Reality and Its Social Perception," chap. 18; Rózsa Kulcsár, "The Socioeconomic Conditions of Women in Hungary," chap. 11; Silva Mežnarić, "Theory and Reality: The Status of Employed Women in Yugoslavia," chap. 12; Ivan Volgyes, "Blue-Collar Working Women and Poverty in Hungary," chap. 13, all in Wolchik and Meyer, *Women, State, and Party,* for discussions of this approach to women's issues in Eastern Europe.

28. Woodward, "The Rights of Women," 250–56 and Gail Kligman, "The Rites of Women: Oral Poetry, Ideology, and the Socialization of Peasant Women in Contemporary Romania," in Wolchik and Meyer, *Women State, and Party,* chap. 19, 325.

29. See David Lane, *The End of Inequality? Stratification under State Socialism* (Harmondsworth, England: Penguin Books, 1971): and *The Socialist Industrial State: Towards a Political Sociology of State Socialism* (Boulder, Colo.: Westview Press, 1976); Walter D. Connor, *Socialism, Politics, and Equality: Hierarchy and Change in Eastern Europe and the USSR* (New York: Columbia University Press, 1979); and Archie Brown and Jack Gray, eds., *Political Culture and Political Change in Communist States* (New York: Holmes & Meier, 1979) for evidence of the persistence of precommunist values and attitudes in a number of areas.

30. Kenneth Jowitt, "An Organizational Approach to the Study of Political Culture in Marxist-Leninist Systems," *American Political Science Review* 68, no. 3 (September 1974): 1171–91.

31. Stites, *The Women's Liberation Movement,* chap. 11; Lapidus, *Women in Soviet Society,* chap. 2; and Beatrice Brodsky Farnsworth, "Bolshevik Alternatives and the Soviet Family: The 1926 Marriage Law Debate," in Atkinson, Dallin, and Lapidus, *Women in Russia,* 139–66.

32. Gregory J. Massell, *The Surrogate Proletariat: Moslem Women and Revolutionary Strategies in Soviet Central Asia* (Princeton, N.J.: Princeton University Press, 1974).

33. Stites, *The Women's Liberation Movement,* 408–409.

34. See Stites, *The Women's Liberation Movement,* 376–91; Lapidus, *Women in Soviet Society;* and Farnsworth, "Bolshevik Alternatives," for discussions of measures adopted during this period.

35. See Wolchik, "Politics, Ideology, and Equality,: Changes in the

Status of Women in Eastern Europe," (Ph.D. dissertation, the University of Michigan, 1978) chap. 6 for an analysis of these appeals in Czechoslovakia.

36. Wolchik, "Politics, Ideology, and Equality," chap 6. See also Bernice Madison, "Social Services for Women: Problems and Priorities," in Atkinson, Dallen, and Lapidus, *Women in Russia*, 307–32; Bogdan Mieczkowski, "Social Services for Women and Childcare Facilities in Eastern Europe," in Wolchik and Meyer, *Women, State, and Party*, chap. 15; Jancar, *Women Under Communism*; Jo Peers, "Workers by Hand and Womb: Soviet Women and the Demographic Crises," in Holland, *Soviet Sisterhood*, chap. 4; and Heitlinger, *Women and State Socialism*, chaps. 11 and 16.

37. Lapidus, *Women in Soviet Society*, 322–34.

38. See Eva Bartová, "Postoje k problemu zeny a rodiny," *Sociologicky casopis* 8, no. 1 (1972) for a summary of popular attitudes toward women's equality in several East European countries. See Siemieńska, "Women, Work and Gender Equality," 309–20, for a recent study of attitudes toward women's roles in Poland.

39. See Lapidus, *Women in Soviet Society*; Jancar, *Women Under Communism*; Kulcsár "Socioeconomic Conditions;" Siemieńska "Women, Work and Gender Equality;" Heitlinger, *Women and State Socialism*, chaps. 9 and 14; Wolchik, "Ideology and Equality" for information and references to studies concerning the distribution of domestic labor in these societies. As Woodward notes in a discussion of gender roles in the family, state policies in certain cases have strengthened rather than diminished the sexual division of domestic labor. While modernization has led to a decrease in family size and changed the form of the family in certain areas of Yugoslavia, for instance, it has had a differential impact on the domestic activities of men and women, for the state has made many of the previous family duties of males irrelevant but has not reduced the importance of the labor women perform within the home. The feminization of agriculture and the tendency for commuting villagers to be male have futher stregthened the identification of women and household work. Woodward, "The Rights of Women," 246–51.

40. See Chalmers Johnson, "Comparing Communist Nations," in Johnson, ed., *Change in Communist Systems* (Stanford: Stanford University Press, 1970), 1–32, and Richard Lowenthal, "Development vs. Utopia in Communist Policy," *Change in Communist Systems*, 33–116, for discussions of some of these unanticipated consequences.

41. See Henry P. David and Robert J. McIntyre, *Reproductive Behavior: Central and Eastern European Experience* (New York: Springer Pub.

Co., 1981); Alena Heitlinger, "Pro-natalist Population Policies in Czechoslovakia," *Population Studies* 30, no. 1 (March 1976): 122–36; and John F. Besemeres, *Socialist Population Politics: Political Implications of Demographic Trends in the USSR and Eastern Europe* (White Plains, N.Y.: M. E. Sharpe, 1980) for discussions of the causes of the fall in the birthrate in these countries.

42. See David and McIntyre, *Reproductive Behavior*, 3–19, and individual chapters for information on specific East European countries. See Besemeres, *Soviet Population Politics*; Lapidus, "Sexual Equality," 131–33; and Peers "Workers by Hand and Womb," for discussions of Soviet population trends and policies.

43. Dudley Kirk, "Albania," in David and McIntyre, *Reproductive Behavior*, 301–02. Yugoslavia also has avoided an explicitly pronatalist approach at the federal level; pronatalist programs exist but are regulated by the republics; ibid, 146–75.

44. Besemeres, *Soviet Population Politics*; David and McIntyre, *Reproductive Behavior*; Robert J. McIntyre, "Demographic Policy and Sexual Equality: Value Conflicts and Policy Appraisal in Hungary and Romania," in Wolchik and Meyer, *Women, State, and Party*, chap. 16; and Heitlinger, *Women and State Socialism*, chaps. 11,12, and 17.

45. See Lapidus, "Sexual Equality," 131–36; and Madison, 316–17; on these provisions and the controversy surrounding them in the Soviet Union.

46. Lapidus, "Sexual Equality," 134; Lynne Attwood, "The New Soviet Man and Woman: Soviet Views on Psychological Sex Differences," in Holland, *Soviet Sisterhood*, chap. 2; Maggie Andrews, "Women's Magazines in the Soviet Union," ibid., chap. 3; Woodward, "The Rights of Women," 247–48; and Wolchik, "Elite Strategy."

47. Excerpts in English from this novel were published as "Alarm Clock in the Cupboard," trans. B. Stillman, *Redbook*, 136 (March 1971): 179–201. See Lapidus, *Women in Soviet Society*; Jancar, *Women Under Communism*; Heitlinger, *Women and State Socialism*; Scott, *Does Socialism Liberate Women?*; Wolchik, "Politics, Ideology, and Equality;" the studies in Parts Two and Three in Atkinson, Dallin, and Lapidus, *Women in Russia*; Wolchik and Meyer, *Women, State, and Policy* Parts II–V; Holland, *Soviet Sisterhood*; Gail Warshofsky Lapidus, ed., *Women, Work and Family in the Soviet Union* (Armonk, N.Y.: M.E. Sharpe, 1982); Alastair McAuley, *Women's Work and Wages in the Soviet Union* (London: Allen and Unwin, 1981); Michael Paul Sacks, *Women's Work in Soviet Russia* (New York: Praeger, 1976); Joel C. Moses, *The Politics of Women and*

Work in the Soviet Union and the United States: Alternative Work Schedules and Sex Discrimination (Berkeley, Calif.: Institute of International Studies, University of California, 1982); Harry G. Shaffer, *Women in the Two Germanies: A Comparative Study of a Socialist and a Non-Socialist Society* (New York: Pergamon Press, 1981) for western studies illustrating these effects.

48. Heitlinger, *Women and State Socialism*, 68–72 and 162–65; Lapidus, *Sexual Equality*, 134–36; Woodward, "The Rights of Women," 255; and Wolchik, "Politics, Ideology, and Equality," chap. 6.

49. See Jancar, "Women in the Opposition," and Renata Siemieńska, "Women and Social Movements in Poland," *Women and Politics* 6, no. 4 (Winter 1986): 5–36, for a discussion of dissident attitudes toward women's issues in Czechoslovakia and Poland. In the Soviet Union, where feminist activists have been divided along religious and secular grounds, attitudes toward gender roles in the family also differ; see Holt, "First Soviet Feminists," 242–51.

50. See Bartová, "Postoje k problemu," Siemieńska, "Women, Work and Gender Equality;" and Wolchik, "Politics, Ideology, and Equality," chaps. 6 and 7, for references to studies illustrating these attitudes.

51. Heitlinger, *Women and State Socialism*; Wolchik, "Politics, Ideology, and Equality," chap. 6.

52. Eva Kanturkova's critique of the current constellation of gender roles has certain similarities to the analyses of Western feminists; however, she calls on women to reject these patterns not so much because they are determined primarily by male experience as because they are determined by the current regime. Her opposition, then, is not so much feminist as a rejection of the broader political system. See Jancar, "Women in the Opposition," 179–81, for a summary of her views.

53. See Morris Bornstein, Zvi Gitelman, and William Zimmerman, *East-West Relations and the Future of East European Politics and Economics* (London and Boston: Allen and Unwin, 1981) for a discussion of these factors.

54. Siemieńska, "Women and Social Movements."

55. See Siemieńska, "Women and Social Movements," and Jancar, "Women in the Opposition," for analyses of Solidarity's positions.

56. See Heitlinger, *Women and State Socialism*; Scott, *Does Socialism Liberate Women?*; and Wolchik, "Politics, Ideology, and Equality," chap. 6, for illustration of these tendencies in Czechoslovakia in the 1960s.

CHAPTER 4

*For reading and commenting on my chapter, many thanks go to Sue Ellen Charlton, Jana Everett, Jane Guyer, Regina Oboler, Jane Parpart, Barrie Thorne, and Lois Wasserspring.

1. Zillah Eisenstein, *Feminism and Sexual Equality: Crisis in Liberal America* (New York: Monthly Review Press, 1984), 89. The state is conceived here as institutions and officials that make extractive and distributive decisions on behalf of all social segments as they pursue various goals that persist actoss time in a certain territory. Important among these goals are the promotion of economic growth and domestic stability.

2. Catharine A. MacKinnon, "Feminism, Marxism, Method, and the State: Toward Feminist Jurisprudence," *Signs: Journal of Women in Culture and Society* 8, no. 4 (1983): 643.

3. Irene Silverblatt, "Andean Women in the Inca Empire," *Feminist Studies* 4, no. 3 (1978): 37–61; Ruby Rohrlich, "State Formation in the Sumer and the Subjugation of Women," *Feminist Studies* 6, no. 1 (1980): 76–102; June Nash, "Aztec Women: The Transition from Status to Class in Empire and Colony," in *Women and Colonization: Anthropological Perspectives*, ed. Mona Etienne and Eleanor Leacock (New York: Praeger, 1980), 137.

4. Engels, *The Origin of the Family, Private Property and the State* (Moscow: Progress Publishers, 1948; originally published in 1884). His emphasis is on women and marriage in prestate societies, the Athenian and German states, and marriage in the Roman state.

5. Karen Sacks, "Engels Revisited: Women, the Organization of Production, and Private Property," *Toward an Anthropology of Women*, ed. Rayna R. Reiter (New York: Monthly Review Press, 1975), 220, 228–33. Also see her *Sisters and Wives: The Past and Future of Sexual Equality* (Urbana: University of Illinois Press, 1982 [Greenwood Press, 1979]), where she elaborates on this argument and on her comparison of state and nonstate societies in Africa. Her conclusions on women and kin groups as "losers" in state formation processes are shared by Rayna Rapp, "Gender and Class: An Archaeology of Knowledge Concerning the Origin of the State," *Dialectical Anthropology* 2 (1977): 309–316; and Rohrlich, "State Formation in Sumer."

6. Heidi Hartmann, "The Unhappy Marriage of Marxism and Feminism: Towards a More Progressive Union," *Women and Revolution: A Discussion of the Unhappy Marriage of Marxism and Feminism*, ed. Lydia Sargent (Boston: South End Press, 1981). She makes this bald (though, as later shown, very plausible) assertion based on the single historical case study of England and Wales.

7. Sherry Ortner, "The Virgin and the State," *Feminist Studies* 4, no. 3 (1978).

R. Reiter (New York: Monthly Review Press,

8. For example, Etienne and Leacock, eds. and authors of the introduction to *Women and Colonization.*

9. Rapp, "Gender and Class," 313.

10. Like Jane F. Collier and Michelle Z. Rosaldo, I find marital exchange to be a particularly insightful social construction. See their "Politics and Gender in Simple Societies," *Sexual Meanings: The Cultural Construction of Gender and Sexuality,* ed. Sherry B. Ortner and Harriet Whitehead (New York: Cambridge University Press, 1981), 275–329. On the ubiquity of *female* exchange, see Gayle Rubin, "The Traffic in Women: Notes on the 'Political Economy' of Sex," in Reiter, *Toward an Anthropology of Women.* Women have been conduits rather than partners in exchange. Even historian Gerda Lerner, who in *The Creation of Patriarchy* focuses on the increasingly elaborate sexual control of women that occurred under state formation in the Near East, grants the importance of prestate marital exchange. Women are exchanged rather than men because of the greater ease in ensuring their loyalty through rape and bonds with offspring. (New York: Cambridge University Press, 1986), 46–48.

Accumulation and attendant behavioral incentives are integrally tied to marital exchange systems. Bridewealth exchange facilitates the accumulation process. Access to women and to "legitimate" sex (to the extent that sex is restricted to marriage) require material accumulation to pay bridewealth to a woman's family to compensate them for her labor and reproductive capacity. Women are accumulated as extra wives, and their labor facilitates husbands' accumulation.

11. Bruce Berman, "Structure and Process in the Bureaucratic States of Colonial Africa," *Development and Change* 15 (1984): 165. Berman can be applauded for rescuing the problems of "mode of production" approaches with a focus on state accumulation efforts.

12. Henry S. Wilson, *The Imperial Experience in Sub-Saharan Africa* (Minneapolis: University of Minnesota Press, 1977), 114–115.

13. Karen Fields, *Revival and Rebellion in Colonial Central Africa* (Princeton, N.J.: Princeton University Press, 1985), cites Kirk-Greene on p. 34. In 1935, the administrator-population ratios were 1:36,000 in Malawi, 1:56,000 in Nigeria, and 1:48,000 in Ghana.

14. Wilson, *The Imperial Experience,* 117.

15. Ibid., 126–127.

16. William B. Cohen, "The French Colonial Service in French West Africa," *France and Britain in Africa: Imperial Rivalry and Colonial Rule,* ed. P. Gifford and William Roger Louis (New Haven: Yale University Press, 1971), 495–97.

17. Robert Heussler, *Yesterday's Rulers: The Making of the British Colonial Service* (Syracuse, N.Y.: Syracuse University Press, 1963), 211.

18. Ibid., xx, 90, 94. British public schools are independent of state control.

19. Helen Callaway, *Gender, Culture and Empire: European Women in Colonial Nigeria* (Urbana: University of Illinois, 1987), 9, 14.

20. T. O. Beidelman, *Colonial Evangelism: A Socio-historical Study of an East African Mission at the Grassroots* (Bloomington, Ind.: Indiana University Press, 1982), chap. 8.

21. Stephen H. Roberts, *History of French Colonial Policy (1870–1925)* (London: P. S. King, Ltd., 1929), 346.

22. Martin Chanock, *Law, Custom and Social Order: The Colonial Experience in Malawi and Zambia* (Cambridge: Cambridge University Press, 1985), 187.

23. Sir Stewart Symes, *Tour of Duty* (London: Collins, 1946), 199–200; Sir Charles Dundas, *African Crossroads* (London: MacMillan, 1955), 19, 66; Sir Philip Mitchell, *African Afterthoughts* (London: Hutchison, 1954), 76.

24. Beidelman, *Colonial Evangelism*, chap. 1, especially 9ff; R. Pierce Beaver, *American Protestant Women in World Missions* (Grand Rapids, Mich.: William B. Eerdmans, 1980) on couples. Islamic religion is outside the boundaries of this analysis (see chapter by Calloway and Creevey in this volume), though I. M. Lewis says that Islam emphasizes patrilineality or at least weakens matrilineality when confronted, just as do Christian and Western influences (*Islam in Tropical Africa*, London: Oxford University Press, 1966), 48.

25. Holger Bernt Hansen, *Mission, Church and State in a Colonial Setting: Uganda, 1890–1925* (London: Heinemann, 1984), 77; Robert W. Strayer, *The Making of Mission Communities in East Africa* (London: Heinemann, 1978), chap. 3; Fields, *Revival and Rebellion*, 100, 120.

26. Chanock, *Law, Custom, and Social Order*, 81.

27. Beidelman, *Colonial Evangelism*, 142, 191; Hansen reports 80% in 1913 for Uganda, *Mission, Church and State*, 273.

28. Hansen, *Mission, Church and State*, 273–78, 302; Strayer, *Making of Mission Communities*, 103. Strayer also analyzes the reluctance on the part of colonial officials to enforce their policy condemnation of Kikuyu female circumcision during the 1920s-1930s crisis as a result of concerns about undermining local authorities upon whom they depended, chap. 8. This theme runs through Chanock as well.

29. Roland Oliver, *The Missionary Factor in East Africa* (London: Longmans, 1952), 53.

30. Ibid., 214.

31. Strayer, *Making of Mission Communities*, 93. For a description of Phelps-Stokes Commission recommendations as they related to gender, as well as of other early programs, see Kathleen Staudt, "Women's Politics, the State, and Capitalist Transformation in Subsaharan Africa," *Studies in Power and Class in Africa*, ed. Irving Markovitz, (New York: Oxford University Press, 1987), 193–208. Two commissions visited Africa, calling for a type of adapted, vocational education like that for American Blacks in the South around the turn of the century and thereafter.

32. Oliver, *The Missionary Factor*, 180.

33. Marcia Wright, "Technology, Marriage and Women's Work in the History of Maize-Growers in Mazabuka Zambia: A Reconñaissance," *Journal of Southern African Studies* 10, no. 1 (1983): 75.

34. Ester Boserup, *Woman's Role in Economic Development* (New York: St. Martin's Press, 1970) analyzes many such programs, along with assumptions of officials. Also see Maud Shimwaayi Muntemba, "Women and Agricultural Change in the Railway Region of Zambia: Dispossession and Counterstrategies, 1930–1970," *Women and Work in Africa*, ed. Edna Bay, (Boulder, Colo.: Westview, 1982), 83–104. The cash crop emphasis on men sometimes produced an actual reversal in husband-wife control over the production process; see Mona Etienne, "Women and Men, Cloth and Colonization: The Transformation of Production-Distribution Relations Among the Baule," in *Women and Colonization*, ed. Etienne and Leacock, 214–38.

35. Lord Lugard's *The Dual Mandate in British Tropical Africa* was quoted in the *Native Affairs Annual Report*, Kenya Colony and Protectorate, (London: His Majesty's Stationary Office, 1929), 57.

36. Lord Hailey, *An African Survey* (London: Oxford University Press, 1956), 872.

37. Chanock, *Law, Custom and Social Order*, 14–15, 179.

38. Ibid., 15, 173; Lucy Mair, *Native Policies in Africa* (London: 1936), 20.

39. Hansen, *Mission, Church and State*, 268.

40. Mair, *Native Policies*, 232.

41. Charles Van Onselen, "The Witches of Suburbia: Domestic Service on the Witwatersrand 1886–1914," in his *Studies in the Social and*

Economic History of the Witwatersrand 1886–1914 vol. 2, New Ninevah (London: Longman, 1982), 10–11.

42. Van Onselen, "The Witches of Suburbia," 15–17. Also see Deborah Gaitskell, "Housewives, Maids or Mothers: Some Contradictions of Domesticity for Christian Women in Johannesburg, 1903–39," *Journal of African History* 24 (1983): 241–256. She argues that "domestic ideology" was "enmeshed with women's spiritual role," and thus "much more a part of the missionary instruction of African women converts . . ."

43. Oliver, *The Missionary Factor*, 289. All along, preaching about equality and brotherhood (however paternalistic the missionary-convert relationship may have been) was troublesome to officials.

44. Ibid., 277, 285.

45. Proffer Gifford and Timothy C. Weiskel "African Education in a Colonial Context: French and British Styles," in *France and Britain in Africa*, ed. Gifford and Louis, 674. W. Bryant Mumford and Maj. G. St. J. Orde-Brown, *Africans Learn to be French* (London: Evans Brothers Ltd. 1936). They report, for 1937, a total of 53,000 students, 5,000 of them girls, 94.

46. Hansen, *Mission, Church and State*, 294.

47. Ibid., 279, 281, 289. Jane Parpart, "Sexuality and Power on the Zambian Copperbelt, 1926–1964," (Boston University Working Paper #120, 1986), 5, 8, and "Class and Gender on the Copperbelt," in *Women and Class in Africa*, ed. Claire Robertson and Iris Berger (New York: Holmes and Meier, 1986), 141–60. Penelope A. Roberts, "The State and the Regulation of Marriage: Sefwi Wiawso (Ghana), 1900–40," in *Women, State and Ideology: Studies From Africa and Asia*, ed. Haleh Afshar (London: Macmillan, 1987), 61. Marja-Liisa Swantz, too, describes how Haya officials attempted to prevent women both from leaving, or if they had already left, from returning in *Women in Development: A Creative Role Denied?* (London: C. Hurst and New York: St. Martins Press, 1985), chap. 2. This did not stop the women, however, from leaving because resourceful means were used to escape.

48. Beidelman, *Colonial Evangelism*, 82, 116; Beaver, *American Protestant Women*, chap. 5.

49. Strayer, *Making of Mission Communities*, 81, 88.

50. Oliver, *The Missionary Factor*, 291.

51. Callaway, *Gender, Culture and Empire*, 15.

52. Jane Bell, M.B.E., "Domestic Science in the Bush," *Corona* 12, no. 5 (1960): 176–78 However, dedicated women in the postwar Colonial Service (when women were finally permitted to enter the British Colonial Ser-

vice), such as Elizabeth O'Kelly with her work on corn mill societies in the Cameroon, helped to strengthen women's economic and organizational activities.

53. G. M. Roddan, C.M.G., "The Key is Woman," *Corona* (1958): 57–59.

54. Chanock, *Law, Custom and Social Order*, 39, 49, 146. Christine M. Geary, "On Legal Change in Cameroon: Women, Marriage, and Bridewealth," (Boston University African Studies Center Working Paper #113, 1986), 2, notes that in French colonies most Africans were subject to customary law for civil matters.

55. Chanock, *Law, Custom and Social Order*, 183. He reminds readers that through marriage, people gained access to land in most economies of Zambia and Malawi. Men lost the use of land through divorce, 145. Parpart, "Sexuality and Power," 2–3.

56. Margaret Jean Hay and Marcia Wright, "Introduction," and eds., *African Women and the Law: Historical Perspectives* (Boston: Boston University Papers on Africa, 7, 1982), xiv. Golden Age is Chanock's term.

57. Martin Chanock, "Making Customary Law: Men, Women, and Courts in Colonial Northern Rhodesia," *African Women and the Law*, 53–67. This is further developed in Chanock, *Law, Custom and Social Order*. Marcia Wright, "Justice, Women, and the Social Order in Abercorn, Northeastern Rhodesia, 1897–1903," *African Women and the Law*.

58. Margaret Jean Hay, "Women as Owners, Occupants, and Managers of Property in Colonial Western Kenya," *African Women and the Law*, 110–25.

59. Berman, "Structure and Process," 183.

60. Jane Guyer, *Family and Farm in Southern Cameroon* (Boston: Boston University African Research Studies #15, 1984), 43–44.

61. Terence O. Ranger, "The Invention of Tradition in Colonial Africa," *The Invention of Tradition*, ed. E. Hobsbawn and Terence O. Ranger (Cambridge University Press, 1983), 258–259.

62. Frank A. Salamone, "Continuity of Igbo Values After Conversion: A Study in Purity and Prestige," *Missiology: An International Review* 3, no. 1 (January 1975): 33–44.

63. Regina Oboler, *Women, Power, and Economic Change: The Nandi of Kenya* (Stanford: Stanford University Press, 1985), 258, 278.

64. Judith Van Allen, "Sitting on a Man: Colonialism and the Lost

Political Institutions of Igbo Women," *Canadian Journal of African Studies* 6, no. 2 (1972), 165–182. Nina Emma Mba, *Nigerian Women Mobilized: Women's Political Activity in Southern Nigeria*, 1900–1965 (Berkeley: University of California Institute of International Studies, Research Series #48, 1982), 46–49, 73, chap. 4.

65. Cited in Mba, *Nigerian Women Mobilized*, 45, although she takes issue with his antistate interpretation. Neither of us would see this as an indigenous variant of the public-private spheres. Women's remarks bear an uncanny resemblance to the peasant behavior James Scott analyzed in *The Moral Economy of the Peasant* (New Haven: Yale University Press, 1976).

66. On the difficulty of attributing and measuring class for women, see selections (including my own, "Stratification: Implications for Women's Politics") in Claire Robertson and Iris Berger, eds., *Women and Class in Africa* (New York: Holmes and Meier, 1986), 197–215; and Lerner's, *The Creation of Patriarchy*, for whom a continuing theme is women's definition by sexual relations, and men's, by property relations. In "Women's Politics, the State and Capitalist Transformation," I discuss the absorption of a public-private ideology among politically active privileged women.

67. Cited in Mba, *Nigerian Women Mobilized*, 168, though the interpretation of Kuti is mine.

68. Parpart, "Sexuality and Power," 10.

69. Gaitskell, "Housewives, Maids or Mothers," citing J. Wells, 255.

70. Parpart, "Sexuality and Power," 19.

71. Parpart "Class and Gender," 149ff; Parpart, "Sexuality and Power," 8; Geary, "On Legal Change," who describes in vivid detail the draconian wheels of state "justice;" Janet MacGaffey, "Women and Class Formation in a Dependent Economy: Kisangani Entrepreneurs," in *Women and Class in Africa*, 161–77.

72. See Staudt, "Stratification," and "Women's Politics, the State and Capitalist Transformation," for analyses of contemporary African politics.

73. James Brain, "Less than Second Class: Women in Rural Settlement Schemes in Tanzania," *Women in Africa: Studies in Social and Economic Change*, ed. Nancy Hafkin and Edna Bay (Stanford: Stanford University Press, 1976), 274.

74. David Hirschmann, "Bureaucracy and Rural Women: Illustrations from Malawi," *Rural Africana* 21 (Winter 1985): 54.

75. M. Crawford Young, "The Colonial State and Its Connection to

Current Political Crisis in Africa," *The Precarious Balance: State and Society in Africa,* ed. Naomi Chazan and Donald Rothchild (Boulder, Colo.: Westview Press, 1987), 57.

76. Goran Hyden is now perhaps best known by his much disputed argument that the state has not yet captured African peasants. See *No Shortcuts to Progress: African Development Management in Perspective* (Berkeley: University of California Press, 1983). I take issue with his obliviousness to gender in "Uncaptured or Unmotivated: Women and the Food Crisis in Africa," *Rural Sociology* 52, no. 1 (Spring 1987): 37–55.

77. Thomas M. Callaghy, "The State as Lame Leviathan: The Patrimonial Administrative State in Africa," *The African State in Transition,* ed. Zaki Ergas (New York: St. Martin's Press, 1987).

78. See selections in *The Precarious Balance.* Comparativist lingo on this phenomenon was long called "penetration."

CHAPTER 5

1. Haleh Afshar, "Women, Marriage and the State in Iran," in Haleh Afshar ed., *Women, State and Ideology: Studies from Africa and Asia* (Albany, N.Y.: State University of New York Press, 1987), 83.

2. Ibid., 86.

3. Azar Tabari and Nahid Yeganeh, eds., *In the Shadow of Islam: The Women's Movement in Iran* (London: Zed Press, 1982); Eliz Sanasarian, "Political Activism and Islamic Identity in Iran," in Lynne B. Iglitzin and Ruth Ross, eds., *Women in the World, 1975–1985: The Women's Decade* (Santa Barbara, Calif.: ABC-Clio Press, 1986), 207–24; Fatna A. Sabbah, *Woman in the Muslim Unconscious* (New York: Pergamon Press, 1984); Azizah al-Hibri, ed., *Women and Islam* (Oxford: Pergamon Press, 1982); Frieda Hussain, *Muslim Women* (New York: St. Martin's Press, 1984); Fatima Mernissi, "Professional Women in the Arab World: The Example of Morocco," *Feminist Issues,* 7, no. 1 (Spring 1987): 47–65; John L. Esposito, *Women in Muslim Family Law* (Syracuse, N.Y.: Syracuse University Press, 1982).

4. Nawal El Saadawi, *The Hidden Face of Eve: Women in the Arab World* (London: Zed Press, 1980); Jane L. Smith, ed., *Women in Contemporary Muslim Societies* (Cranbury, N.J.: Associated University Presses, 1980); Lois Beck and Nikki Keddie, eds., *Women in the Muslim World* (Cambridge: Harvard University Press, 1978); Fatima Mernissi, *Beyond the Veil: Male-Female Dynamics in a Modern Muslim Society* (New York: John Wiley, 1975); Joseph Ginat, *Women in Muslim Rural Society: Status and Role in Family and Community* (New Brunswick: Transaction Books, 1982); John

L. Esposito, *Islam and Development: Religion and Sociopolitical Change* (Syracuse, N.Y.: Syracuse University Press 1980).

5. See Donald E. Smith, *Religion and Political Development* (Boston: Little, Brown and Co., 1970), 1–10, 246–79; and *Religion and Political Modernization* (New Haven, Conn.: Yale University Press, 1974), 3–28.

6. Ahmad Khurshid, *Family Life in Islam*. (Leicester: The Islamic Foundation, 1974), 16.

7. Noel Coulson and Doreen Hinchcliffe, "Women and Law Reform in Contemporary Islam," in Beck and Keddie, *Women in the Muslim World*, 37–51.

8. Ibid., 38.

9. Ibid., 39. See also John L. Esposito, *Women in Muslim Family Law*.

10. Coulson and Hinchcliffe, "Women and Law Reform," 44–45.

11. The principal brotherhoods sending missionaries to Senegal were the Qadriyya and the Tidjaniiya but, in 1886, a Qadiri religious leader (*marabout*) founded the Muridiyya order which was to become the most politically powerful religious group in Senegal in the twentieth century.

12. See Lucy Creevey (Behrman), *Muslim Brotherhoods and Politics in Senegal* (Cambridge: Harvard University Press, 1970). For detail on the spread of sufism in North and West Africa, see J. Spencer Triminham, *Islam in West Africa* (Oxford: Clarendon Press, 1959); Octave Depont and Xavier Coppolani, *Les Confreries religieuses musulmanes* (Alger: Adolphe Jourdan, 1897); and A. LeChatelier, *L'Islam dans l'Afrique Occidentale* (Paris: G. Steinheil, 1899).

13. See Lucy Creevey (Behrman), "The Islamization of the Wolof by the End of the Nineteenth Century," Daniel McCall, Norman Bennett and Jeffrey Butler, eds., *Western African History: Boston University Papers on Africa*, vol. IV (New York: Praeger, 1969).

14. See Ruth S. Morgenthau, *Political Parties in French-Speaking West Africa* (Oxford: Clarendon Press, 1964); Edward J. Schumacher, *Politics, Bureaucracy and Rural Development in Senegal* (Berkeley, Calif.: University of California Press, 1975); Creevey, *Muslim Brotherhoods and Politics in Senegal*; Lucy Creevey (Behrman), "Muslim Politics and Development in Senegal," *The Journal of Modern African Studies* 15, no. 2 (June 1977): 261–77; Lucy Creevey, "Muslim Brotherhoods and Politics in Senegal in 1985", *The Journal of Modern African Studies* 23, no. 4 (December 1985): 715–21.

15. See Sheldon Gellar, *Senegal: An African Nation between Islam*

and the West (Boulder, Colo.: Westview Press, 1982).

16. Ibid., 88–92.

17. Ibid., 123.

18. See Bernhard Venema, "The Wolof of Senegal: Social Structure and Rural Development in Senegal," Wageningen, The Netherlands: PUDOC, 1978; David P. Gamble, *The Wolof of Senegambia: Ethnographic Survey of Western Africa* (London: International African Institute, 1967); William Bascom and Melville Herskovits, eds., *Continuity and Change in African Cultures* (Chicago: University of Chicago Press, 1959), See also Lucy Creevey, ed., *Women Farmers in Africa: Rural Development in Mali and the Sahel* (Syracuse: Syracuse University Press, 1986).

19. See for example L. Tautain, *Etudes critiques sur l'éthologie et l'ethnographie des peuples du bassin du Sénégal* (Paris: Ernest Lerous, 1885); and G. Mollien, *Voyage dans l'intérieur de l'Afrique aux sources de Sénégal et de la Gambie fait en 1818* (Paris: Courcier, 1820).

20. See Ruth Leger Sivard, *Women . . . A World Survey* (Washington, D.C.: World Priorities, 1985).

21. Gellar, *Senegal*, 101–103.

22. John Waterbury, "The Senegalese Peasant: How Good is Our Conventional Wisdom?" and Sheldon Gellar, "Circulaire 32 Revisited: Prospects for Revitalizing the Senegalese Cooperative Movement in the 1980's," in Mark Gersovitz and John Waterbury, eds., *The Political Economy of Risk and Choice in Senegal* (London: Frank Cass, 1987). See also Bernhard Venema, "The Changing Role of Women in Sahelian Agriculture," in Creevey, *Women Farmers in Africa*, 80–94.

23. Egyptian women benefited from laws regularizing their marriage and divorce rights as early as between 1920–1929. See Coulson and Hinchcliffe, "Women and Law Reform," 291. Women obtained the right to vote in Egypt in 1956.

24. John Alden Williams, "Veiling in Egypt, a Political and Social Phenomenon," in Esposito, *Islam and Development*, 74.

25. For example, comparisons of the zones where Muslim leaders are the most powerful show that not only do significantly fewer girls receive education than in other areas, but significantly fewer boys do as well.

26. See Ester Boserup, *Woman's Role in Economic Development* (New York: St. Martin's Press, 1970).

27. Sir Herbert Palmer, *Sudanese Memoirs: Being Mainly Translations of a Number of Arabic Manuscripts Relating to the Central and West-*

ern Sudan (Lagos: Government Printer, 1928), 98–134.

28. S. J. Hogben and A.H.M. Kirk-Greene, *The Emirates of Northern Nigeria* (London: Oxford University Press, 1966), 188.

29. Ibid., 190–93. Palmer, *Sudanese Memoirs*, 111–112.

30. A. D. H. Bivar and Mervyn Hiskett, "The Arabic Literature of Nigeria to 1804: A Provisional Account," *Bulletin of the School of Oriental and African Studies* 25, no. 1 (1962): 152–58.

31. See Hogben and Kirk-Greene, *Emirates*, 92–93, 314–15; Sir Herbert Palmer, "Review of Y. Urvoy, Histoire de l'Empire du Bornu," *Africa* 20, no. 2 (April 1950): 161–63; and M.G. Smith, *The Affairs of Daura: History and Change in a Hausa State 1800–1958* (Berkeley, Calif.: University of California Press, 1978), 53–54.

32. Mervyn Hiskitt, "Kitab al-Farq: A Work on the Habe Kingdoms Attributed to Uthman dan Fodio," *Bullitin: School of Oriental and African Studies* 23, no. 3 (1960): 553–79.

33. Robert Heussler, "Indirect Rule in Northern Nigeria," *South Altantic Quarterly* 47, no. 3 (Summer 1968): 506. Excellent detailed accounts of Indirect Rule and the British Colonial Period are found in C. S. Whitaker, *The Politics of Tradition, Continuity and Change in Northern Nigeria, 1946–1966* (Princeton, N.J.: Princeton University Press, 1970); and M.G. Smith, *The Affairs of Daura*.

34. Sir Fredrick Lugard, *The Dual Mandate in British Tropical Africa*, 4th ed., (London: William Blackwood, 1929).

35. Barbara J. Callaway and Enid Schildkrout, "Law, Education and Social Change: Implications for Hausa Muslim Women in Nigeria," in Iglitzin and Ross, *Women in the World*, 181–207.

36. Barbara J. Callaway, *Muslim Hausa Women in Nigeria: Tradition and Change* (Syracuse, N.Y.: Syracuse University Press, 1987), chap. 4 and 5.

37. Abul A'la Mawdudi, *Human Rights in Islam* (Leicester: The Islamic Foundation, 1976), 36–37.

38. Barbara J. Callaway, "Women and Political Participation in Kano City," *Comparative Politics*, 19, no. 4 (July 1987): 379–393.

39. Callaway, *Muslim Hausa Women*.

40. Callaway and Schildkrout, "Law, Education and Social Change."

41. Ibid.

42. Callaway, *Muslim Hausa Women*, 107.

43. Ibrahim A. Ragab, "Islam and Development," *World Development* VIII, no. 7–8 (July/August 1980): 513–22.

44. Esposito, *Women in Muslim Family Law*, 10–134.

CHAPTER 6

*Thanks to Jill K. Conway and Donna Robinson Divine for their comments on an earlier draft.

1. For discussion of the changing approach to the state, see the collection of essays edited by Peter Evans, Dietrich Rueschemeyer, and Theda Skocpol, *Bringing the State Back In* (Cambridge: Cambridge University Press, 1985), especially the essays by Skocpol, "Bringing the State Back In: Strategies of Analysis in Current Research," 3–37; and Alfred Stepan, "State Power and the Strength of Civil Society in the Southern Cone of Latin America," 317–43; as well as the review essay by Stephen D. Krasner, "Approaches to the State: Alternative Conceptions and Historical Dynamics," *Comparative Politics* 16, no. 2 (January 1984): 223–46.

2. For the initial formulation of these ideas, see Jill K. Conway, Susan C. Bourque, and Joan W. Scott, "Introduction: The Concept of Gender," *Daedalus* 116, no. 4 (Fall 1987): xxi–xxx. A number of essays in this issue elaborate various aspects of gender and the state. See in particular the essays by Mary G. Dietz, "Context is All: Feminism and Theories of Citizenship," 1–24; Jill Conway, "Politics, Pedagogy, and Gender," 137–52; and Susan C. Bourque and Kay B. Warren, "Technology, Gender, and Development," 173–98.

3. Conway, Bourque, and Scott, "Introduction," xxi.

4. Michelle Z. Rosaldo, "The Use and Abuse of Anthropology: Reflections on Feminism and Cross-Cultural Understanding," *Signs: Journal of Women in Culture and Society* 5, no. 3 (1980): 389–417.

5. Joan W. Scott, "Gender: A Useful Category of Historical Analysis," *American Historical Review* 91, no. 5 (December 1986): 1069.

6. Irene Silverblatt, *Moon, Sun and Wiches: Gender Ideologies and Class in Inca and Colonial Peru* (Princeton, N.J.: Princeton University Press, 1987).

7. In effect, Silverblatt has rewritten the Malinche myth of Indian women's treachery by consorting with the Spanish conquerors against their own people. Her research suggests male collusion with the conquerors.

8. Another untold story is how the conquered presented their plight to the Spanish crown. Guaman Poma, one of Silverblatt's chief sources, phrases his tale of wrongdoing in terms of the conquistadors' violation of women on the basis of the rules established by the Spanish crown. Was Guaman Poma's emphasis on the mistreatment of women consciously crafted for sympathetic ears? Was it an appeal to the Spanish Crown's notions of chivalry and hence the manipulation of gender ideologies?

9. For discussion of this phenomenon, see Kathleen Staudt, *Women, Foreign Assistance and Advocacy Administration* (New York: Praeger, 1985); Amartya Sen, "Women, Technology and Sexual Divisions," (Santo Domingo: U.N./INSTRAW, 1985); and Carmen Diana Deere, "The Latin American Agrarian Reform Experience," in Carmen Diana Deere and Magdalena Leon, eds., *Rural Women and State Policy: Feminist Perspectives on Latin American Agricultural Development* (Boulder, Colo.: Westview Press, 1987), 165–90.

10. Staudt, *Women, Foreign Assistance*, 5.

11. Carmen Diana Deere and Magdalena Leon, "Conclusion," *Rural Women and State Policy*, 262.

12. Deere, "Latin American Agarian Reform," 166.

13. Ibid, 175.

14. My own work in rural Peru revealed that male peasant community leaders on occasion subverted the attempts of the central government at gender equity. See Susan C. Bourque, "Experiments with Equality: Complexities in Peruvian Public Policy," *Journal of Asian and African Studies* 20, nos. 3 and 4 (1985): 156–68; and Susan C. Bourque and Kay B. Warren, "Multiple Arenas for State Expansion: Class, Ethnicity and Sex in Rural Peru," *Ethnic and Racial Studies* 3, no. 3 (July 1980): 264–80.

15. Lourdes Arizpe and Carlota Botey, "Mexican Agricultural Development Policy and Its Impact on Rural Women," *Rural Women and State Policy*, 67–83.

16. Arizpe and Botey, "Mexican Agricultural Development," 73.

17. Deere and Leon, "Conclusion," 262.

18. Acknowledging the limits of dependency theory does not deny its signal contribution to the study of comparative politics, or detract from the continuing influence of such theorists in our thinking about Latin American politics. See, for example, the assessment by Arturo Valenzuela, "Political Science and the Study of Latin America" (paper presented at the Latin American Studies Association Meeting, Albuquerque, New Mexico, April

1984). For an overview of the development of dependency theory and its variations, see Ronald H. Chilcote, *Theories of Development and Underdevelopment* (Boulder, Colo.: Westview Press, 1984).

19. In Latin American politics, the focus on the internal political cultures might be traced to the initial formulation of bureaucratic authoritarianism by Guillermo O'Donnell. O'Donnell asked, how can we account for the failure of democracy in the most economically advanced countries of Latin America? He found his explanation in the aspirations of the technocratic elites to enjoy the perquisites of their status at the level of their counterparts in Western Europe or the United States. Those values and attitudes outweighed their commitments to democracy and led them to support military intervention in both Argentina and Brazil. O'Donnell's insights opened up the field, and sparked a wide range of questions about the state. Guillermo A. O'Donnell, *Modernization and Bureaucratic Authoritarianism: Studies in South American Politics*, 2nd edition (Berkeley: Institute of International Studies, 1979).

20. To briefly summarize each, for liberals state elites reflect the balance of interest in civil society, for Marxists state elites mirror the interests of dominant economic groups. For an excellent discussion of the variation among Marxist positions on the relative autonomy of the state, see Nora Hamilton, *The Limits of State Autonomy: Post-Revolutionary Mexico* (Princeton, N.J.: Princeton University Press, 1982), chapter 1.

21. Skocpol, "Bringing the State Back In," 22.

22. Merilee S. Grindle, *State and Countryside: Development Policy and Agrarian Politics in Latin America* (Baltimore, Md.: Johns Hopkins University Press, 1986), 3. While Grindle argues that Mexican state elites redefined rural development in the 1970s, she emphasizes that their options were clearly constrained by the economic and political power of the large capitalist farmers, a group that, to a great extent, state policy created in the first place.

23. Elena Urrutia, "Beatriz Paredes, gobernadora," *fem* 11, no. 51 (March 1987): 6–8.

24. Skocpol, "Bringing the State Back In," 22.

25. Alfred Stepan, *Rethinking Military Politics: Brazil and the Southern Cone* (Princeton, N.J.: Princeton University Press, 1988), xii, 33.

26. A member of *El Poder Femenino* recounts their tactics as follows: "We wrote letters [to leading members of the military] pleading with them to save our families from the chaos and violence perpetrated by the Unidad Popular [Allende government]. In the letters we not only questioned their duty as soldiers, but their virility, their machismo. We put it in very strong

terms. . . . We threw wheat in the soldiers' barracks to imply that they were 'chickens.' Several women also contemplated painting the barracks a light color blue so that 'baby boys' would come out. If we had to humiliate them to make them act then we would do so." Maria de los Angeles Crummett, "El Poder Femenino: The Mobilization of Women Against Socialism in Chile," *Latin American Perspectives* 4, no. 4 (Fall 1977): 107.

27. Elsa Chaney, *Supermadre: Women in Politics in Latin America* (Austin, Tex.: University of Texas Press, 1979); Nicholas Fraser and Marysa Navarro, *Eva Peron* (New York: W. W. Norton, 1980).

28. Ximena Bunster-Burotto, "Surviving Beyond Fear: Women and Torture in Latin America," in *Women and Change in Latin America*, June Nash, Helen Safa, and Contributors (South Hadley, Mass.: Bergin and Garvey, 1986), 297–325.

29. Patricia Chuchryk, "Subversive Mothers: The Opposition to the Military Regime in Chile," in this volume. This argument is skillfully developed by Marysa Navarro, "The Personal is Political: The Madres of the Plaza de Mayo," in Susan Eckstein, ed., *Power and Popular Protest* (Berkeley, Calif.: University of California Press, forthcoming, 1989). For an excellent review of women's participation in human rights groups in Argentina, Chile, and Guatemala, see Jennifer G. Schirmer, " 'Those who die for life cannot be called dead': Women and Human Rights Protest in Latin America," in *Human Rights Yearbook*, Vol. 1 (Spring 1988).

30. Scott Mainwaring and Eduardo Viola, "New Social Movements, Political Culture and Democracy: Brazil and Argentina in the 1980s," *Telos* 17, no. 3 (Fall 1984): 17–52.

31. See for example the study by Cecilia Blondet, *Muchas vidas construyendo una indentidad*, Mujeres pobladoras de un barrio limeño; Documento de Trabajo, no. 9 (Lima, Peru: Instituto de Estudios Peruanos, 1986). Additional data can be found in Susan C. Bourque, "Women and Development: Redrawing the Urban Map in Latin America," in K. Lynn Stoner, ed., *Latinas of the Americas* (New York: Garland Press, 1988); Nora Galer, Virginia Guzman, and Maria Gabriela Vega, eds., *Mujer y Desarrollo* (Lima, Peru: Centro de la Mujer Peruana Flora Tristán, 1985); and Violeta Sara-Lafosse, *Comedores comunales: la mujer frente a la crisis* (Lima, Peru: Grupo de Trabajo Servicios urbanos y mujeres de bajos ingresos, 1984).

32. There is an extensive bibliography on women and politics in Peru. See for example Bourque, "Experiments with Equality; "Urban Activists: Paths to Political Consciousness in Peru," in Susan C. Bourque and Donna Robinson Divine, eds., *Women Living Change* (Philadelphia: Temple University Press, 1985), 25–56; Chaney, *Supermadre;* Virginia Vargas, "El movimiento feminista en el Peru: balance y perspectivas" (paper delivered

at the Annual Meeting of the Latin American Studies Association, Washington, D.C., March 1982). For coverage of feminist activity, see the Peruvian magazine, *Viva*, published by the Centro Flora Tristán. Of special interest is the March 1985 issue, "Feministas al Parlamento."

33. Sonia Alvarez, "Contradictions of a 'Women's Space' in a Male-Dominant State: The Political Role of the Commissions on the Status of Women in Post-Authoritarian Brazil," in Kathleen Staudt, ed., *The Bureaucratic Mire: Women's Programs in Comparative Perspective*, (Philadelphia: Temple University Press, 1989).

34. Mainwaring and Viola, "New Social Movements," 39.

CHAPTER 7

*This is a revised version of a paper presented at the XIII International Congress of the Latin American Studies Association, Boston, October 23–25, 1986. I would like to thank the Social Sciences and Humanities Research Council of Canada for funding the initial research, and the University of Lethbridge Faculty Research Fund for making a return field trip in 1987 possible. I would also like to thank the editors for their useful comments on an earlier draft of this paper. However, without the assistance of many Chilean women, this paper could not have been written. First I owe my thanks to those women of the *Agrupaciones* who allowed themselves to be interviewed, and who at times did so with some reservation. I am also indebted to the friend and colleague who, with a great deal of difficulty, conducted some of these interviews. Long discussions with another friend and colleague, a long time member of two of the organizations discussed in this chapter, provided a number of important insights. Although, for obvious reasons these individuals cannot be identified, their contributions are gratefully acknowledged.

1. Penny Lernoux, *Cry of the People* (New York: Penguin Books, 1982), 142.

2. In "One Decade of State Repression in Chile: A Preliminary Analysis" (in Arch Ritter, *Latin America and the Caribbean: Geopolitics, Development and Culture—Conference Proceedings*, Ottawa: Canadian Association for Latin American and Caribbean Studies, 1984), J. Arancibia, M. Charlin, and P. Landstreet suggest that during the first ten years of military rule, four distinct phases of repression can be identified.

3. Arancibia, Charlin and Landstreet, "One Decade of State Repression in Chile," 32.

4. Cited in John Dinges, "The Rise of the Opposition," *NACLA Report on the Americas* 17, no. 5 (Sept./Oct. 1983): 16.

5. Cited in Ibid., 36.

6. Cited in Ibid., 31.

7. Jon Barnes, "Appendix: Human Rights and the Pinochet Decade," in Phil O'Brien and Jackie Roddick, *Chile: The Pinochet Decade* (London: Latin American Bureau, 1983), 111. An article in the Caracas daily *El Universal* (August 26, 1983) quoted a minister in Pinochet's cabinet as saying, "In Chile, no one has disappeared . . . the lists that have been presented are false and contain the names of persons who wanted to abandon their families and leave the country or names of persons who never really existed." (Cited in Rosa del Olmo, "Women and the Search for the Detained/Disappeared Persons of Latin America," *Resources for Feminist Research* 15, no. 1 (March 1986): 42.

8. There are several of these associations: the Association of the Relatives of the Detained and Disappeared, the Association of Political Prisoners, the Association of the Exiled, and the Association of the Politically Executed. The members of all these groups are primarily women and while I would suggest that the observations made in this paper apply equally to all of these groups, most of the interviews were conducted with members of the Association of the Relatives of the Detained and Disappeared, henceforth referred to as the *Agrupación*.

9. "La Mujer chilena se moviliza activamente en la lucha general para la libertad y la democracia", *Chile-America* nos. 54–55 (June-July 1979): 18.

10. A recent study places their current membership at 380. See María de la Luz Silva, *La Participación Politica de la Mujer: Las Organizaciones de Mujeres* (Buenos Aires: Friedrich-Naumann-Stiftung Foundation, 1986), 146.

11. This has changed in recent years, especially since 1986. There is some evidence to suggest that women's organizations have been added to the list of those targeted for military repression.

12. In August 1983 I was permitted to attend a meeting of the *cabezas del grupo*. I conducted a group interview which lasted roughly one and one half hours, at which time I left so that they could conduct their regular business without an outsider present.

13. MEMCH 83 was formed to coordinate women's activities as part of the mobilization around the Days of Protest (beginning May 11, 1983) in response to pleas made by Olga Poblete and Elena Caffarena, two of the original members of the *Movimiento Pro-Emancipación de la Mujer Chilena* (1935), at a meeting organized to launch the publication of a collection of documents authored by the leaders of the first MEMCH. See the discussion of MEMCH 83 below.

14. Silva, *La Participación Política de la Mujer,* 146.

15. In Chilean political culture, to be political has generally meant to be partisan. There is a long-standing historical precedent, however, for women's groups in Chile to reject partisan labels and attempt to maintain autonomy from political parties. See Julieta Kirkwood, *"Ser Política en Chile: Las Feministas y los Partidos"* (Santiago: Programa FLACSO, Documento de Trabajo no. 143, 1982).

16. There has been much discussion internally whether or not this kind of work is paternalistic. They have concluded, however, that even if only one family has one of its needs looked after, then the members of that family can more easily continue the struggle.

17. For an excellent discussion of the Madres de la Plaza de Mayo, see Marysa Navarro, "The Personal is Political: The Madres de la Plaza de Mayo" (presented at the XIII International Congress of the Latin American Studies Association, Boston, October 23–25, 1986) and forthcoming in Susan Eckstein, ed., *Power and Popular Protest* (Berkeley, Calif.: University of California Press, 1989).

18. del Olmo, "Women and the Search for the Detained/Disappeared Persons of Latin America," 42.

19. Silva, *La Participación Política de la Mujer,* 154; "¿Dónde Estan?: Entrevistas con mujeres de la Agrupación de Familiares de los Detenidos -Desaparecidos," *Revista Furia* (Chile) no. 3 (March 1982): 19.

20. "La mujer chilena se moviliza," *Chile-America,* 19.

21. In October 1986 Amnesty International initiated its Carmen Bueno campaign designed to draw attention to the issue of the detained-disappeared in Chile. Carmen Bueno disappeared in 1974.

22. See Thomas E. Skidmore and Peter H. Smith, *Modern Latin America* (New York: Oxford University Press, 1984), 65. The authors argue that "the social role of females has typically been confined to the private sphere, particularly the family, and here women have often reigned supreme." These and other writers have rendered women's political achievements invisible. See Ronaldo Munck, *Politics and Dependency in the Third World: The Case of Latin America* (London: Zed Books, 1985), 127, who suggests that, "it remains a fact that women as a whole have had an only limited history of political activity in Latin America." It should be pointed out as well that many Latin American scholars and analysts continue to leave women entirely out of their political commentaries and analyses. See, for example, Manuel Antonio Garretón, "Political Process in an Authoritarian Regime: The Dynamics of Institutionalization and Opposition in Chile, 1973–1980," in Arturo Valenzuela and J. Samuel Valenzuela, eds., *Military*

Rule in Chile: Dictatorship and Opposition (Baltimore: Johns Hopkins University Press, 1986).

23. Carolyn M. Elliot, "Theories of Development: An Assessment," *Signs: Journal of Women in Culture and Society* 3, no. 1 (Autumn 1977): 5.

24. Círculo de Estudios de la Mujer, "La Mujer en el Discurso Oficial de Pinochet," "Un pequeño romance," and "Algunas Ideas Acerca de los Factores que Influirian en el Comportamiento Conservador de la Mujer Campesina," all mimeographed in Santiago in 1980. The notion of women as politically conservative is not limited to Latin America. See Thelma McCormack, "Toward a Non-Sexist Perspective on Social and Political Change" in Marcia Millman and Rosabeth Moss Kanter, eds., *Another Voice: Feminist Perspectives on Social Life and Social Science* (Garden City, N.Y.: Anchor Press, 1975) for a useful analysis and discussion of the political science literature.

25. Jane Jaquette, "Female Political Participation in Latin America," in Lynne B. Iglitzin and Ruth Ross, eds., *Women in the World: A Comparative Study* (Santa Barbara: ABC-CLIO Press, 1975).

26. This is pointed out by del Olmo, "Women and the Search for the Detained/Disappeared Persons of Latin America," 43.

27. See Skidmore and Smith (*Modern Latin America*, 64) who suggest that "if we are to judge by the conventional accounts, women have played only minor roles in the economic and political transformation of Latin America. That is certainly true if we look at the prominent public positions."

28. Chapter 1 of this volume.

29. Sonia Alvarez, *The Politics of Gender in Latin America: Comparative Perspectives on Women in the Brazilian Transition to Democracy,* (Ph.D dissertation, Yale University, 1986), 588.

30. María de los Angeles Crummett, "*El Poder Femenino:* The Mobilization of Women Against Socialism in Chile," *Latin American Perspectives* 4, no. 4 (Fall 1977): 110.

31. Lourdes Benería and Gita Sen, "Class and Gender Inequalities and Women's Role in Economic Development—Theoretical and Practical Implications," *Feminist Studies* 8, no. 2 (Spring 1982): 164.

32. For greater discussion and analysis of EPF see Crummett, "*El Poder Femenino*"; Elsa Chaney, "The Mobilization of Women in Allende's Chile", in Jane S. Jaquette, ed., *Women in Politics* (New York: John Wiley and Sons, 1974); Michele Mattelart, "La Mujer y la Linea de Masa de la Burguesía: El Caso de Chile," in María del Carmen Elí de Leñero, ed., *La Mujer*

en America Latina, vol. 2 (Mexico City: Sep/setentas, 1975.)

33. At the same time, the government also created the National Secretariat of Youth. Scholars often point to the creation of these two organizations as evidence of the Chilean state's corporatism, but on this there is little agreement. Thomas Sanders, for example, argues that Chile is semi-corporatist ("Military Government and National Organization," in Howard Handelman and Thomas G. Sanders, eds., *Military Government and the Movement Toward Democracy in South America*, [Bloomington, Ind.: Indiana University Press, 1981) while Arturo and J. Samuel Valenzuela suggest that the Chilean state does not conform to a corporatist model given that the ". . . whole thrust of the Chilean regime has been to exclude organized groups from any policy-making role in the name of social and economic liberalism" (*Military Rule in Chile*, 4).

34. At the same time it is important not to *overestimate* their influence. Many women are obligated by financial necessity to become members of CEMA given that income generating skills are taught in the centers, food often distributed and the women's handicrafts marketed through CEMA stores. This does not necessarily mean that members accept the ideological package or support the military.

35. Norbert Lechner and Susana Levy, "Notas Sobre la Vida Cotidiana III: El Disciplinamiento de la Mujer" (Santiago: Programa FLACSO, Materia de Discusión no. 57, July 1984), 2.

36. For a much more complete discussion of the SNM and CEMA-Chile see Giselle Munizaga, "El Discurso Público de Pinochet, 1973–1976" (Buenos Aires: CLACSO, 1983); Cristina Larraín, *Catastro de Organizaciones Femeninas del Gobierno* (Santiago: Instituto Chileno Estudios Humanisticos, 1982); Lechner and Levy, "Notas Sobre la Vida Cotidiana III"; "El Lugar de la Mujer en el Mundo de Pinochet," *Revista Furia* (Chile) no. 3 (March 1982); and Patricia Chuchryk, *Protest, Politics, and Personal Life: The Emergence of Feminism in a Military Dictatorship*, (Ph.D. dissertation, York University, Toronto, Canada, 1984). It is also important to emphasize that motherhood does not exempt women from torture, imprisonment, and sometimes death. See Ximena Bunster-Burotto, "Surviving Beyond Fear: Women and Torture in Latin America", in June Nash, Helen Safa, and Contributors, *Women and Change in Latin America* (South Hadley, Mass.: Bergin and Garvey, 1986), 297–325.

37. One of the issues on the agenda of a conference organized b, women unionists in June 1987 was the subjection of prospective female employees to gynecological examinations, often by untrained personnel, to ascertain that they are not pregnant.

38. Lois Wasserspring, "Women and the State in Latin America," (Wellesley, Mass.: Wellesley College, 1987), p. 19.

39. See Asunción Lavrin, "The Ideology of Feminism in the Southern Cone, 1900–1940" (The Wilson Center, Latin American Program, Washington, D.C., Working Paper no. 169, 1986); Julieta Kirkwood, "Ser Política en Chile: Las Feministas y los Partidos" (Santiago: Programa FLACSO, Documento de Trabajo no. 143, 1982). For a discussion of how women have traditionally conceptualized their political roles as extensions of their domestic roles, see Elsa Chaney, *Supermadre: Women in Politics in Latin America* (Austin, Tex. University of Texas Press, 1979.) See also the work of historian Temma Kaplan, who documents women's participation in neighborhood based political activity in Europe during the First World War, in "Female Consciousness and Collective Action: The Case of Barcelona, 1910–1918," *Signs: Journal of Women in Culture and Society*, 7, no. 3 (Spring 1982): 545–66 and "Women and Communal Strikes in the Crisis of 1917–1922," in Renate Bridenthal and Claudia Koonz, eds., *Becoming Visible: Women in European History*, Second Edition (Boston: Houghton Mifflin, 1986).

40. Marysa Navarro, "The Personal is Political." Jane Jaquette comments that "[t]he example of the *Madres* has been used to recast conventional theories of female political participation that see women as 'passive', 'feminine' values as apolitical, and ethical considerations as irrelevant to politics" in "Women, Feminism and the Transition to Democracy in Latin America" (Paper presented at the XIII International Congress of the Latin American Studies Association, Boston, October 23–25, 1986), 12.

41. "¿Dónde Estan?" *Revista Furia*, 20.

42. See Jaquette, "Women, Feminism and the Transition to Democracy"; Navarro, "The Personal is Political"; and Marjorie Agosin, "Whispers and Triumphs: Latin American Women Writers Today," *Women's Studies International Forum*, 9, no. 4 (1986): 427–33 who make similar points.

43. Navarro, "The Personal is Political," 26.

44. See del Olmo, "Women and the Search for the Detained/Disappeared Persons of Latin America," who suggests that this is not an unusual consequence.

45. See Riet Delsing, Andrea Rodó, Paulina Saball, and Betty Walker, "Tipología de Organizaciones y Grupos de Mujeres Pobladoras," (Santiago: Documentación, Estudios, Educación—SUR, Documento de Trabajo no. 17, April 1983), 32, who made similar observations.

46. "¿Dónde Estan?" *Revista Furia*, 19.

47. Adriana Santa Cruz, "Movimiento de la Mujer: Cauce a una Aspiración Justa," *Análisis* 59 (July 1983): 34.

48. For a more complete discussion of these and other groups see

Chuchryk, *Protest, Politics, and Personal Life.*

49. As will be discussed below, it is precisely this focus on the politicization of daily life which has led to women's reconceptualization of what constitutes politics. See Virginia Vargas, "El Aporte de la Rebeldía de las Mujeres," (paper presented at the XIII International Congress of the Latin American Studies Association, Boston, October 23–25, 1986); and Jaquette, "Women, Feminism and the Transition to Democracy."

50. It is interesting to note that *Acción Femenina* (AF) was formed in October 1985 by some women who left MOMUPO because they thought MOMUPO was too "political". AF does not define itself as a feminist group although there are feminists who participate in it. In an interview with one of its members, it was pointed out to me that one of the goals of the group is to develop feminist consciousness.

51. Given the nature of Chilean political culture, calling oneself a socialist usually means membership in one of the various sections of the Socialist Party.

52. This issue emerged in response to Pinochet's 1980 Constitution which provides for elections in 1989, and, not surprisingly, for his right to present himself as the only presidential candidate for re-election for a term of nine years.

53. It is important to point out that *La Morada* and the groups which share its space are in Chile referred to pejoratively as "militant" feminist organizations (that is, the groups which "go too far"). As a result, other women's groups sometimes go to extraordinary efforts to distinguish themselves from the feminists of *La Morada.*

54. We don't exactly know how many, given women's concentration in the informal labor market. See Ximena Díaz and Eugenia Hola, "Modes de inserción de la mujer de los sectores populares en el trabajo informal urbano" (Santiago: Centros de Estudios de la Mujer, 1985).

55. See Luis Razeto, Arno Klenner, Apolonia Ramirez, and Roberto Urmeneta, *Las Organizaciones Económicas Populares* (Santiago: Academia de Humanismo Cristiano, 1983).

56. See Delsing et al., "Tipología de Organizaciones."

57. Frenando I. Leiva and James Petras, "Chile's Poor in the Struggle for Democracy," *Latin American Perspectives* 13, no. 4 (Fall 1986): 5.

58. Carmen Tornaría, "Women's Involvement in the Democratic Process in Uruguay," *The Latin American Women's Movement: Reflections and Actions* (Santiago and Rome: ISIS International Women's Information and Communication Service, 1986), 25–26. Although Tornaría makes her com-

ment with reference to Uruguay, it is no less true of Chile. Jaquette ("Women, Feminism and the Transition to Democracy," p. 32) suggests that Latin American feminism challenges traditional notions of the public and private.

59. Horacio Walker, *The Transformation of Practices in Grass Roots Organizations: A Case Study in Chile,* (Ph.D. dissertation, University of Toronto, 1986), 100.

60. Ibid., 65.

61. Ibid., 95.

62. The implication of the demand to be a person, of course, is that being a woman is somehow less than being a person.

CHAPTER 8

*I would like to thank the American Institute of Indian Studies for funding my fieldwork in India in 1982 and the Research Unit on Women's Studies, S.N.D.T. Women's University, with which I was affiliated. An earlier version of this paper was presented at the 1985 Annual Meeting of the American Political Science Association.

1. Louise A. Tilly, "Women's Collective Action and Feminism in France, 1870–1914," in *Class Conflict and Collective Action,* ed. Louise A. Tilly and Charles Tilly (Beverly Hills, CA: Sage Publications, 1981), 214.

2. Collective action refers to the "struggle over control of resources among groups" and is defined as "a group's application of pooled resources to common ends," Louise A. Tilly, "Paths of Proletarianization: Organization of Production, Sexual Division of Labor, and Women's Collective Action," *Signs: Journal of Women in Culture and Society* 7, no. 2 (Winter 1981): 402.

3. In Ann S. Orloff and Theda Skocpol, "Why not Equal Protection? Explaining the Politics of Public Social Spending in Britain 1900–1911 and the United States 1880–1920," *American Sociological Review* 49, no. 6 (Dec. 1984): 730–31. See also Theda Skocpol, *States and Social Revolutions: A Comparative Analysis of France, Russia and China* (Cambridge: Cambridge University Press, 1979).

4. Dietrich Rueschemeyer and Peter B. Evans, "The State and Economic Transformation: Toward an Analysis of the Conditions Underlying Effective Intervention," in Peter B. Evans, Dietrich Rueschemeyer and Theda Skocpol, eds., *Bringing the State Back In* (Cambridge University Press, 1985), 46–47.

5. Ibid., 47.

6. See Chapter 1 of this volume.

7. This distinction comes from Maxine Molyneux, "Mobilization Without Emancipation? Women's Interests, the State, and Revolution in Nicaragua," *Feminist Studies* 11, no. 2 (Summer 1985): 232–33. Practical gender interests arise out of women's needs within particular gendered and class contexts. Strategic gender interests are objectives designed to overcome gender subordination.

8. Hugh Heclo, "Toward a New Welfare State?" in *The Development of Welfare States in Europe and America,* ed. Peter Flora and Arnold J. Heidenheimer (New Brunswick, N.J.: Transaction Books, 1981), 383–406.

9. Frances Fox Piven, "Women and the State: Ideology, Power, and the Welfare State," *Socialist Review* 14, no. 2 (March–April 1984): 11–19. Elise Boulding, "Integration into What? Reflections on Development Planning for Women," in *Women and Technological Change in Developing Countries,* ed. Roslyn Dauber and Melinda L. Cain (Boulder, Colorado: Westview Press, 1981), 9–32; Kathleen E. Ferguson, *The Feminist Case Against Bureaucracy* (Philadelphia: Temple University Press, 1984).

10. The term "informal sector" refers to the economic activities of small producers, vendors, and service workers in the Third World whose enterprises are not regulated or unionized in contrast to the large-scale "formal sector" enterprises. Women are concentrated in the least remunerative informal sector activities. See Kate Young and Caroline Moser, eds., *Women and the Informal Sector: Bulletin of the Institute of Development Studies* 12, no. 3 (July 1981). These Indian associations see themselves as organizations of self-employed women, but some of them are dependent workers in putting-out systems. Pushpa Sundar, "Women's Employment and Organization Modes," *Economic and Political Weekly* 18, no. 48 (Nov. 26, 1983): M171-M176.

11. Rueschemeyer and Evans, "State and Economic Transformation," 47.

12. Francine R. Frankel, *India's Political Economy, 1947–1977 The Gradual Revolution* (Princeton, N.J.: Princeton University Press, 1978).

13. Ibid., 549.

14. Ibid., xiii.

15. Bharat Patankar and Gail Omvedt, "The Bourgeois State in Post-Colonial Social Formations," *Economic and Political Weekly* 12, no. 53 (Dec. 31, 1977): 2165–2177. The class basis of the Indian state put forward by

Marxists ranges from capitalist, to merchant, to capitalist and landlord, to even more heterogeneous groupings. For example, see Barbara Harriss, *State and Market* (New Delhi: Concept Publishing Co., 1984).

16. Patankar and Omvedt, "The Bourgeois State," 2175.

17. Ibid.

18. Lloyd I. and Susanne Hoeber Rudolph, *In Pursuit of Lakshmi: The Political Economy of the Indian State,* (Chicago: University of Chicago Press, 1987).

19. Rajni Kothari, "The Non-Party Political Process," *Economic and Political Weekly* 19, no. 5 (February 4, 1984): 218. See also "Decline of the Moderate State" and other essays in *State Against Democracy: In Search of Humane Goverance* (Delhi: Ajanta Publications, 1988), 15–36.

20. Along similar lines Ashis Nandy argues, "These three reasons of state—security, development and modern science—are creating internal colonies, new hierarchies and recipient cultures among the people, so that a small elite can live off both economic and psychosocial surpluses extracted from the people as a part of the process of modernisation." ("Culture, State, and the Rediscovery of Indian Politics," *Economic and Political Weekly* 19, no. 49 [December 8, 1984]: 2081.)

21. Pranab Bardhan, *The Political Economy of Development in India,* (Oxford, England: Basil Blackwell Publisher Ltd., 1984).

22. Atul Kohli, *The State and Poverty in India: The Politics of Reform* (Cambridge: Cambridge University Press, 1987).

23. Kothari, "Decline of the Moderate State," 35.

24. Kothari, "The Non-Party Political Process," 219.

25. Ibid., 222.

26. Committee on the Status of Women in India, *Towards Equality* (New Delhi: Government of India, 1974). For an overview of this research, see Vina Mazumdar and Kumud Sharma, "Women's Studies: New Perceptions and the Challenges," *Economic and Political Weekly* 14, no. 3 (1979): 113–20. The most recent example of this approach is the National Commission of Self Employed Women, chaired by Ela Bhatt, whose report *Shram Shakti* (labor power) was issued in June 1988.

27. P. M. Mathew, "Women's Industrial Employment in Kerala, India," *Bulletin of Concerned Asian Scholars* 18, no. 3 (July-Sept. 1986): 43–58; Florence McCarthy and Shelley Feldman, "Rural Women Discovered: New Sources of Capital and Labour in Bangladesh," *Development and*

Change 14, no. 2 (April 1983): 211–36.

28. See Madhu Kishwar and Ruth Vanita, eds., *In Search of Answers: Indian Women's Voices From Manushi* (London: Zed Books Ltd., 1984).

29. Ibid., 42.

30. These programs provide low interest business loans to the self-employed poor with the rationale that such programs enable the poor to get out of the clutches of moneylenders and to increase their productivity and income. Jana Everett and Mira Savara, "Bank Loans to the Poor in Bombay: Do Women Benefit?" *Signs: Journal of Women in Culture and Society* 10, no. 2 (Winter 1984): 272–90.

31. For an argument that women's participation in welfare programs in the U.S. should be seen as a form of political participation, see Barbara J. Nelson, "Women's Poverty and Women's Citizenship: Some Political Consequences of Economic Marginality," *Signs: Journal of Women in Culture and Society* 10, no. 2 (Winter 1984): 209–31.

32. Jan Breman, " 'I am the Government Labour Officer . . . ' State Protection for Rural Proletariat in South Gujarat," *Economic and Political Weekly* 20, no. 24 (June 15, 1985): 1043–1055.

33. Ibid., 1048.

34. Ibid., 1054–55.

35. The three organizations studied were selected because they are the largest and most well-documented women's organizations of urban informal sector workers. Informal sector activity is the most common source of income for urban women. These organizations are not necessarily representative of all organizations working with lower class women. Information in this section is based on Devaki Jain, *Women's Quest For Power* (Bombay: Vikas, 1980); Jennefer Sebstad, *Struggle and Development Among Self Employed Women: A Report on the Self Employed Women's Association, Ahmedabad, India* (Washington D.C.: U.S.A.I.D. Office of Urban Development, 1982); Hilde Jeffers, "Organizing Women Petty Traders and Producers: A Case Study of Working Women's Forum, Madras," (masters thesis, Department of City and Regional Planning, University of California, Berkeley, 1981); M. Mistey et al., "A Study of the Repercussions of Bank Loans to Annapurnas Financed by the Multi-Service Agency of the Bank of Baroda" I-IV (masters thesis, College of Social Work, Bombay University, 1979); Maitreyi Krishna Raj, *Approaches to Self-Reliance for Women: Some Urban Models* (Bombay: Research Unit on Women's Studies, S.N.D.T. Women's University, 1980); Everett and Savara "Bank Loans to the Poor"; and on interviews conducted with the three association leaders: Jaya Arunachalam, New Delhi, September 4, 1982; Ela Bhatt, Ahmedabad, October 25–26, 1982; and Prema Purao, Bombay, August–November, 1982.

36. The selection of organizations was based on the availability of documentation and on an effort to include regional and ideological diversity. Many of the sources are journalistic accounts by participants or sympathetic observers. For a more extensive examination of women's participation in these movements, see Jana Everett, "We Were in the Forefront of the Fight: Feminist Theory and Practice in Indian Grass-Roots Movements." *South Asia Bulletin* 6, no. 1 (Spring 1986): 17–24. For an overview of women in collective action worldwide, see Eleanor B. Leacock, ed., "A Conference Report: A Decade of Women's Collective Action: Anthropological Perspectives," Mijas, Spain, 1985. *IWAC Bulletin I*, International Women's Anthropology Conference, Inc. (February, 1986).

37. Kothari, "The Nonparty Political Process," 220.

38. Mira Savara and Sujatha Gothoskar, "An Assertion of Womanpower," in Kishwar and Vanita, *In Search of Answers*, 134–48; Gail Omvedt, "Women and Rural Revolt in India," *Journal of Peasant Studies* 5, no. 3 (April 1978): 370–403; Amrita Basu, "Two Faces of Protest: Alternative Forms of Women's Mobilization in West Bengal and Maharashtra," in *The Extended Family: Women and Political Participation in India and Pakistan*, ed., Gail Minault (Columbia, Mo.: South Asia Books, 1981), 217–62.

39. Uma Bhatt, "Give Us Employment, not Liquor: Anti-Liquor Movement in Uttarakhand," *Manushi* 4, no. 6 (1984): 2–7; Gopa Joshi and Sunderlal Bahuguna, "Protecting the Sources of Community Life," in *In Search Of Answers*, 125–33; Shobhita Jain, "Women and People's Ecological Movement: A Case Study of Women's Role in the Chipko Movement in Uttar Pradesh," *Economic and Political Weekly* 19, no. 41 (Oct. 13, 1984): 1788–94.

40. Burnad Fatima, "Despite Heavy Odds: Organizing Harijan Women in Tamil Nadu Villages," *Manushi* 4, no. 1 (1983): 33–6; Institute of Social Studies, *Catalogue of Agencies Reaching Poorest Women in India* (New Delhi: Swedish International Development Authority, 1981), 127–128.

41. Maria Mies, "Landless Women Organize: Case Study of an Organization in Rural Andhra," *Manushi* 3, no. 3 (1983): 2–16; Sudesh Vaid, "Breaking Fear's Silence," in *In Search of Answers*, 120–24.

42. Manimala, " 'Zameen Kenkar? Jote Onkar!' [Who owns the land? The person who works it!] Women's Participation in the Bodhgaya Land Struggles," *In Search of Answers*, 149–176; Institute of Social Studies, *Catalogue of Agencies*, 18–19.

43. Mira Savara, "Issues and Struggles of Tribal Women in Thane District, Maharashtra, India" (paper presented at the International Union of Anthropological and Ethnological Sciences, Vancouver, Canada, 1983); Insti-

tute of Social Studies, *Catalogue of Agencies*, 80–81.

44. J. Craig Jenkins, "Resource Mobilization Theory and the Study of Social Movements," *Annual Review of Sociology* 9 (1983): 527–53.

45. Kothari, "The Non-Party Political Process," 222.

46. D. L. Sheth, "Grass-roots Initiatives in India," *Economic and Political Weekly* 19, no. 6 (Feb. 11, 1984): 262.

47. Joan M. Nelson, *Access to Power: Politics and the Urban Poor in Developing Nations* (Princeton, N.J.: Princeton University Press, 1979).

48. Renana Jhabwala, "Neither a Complete Success nor a total Failure: SEWA Organizes Bidi Workers," *Manushi* 4, no. 4 (1984): 18–22.

49. Manimala, "Women's Participation in the Bodhgaya Land Struggles," p. 174. The practice of giving titles in women's names only did not continue, but joint titles were given. See Govind Kelkar and Chetna Gala, "Chhatra Yuva Sangharsh Vahini and Women's Liberation in Bodh Gaya, Bihar," (New Delhi: mimeo, 1988).

50. Jain, *Women's Quest for Power*, 15; Nirmala Banerjee, "The Weakest Link," *Bulletin of the Institute of Development Studies* 12, no. 3 (July 1981): 36–40.

51. State Bank of India, *Impact of Credit on Weaker Sections: A Report Based on Eight Case Studies* (Bombay, 1978).

52. See references in note 35.

53. Samuel P. Huntington and Joan M. Nelson, *No Easy Choice: Political Participation in Developing Countries* (Cambridge, Mass.: Harvard University Press, 1976).

54. Uttarkhand represents an exception to this generalization and the mass base for the Chipko and Anti-Alcohol movements appears to be mainly female (in part because many men have migrated to cities for work).

55. Frankel, *India's Political Economy*, 549.

56. Leslie J. Calman, *Protest in Democratic India: Authority's Response to Challenge* (Boulder, Colo.: Westview Press, 1985).

57. Amrita Basu, "Two Faces of Protest," 225.

58. Kohli, *The State and Proverty in India*, 41–45.

59. Kothari, "NGOs, the State and World Capitalism," *Economic and Political Weekly*, 21, 50 (Dec. 13, 1986): 2182.

CHAPTER 9

1. Eric A. Nordlinger, "Taking the State Seriously" in Myron Weiner and Samuel Huntington, eds., *Understanding Political Development: An Analytic Study* (Boston: Little, Brown and Co., 1987), 362.

2. As Staudt indicates, this argument has been put forward by a number of feminist scholars including Rayna Rapp, "Gender and Class: An Archaeology of Knowledge Concerning the Origin of the State," *Dialectical Anthropology* 2 (1977): 309–16.

3. Judith Stacey, *Patriarchy and Socialist Revolution in China* (Berkeley: University of California Press, 1983).

4. Lois Wasserspring, "Women and the State in Latin America," (Wellesley, Mass.: Wellesley College, Mimeo, 1987).

5. Linda Gordon, "Family Violence, Feminism, and Social Control," *Feminist Studies* 12, no. 3 (Fall 1986): 453–78.

6. Sonia E. Alvarez, "Politicizing Gender and Engendering Democracy," in Alfred Stepan, ed., *Democratizing Brazil* (New York: Oxford University Press, 1989), 205–251.

7. Ruth Milkman, *Gender at Work: The Dynamics of Job Segregation by Sex During World War II* (Urbana, Ill.: University of Illinois Press, 1987).

8. The terms are drawn from Victor Azarya and Naomi Chazan, "Disengagement from the State in Africa: Reflections on the Experience of Ghana and Guinea," *Comparative Studies in Society and History* 29, no. 1 (Jan. 1987): 106–31. In specific empirical instances women's responses may contain elements of both engagement and disengagement, and of both access and transformation. Furthermore, goals and effects must be distinguished: for example, women seeking state transformation may achieve access or vice versa.

9. Exceptions include Azarya and Chazan, "Disengagement from the State in Africa", and James C. Scott, "Everyday Forms of Peasant Resistance," *Journal of Peasant Studies* 13, no. 2 (Jan 1986): 5–35.

10. Sidney Verba and Lucien W. Pye, eds., *The Citizen and Politics: A Comparative Perspective* (Stanford, Conn.: Greylock Publishers, 1978), 1.

11. Azarya and Chazan, "Disengagement from the State in Africa," 117.

12. Maria Mies, *Patriarchy and Accumulation on a World Scale: Women in the International Division of Labour* (London: Zed Books, 1986).

13. Irene Silverblatt, *Moon, Sun, and Witches: Gender Ideologies and Class in Inca and Colonial Peru* (Princeton, N.J.: Princeton University Press, 1987).

14. Charles Tilly, Louise Tilly, and Richard Tilly, *The Rebellious Century, 1830–1930* (Cambridge, Mass.: Harvard University Press, 1975).

15. On the first wave of feminism in different states around the world, see Ellen DuBois, *Feminism and Suffrage: The Emergence of an Independent Women's Movement in America, 1848–1869* (Ithaca, N.Y.: Cornell University Press, 1978); Joni Lovenduski, *Women and European Politics: Contemporary Feminism and Public Policy* (Amherst, Mass.: University of Massachusetts Press, 1986); Kumari Jayawardena, *Feminism and Nationalism in the Third World* (London: Zed Books, 1986); Asunción Lavrin, ed., *Latin American Women: Historical Perspectives* (Westport, Conn.: Greenwood Press, 1978).

16. Alvarez, "Politicizing Gender and Engendering Democracy," 3.

17. Ibid.

INDEX

A

Abortion, 29, 55, 87, 116, 189
Accumulation, 67, 68, 69, 74–75,
    85, 178, 212n.10
Afigbo, A. E., 81–82
Africa, 11, 17, 66–113, 180–81, 186
Afshar, Haleh, 87
Agricultural policy, 72, 74, 101,
    118–123; feminization of agricul-
    ture, 54, 78, 96, 170, 208n.39
Agrupación de Familiares de
    Detenidos-Desaparecidos,
    133–36, 140, 150
Albania, 46, 48, 49, 58
Alcoholism, 163, 168
Annapurna Mahila Mandal, 161,
    164, 165, 168
Anti-alcohol movement, 163, 167,
    168, 169
Alvarez, Sonia, 128, 182, 187
Argentina, 122, 125, 126, 127, 128, 134
Aristotle, 23
Arizpe, Lourdes, 120
Arunachalam, Jaya, 164
Asia, 55, 152–76
Association of African Women for
    Research and Development, 98

Australia, 31
Azarya, Victor, 185
Aztec, 67

B

Baranskaya, Natalia, 60
Bardaglio, Peter, 9
Bardhan, Pranab, 157
Barrett, Michele, 10
Basu, Amrita, 174
Berman, Bruce, 69, 80
Bhatt, Ela, 164–65, 169
Birth control, 29, 110, 116, 128, 144
Birth rates, 57–59, 64, 182
Bodhgaya movement, 163, 165, 167,
    168
Bodin, Jean, 23, 24
Bolsheviks, 47, 50
Boris, Eileen, 9
Botey, Carlota, 120
Brain, James, 83
Brazil, 122, 124–25, 126, 127, 128, 130
Breman, Jan, 160
Bridewealth, 55, 68, 71, 73, 75, 83,
    91–93, 212n.10
Britain, 25, 39, 41

British colonialism, 69–72, 74–78, 79, 103, 104, 111, 155
Bulgaria, 50, 58
Bunster-B., Ximena, 126
Bureaucracies, 11, 29–32, 42, 83, 154, 172, 182–83. *See also* State, officials

C
Callaghy, Thomas, 85
Callaway, Helen, 70–71
Cameroon, 80
Canada, 41
Capitalism, 9, 11, 21, 26, 39, 69, 145, 155, 160, 163, 170, 173, 184, 194n.26. *See also* Development
Chaney, Elsa, 141
Chanock, Martin, 79
Chazan, Naomi, 185
Child care, 39–40, 42, 55, 56, 63, 128, 139, 144, 161
Chile, 18,125–27,130–51
China, 181, 186, 189
Chipko movement, 163. *See also* Forest protection
Chuchryk, Patricia, 126–27
Class: 2, 3–4, 5, 10, 18, 26, 76, 116, 119, 175, 217n.66; cross-class alliance, 126, 161–72; divisions, 4, 10, 46, 81, 82, 152–76, 189, 193–94n.25, 199n.31; domination in state, 4, 26–27, 157–58; gender conceptually subordinate to, 47; structuring politics, 4. *See also* Marxism; State autonomy
Collective action, 161, 152–54, 170–71, 173, 175–76, 233n.2. *See also* Feminist movements; Women's organizations
Colonialism, 16, 17, 66–85, 105. *See also* British colonialism; French colonialism
Communist parties, 48–52, 135, 158, 164, 174. *See also* Political party

commitment to female emancipation
Congress party, 155–56, 164
Constitution, 29, 109–110
Consumer goods, 32, 53, 56, 62–63, 78, 185
Corporatism, 38, 157, 201n.55, 230n.33
Costa Rica, 134
Coulson, Noel, 91
Credit for women, 160–62, 164, 166, 168, 171
Crummett, Maria de los Angeles, 126
Czechoslovakia, 46, 49, 50, 58, 61, 62

D
Daniels, Cynthia, 9
Deere, Carmen Diana, 119–20
Delphy, Christine, 40
Dependency theory, 5, 12, 62, 68, 69, 121, 174, 184, 192n.9, 223–24n.18
Development, 2, 6, 7–8, 14–15, 18, 40, 42, 48, 52–53, 57–58, 64, 71, 111, 121, 148, 157, 178, 184; ideologies of, 74, 124
Domestic labor, 27, 75–79
Double day, as policy induced, 53–56

E
Echeverría, Luis, 123
Economic crisis, 11, 62–64, 69, 84, 100, 112, 144, 148, 181
Economic development. *See* Development
Education, 53, 54, 71, 73, 76–77, 87, 95, 98–99, 100, 103, 105, 107–8, 109, 132–33, 142, 214n.31
Egypt, 100
Eisenstein, Zillah, 9, 10, 27
Elshtain, Jean Bethke, 22, 24, 40–41, 202,nn.63–64

Engels, F., 4, 47, 67, 68
Equality, different beliefs about, 61;
    See also Law; Legal equality
Ethnicity, 7, 10, 18, 28, 58, 78, 94,
    103, 105, 116
Europeans: colonizers, 69–72,
    75–79; Eastern, 16, 20, 44–65,
    180–81, 182; state in Africa,
    66–78; Western, 6, 16, 20–43,
    180–81, 186
Evans, Peter, 153, 156, 174

F

Family policy, 15, 29, 45, 54, 55, 56,
    71, 73, 89–90, 97–98, 105, 106;
    Christian, 76; Islamic, 88–94, 98,
    107, 109–110; strengthening of, 18,
    56–61, 63–64, 65, 73, 76, 82. *See
    also* Marriage; Religion
Feminism: 1, 2, 7–12, 35–41, 50, 100,
    146–47, 150, 178, 186,
    232nn.50,53; liberal, 8, 9, 13, 22,
    26, 32, 35–37, 40, 42; movements,
    2, 8, 25–26, 52, 60–61, 115, 133,
    140, 143, 144, 145, 146–47, 187;
    radical, 35–39; Socialist, 35–39,
    145, 201nn.49,54; state, attention
    to, 7–8, 35–41; structural, 9; Third
    World, 7; Western, 1–2, 10, 25, 87,
    154–55, 175, 186. *See also* Gender
    ideology; Politics, definition of;
    Socialist countries; Women's
    organizations
Ferguson, Kathy, 31, 36
Forest protection, 163, 167, 168, 171
France, 25, 40, 41
Frankel, Francine, 156, 158, 173
French colonialism, 69–72, 76–78,
    80, 93–94, 96, 97, 100, 101, 104, 111

G

Geisel, Ernesto, 124
Gellar, Sheldon, 96, 98

Gender: equality, 63, 119, 189–90;
    ideology, 4, 13, 14–15, 51, 66, 72,
    77, 82, 84, 223n.8; imagery, 18, 21,
    56, 59, 116, 120, 125, 224–25n.26;
    interests, 8, 11; relations, 2, 4, 5,
    38, 54, 57, 88, 115, 180, 192n.9;
    state and, 8, 115, 179–184. *See also*
    Feminism; Households; Mother-
    hood; Public-private distinction;
    Women's interests
Germany: East, 46, 58; West, 50
Gersovitz, Mark, 99
Ghana, 77
Ghandi, Mahatma, 155
Glasnost, 49, 63
Gorbachev, Mikhail, 49, 52, 62, 63
Gordon, Linda, 182
Gramsci, Antonio, 28, 198n.21
Grass-roots organizations, 146,
    162–63, 172
Grindle, Merilee, 122–24
Guatemala, 125, 126, 134

H

Hailey, Lord, 74
Hartmann, Heidi, 68
Hay, Margaret Jean, 80
Heper, Metin, 30
Hinchcliffe, Dorothy, 91
Hirschmann, David, 83
Historically specific research, 5–6,
    12, 68, 115, 178, 184
Hobsbawn, E., 80
Honduras, 120
Households: division of labor, 4, 11,
    39, 54, 55, 57, 60, 63, 74, 208n.39;
    female heads, 119–120; income
    distribution within, 81, 92–93, 96,
    99, 119, 214n.34
Huessler, Robert, 70
Hungary, 46, 58
Human rights movements, 108, 124,
    125, 126, 131–36, 143, 225n.29

I

Ideology. *See* Gender ideology; State ideology
Incas, 67, 116–18
India, 18–19, 37, 152–176, 186, 187, 189
Informal sector, 107, 160–170, 181, 234n.10, 236n.35
International development agencies, 2
International relations context of states, 6, 22, 23, 25, 28, 33, 42 62, 179, 202n.55
International Women's Day, 56, 143, 147
Iran, 29, 87–88
Islam. *See* Religion, Islam

J

Jaquette, Jane, 136, 231n.40
Jowitt, Kenneth, 54

K

Kanturkova, Eva, 62, 210n.52
Kashtakari Sangathana movement, 163
Kenya, 72, 78, 80, 81
Khoumeni, Ayatollah, 87–88
Kishwar, Madhu, 159
Kohli, Atul, 157–58, 174
Kothari, Rajni, 157–58, 174–75

L

Labor force participation, 27, 46, 53, 54, 58, 64, 75, 98–99, 107, 148, 180, 183; in agriculture, 72, 78, 98, 119–120; wages, 39, 40, 147, 160; women as labor reserve 53, 72
Lapidus, Gail, 47, 56
Latin America, 18, 114–151, 183, 187
Law, 9, 25, 47, 79, 80–81, 97, 109–110, 116, 128; customary law,
78, 79, 80, 97, 109, 110; plural legal systems, 80, 97–98, 104, 109, 110; legal equality, 47, 55, 57; as leverage, 79; Sharia, 29, 89–90, 101, 103, 106, 109, 110, 112. *See also* Family law; Gender equality; Religion
Legitimacy, state, 21, 26–27, 29, 43
Leon, Magdalena, 119
Lerner, Gerda, 212n.10
Liberal pluralism, 3–4, 9, 13, 21, 22, 25, 28, 41, 43, 90, 111, 123, 156, 199n.3
Locke, John, 27
Literature (novels), 60
Lugard, Lord, 69, 74, 104

M

Machiavelli, Niccolò, 23, 24, 197n.7
MacKinnon, Catharine, 8, 9
Madres de la Plaza de Mayo, 125, 126, 134, 141, 231n.40
Mainwaring, Scott, 128
Malawi (Nyasaland), 79, 80, 83–84
Male control: institutionalized, 5, 9, 14, 16, 69, 74–75, 91, 106, 180, 194n.26; redistribution as threat, 57, 79, 80, 81, 112, 120, 195n.33, 202n.63, 223n.14; violence, *see* Sexual violence
Marianismo. *See* Motherhood
Marital exchange, 67, 212n.10. *See also* Bridewealth; Family law; Marriage
Marriage, 29, 37, 38, 71–77, 80, 83, 87, 103, 107, 110; adultery, 77–78; divorce, 73, 80, 91, 139. *See also* Family law; Religion
Marxism, 3–4, 21, 47, 90, 137; feminist, 4, 10, 52, 201n.49; instrumental, 4; state and, 3, 9, 156–57, 174; structural, 4. *See also* Class; Feminism, socialist; Socialist countries

Maternity policy, 16, 56, 59, 61, 63, 143, 189; compulsory pregnancy tests, 139, 143, 230n.37; mortality, 107
Mauritania, 86
Mba, Nina, 82
Media: feminist, 143–44, 145, 159, 226n.32; official, 54, 55, 56, 59, 138–39
Men as administrative targets, 74–75
Mernissi, Fatima, 11
Mexico, 67, 120,122–23, 182, 222n.7
Mill, John Stuart, 41
Military, 23, 32, 105, 123–26, 130–151, 183; enfranchising women, 109; women in, 11, 34; women's protests and, 125–26, 130–151, 187
Militarization of state, 7, 18, 23, 32–34, 129, 182, 196–97n.6, 200nn.41,43
Missionaries. *See* Religion, Christian missionaries, Muslim missionaries
Modernization. *See* Development
Molyneaux, Maxine, 8–9, 10. *See also* Women's interests
Motherhood, 18, 41, 55–56, 57–59, 126, 129, 131, 136–142, 150, 183. *See also* Gender imagery
Mothers, 18, 80; allowances for, 59; as organizational orientation, 130–151, 188
Morality, 24, 71, 76, 77, 78, 82, 92
Movimiento Pro-Emancipación de la Mujer Chilena (MEMCH), 133, 227n.13
Mujeres Democraticas, 131–33, 136, 150
Mueller, Adele, 7

N

Nationalism, 18, 21, 25, 27–28, 32, 68, 83, 90, 96, 105, 112, 138, 185

Navarro, Marysa, 140, 141
Nazi, 46
Nehru, Jawaharlal, 156
Nelson, Joan, 166
Nigeria, 17, 71, 80, 81–82, 86–87, 101–112

O

Oboler, Regina, 81
Oliver, Roland, 73, 74
Omvedt, Gail, 156–57, 158, 174
Orloff, Ann Shula, 14
Ortner, Sherry, 68

P

Pakistan, 29
Parpart, Jane, 79, 82–83
Paredes, Beatriz, 123
Patankar, Bharat, 156–57, 158, 174
Patron-client ties, 160, 166, 170, 173
Perestroika, 62
Peru, 120, 127, 128, 129, 186. *See also* Incas
Pinochet, General, 18, 127, 131, 138–39, 150,232n52; Lucía Hiriat de Pinochet, 138
Piven, Frances Fox, 9, 154
Pluralism. *See* Liberal pluralism
Poder Femenino, 125–27, 137
Poggi, Gianfranco, 6, 24
Poland, 46, 50, 52, 53, 58, 61, 63. *See also* Solidarity
Political culture, 114, 116, 121, 129, 224n.19
Political party: commitment to female emancipation, 45, 50–51, 105, 188–89; as policy-making body, 48–50; women in, 51, 60, 63, 65, 171; sectarianism, 148
Political science, vii, 1, 2, 66, 115, 129, 178, 218n.78. *See also* State conceptualizations
Political theory, 23, 27. *See also*

Political theory, *continued*
Feminism; Liberal pluralism;
Marxism; Public-private distinc-
tion; State conceptualizations
Politics, definition of, 3, 12, 14–15,
28, 51, 81, 127, 128, 135, 136, 145,
149, 153, 155, 158, 160, 166, 180,
182, 232n.49; symbolic content,
18, 67, 82, 116, 169, 183
Polygyny, 73, 74. *See also* Law,
Sharia; Religion, Islam
Population policy. *See* Birth control;
Birth rates;Pronatalism
Production, 3, 80. *See* Development;
Labor force participation
Pronatalism, 57–59, 61, 139, 183
Property laws, 25, 26, 80, 91–93,
96–97, 98, 99, 102, 119–120,
122–23, 216n.55
Prussia, 25
Public policies, 2, 14, 42, 45, 49–59,
64, 116, 179–181, 186–87. *See also*
Abortion; Agricultural policy;
Birth control; Development;
Education; Family policy; Law;
Maternity; Pronatalism; State
welfare
Public-private distinction, 2, 8, 11,
15, 16, 17, 18, 20–26, 32, 37, 40,
42, 60, 66, 71, 78, 82, 103, 108, 131,
136–37, 148–49, 180, 202n.64,
233n.58. *See also* Politics,
definition of
Purao, Prema, 164, 168
Pye, Lucien, 185

Q
Qu'ran. *See* Law, Sharia; Religion,
Islam

R
Ranger, T. O., 80
Rapp, Rayna, 68

Religion, 10, 21–22, 28–29, 45–46,
80–81, 84, 131,146, 210n.49;
Catholicism, 74, 81, 95, 134;
Christian, 84, 90, 112; Christian
missionaries, 17, 68, 70, 71, 72–76,
104, 105, 111; Church human
rights protests, 131, 134; Islam, 11,
17–18, 29, 86–113, 182–83,
213n.24, 215n.42; Muslim
missionaries, 93, 101–2, 110–11;
political interests of, 17, 88, 90;
Protestants, 23, 75; secularism,
17, 88, 94, 109, 111 *See also* Family
law; Ideology
Reardon, Betty, 33–34
Reproduction, 3, 17, 18, 57, 82, 139,
183, 186; Marxist inattention to,
47; state emphasis on, 3, 57. *See
also* Birth control; Child care;
Households; Maternity policy;
Motherhood; Pronatalism; Public
policies
Revolution, 10–11, 181. *See also*
Socialist countries
Roberts, Stephen, 71
Romania, 41, 50, 58, 63
Rosaldo, Michelle, 116
Rudolph, Lloyd and Susanne, 157
Rueschemeyer, Dietrich, 153, 156,
174
Rural areas, 162–174
Ryotu Coolie Sangham movement,
163

S
Sacks, Karen, 67
Salamone, Frank, 80–81
Savara, Mira, 159
Schirmer, Jennifer, 38–39
Scott, Joan, 116
Seclusion for women, 92, 98, 100,
102, 106; restrictions on female
movement, 77, 83, 215n.47. *See
also* Family law, Sharia; Religion,
Islam

Self-Employed Women's Association, 161–62, 164, 165, 166–67, 168
Senegal, 17, 86–87, 93–101, 110–12
Sexual behavior, 71, 73, 76, 77, 116–18
Sexual violence, 37, 55, 116, 128, 163, 165, 168, 169, 186, 187, 223n.8
Shahada movement, 162–63, 167, 168
Siemienska, Renata, 63
Silverblatt, Irene, 116–18, 186, 222–223nn.7,8
Sivard, Ruth, 98
Skocpol, Theda, 6, 14, 153
Slavery, 94, 102, 103
Smith, Donald E., 88
Socialist countries, 4, 11, 16–17, 44–65, 121, 180–81. *See also* Europe, Eastern; Marxism; Revolution
Solidarity, 61–62, 63
South Africa, 75, 82, 189
Sovereignty, 24
Spain, 29; Spanish colonialism, 186
Stacey, Judith, 181
State: autonomy, 2, 4, 5, 10, 12, 25, 30, 157, 176, 184; conceptualizations, 1, 3–6, 7–12, 20–43, 84–85, 115, 121–22, 153, 156–160, 188–190, 211n.1, 224n.20; formation and impact, as gendered, 68, 116–18, 179, 180; ideologies, 3, 5, 6, 14–15, 21, 28, 39, 45, 70, 71–72, 78, 178–79; as mediator, 4, 9, 68; officials, 11, 12, 14, 17, 29–32, 54, 57–58, 65, 66, 68, 70, 71–72, 74, 83–84, 120, 121–24, 127, 172, 177, 180–81, 199n.32, 224nn.19,22; as patriarchal and masculine, 8, 9, 24, 27, 40, 84, 145, 159; protection, 11, 40, 165, 167; relations with society, 2–3, 5–6, 15, 19, 79–85, 152–176, 178, 184–88; welfare, 9, 10, 16, 22, 35–41, 183. *See also* Law; Legitimacy, state; Politics,

definition of; Public policies; Religion, Islam; Women's absence from state; Women's political voice
Staudt, Kathleen, 28, 119
Statist approaches, 3, 4, 5, 157, 177. *See also* State conceptualizations; Weber, Max
Stepan, Alfred, 122, 124, 127
Sumer, 67
Switzerland, 25

T

Tanzania (Tanganyika), 71, 72, 83
Tilly, Louise, 152, 186
Torture, 124, 126, 140, 144, 183, 188, 230n.36. *See also* Human rights movements; Militarization of the state; Sexual violence
Trade unions, 27, 131, 143

U

Uchendu, Victor, 80–81
Uganda, 76, 77, 78
United Nations Decade, 7, 12
U.S.S.R., 16, 44–65, 182
United States, 1, 8, 10, 31, 40, 41, 154
Urbanization, 94, 128, 161–62, 164–174, 179
Uruguay, 122

V

Verba, Sidney, 185
Victorian ideas, 72, 76, 83. *See also* Gender ideology; Motherhood
Violo, Eduardo, 128

W

Walker, Horacio, 149
Wasserspring, Lois, viii, 139
Waterbury, John, 99
Weber, Max, 5, 31, 153

Welfare. *See* Public policies; State welfare; Women, welfare state
Western feminism. *See* Feminism
Women: absence from state, 12, 13, 20–29, 50–51, 63, 71–72, 84–85, 99, 195n.34; age differences among, 133; autonomy from state, 81–82, 154–55, 175; class differences among, 1, 10, 82; their interests, 5, 6, 8–9, 12, 15, 17, 19, 21, 32, 103, 154, 172, 174–75, 184, 187–88, 193n.17; leaders, 9, 50, 98, 123, 164, 171; their organizations, 4, 19, 50, 52, 59, 60–61, 82, 114, 119, 127, 128, 130–151, 152–176, 182; political voice, 13, 18, 51, 81, 128; self-respect, 61, 141–42, 149–150, 169, 171; work, rural-urban differences, 46, 161–172; and welfare state, 20, 35–42, 154–55, 181–82, 200–201n.48. *See also* Class; Feminism; Gender; Human rights movements; Labor force participation; Motherhood; Public policies; State-society relations
Women in Development, 7, 192n.13
Women's bureaus/programs, 83, 120, 123, 128, 138, 149, 182, 235n.26
Woolf, Virginia, 33
Working Women's Forum, 161–65
Wright, Marcia, 74, 80

Y
Young, Crawford, 84
Yugoslavia, 48, 49, 51, 52, 53, 60

Z
Zaire (Belgian Congo), 75, 83, 192n.13
Zambia (Northern Rhodesia), 74, 79, 82, 83
Zimbabwe, 34

DATE DUE